VISUAL QUICKSTART GUIDE

HTML

FOR THE WORLD WIDE WEB
2ND EDITION

by Elizabeth Castro

Peachpit Press

Visual QuickStart Guide
HTML for the World Wide Web, 2nd Edition
Elizabeth Castro

Peachpit Press
2414 Sixth Street
Berkeley, CA 94710
(510) 548-4393
(510) 548-5991 (fax)

Find us on the World Wide Web at: http://www.peachpit.com
Or contact Liz directly at lcastro@cookwood.com

Peachpit Press is a division of Addison Wesley Longman

ISBN: 0-201-68862-X

0 9 8 7 6 5 4 3

Printed in the United States of America

Special thanks to:

Nolan Hester at Peachpit Press for his great suggestions and for his patience when I added new sections (and more pages) at the second-to-last moment.

Andreu Cabré for his feedback, for his great Photoshop tips, and for sharing his life with me.

Llumi and **Xixo** for chasing cherry tomatoes and each other around my office and for helping me think up examples of HTML documents.

Table of Contents

Table of Contents

Introduction

Why would you want to publish an HTML page? Simply, to communicate with the world. The World Wide Web is the Gutenberg press of our time. Practically anyone can publish any kind of information, including graphics, sound and even video, on the Web, opening the doors to each and every one of the millions of Internet users. Some are businesses with services to sell, others are individuals with stories to share. You decide how your page will be.

Recently, several programs have been released that let you create Web pages without learning HTML (Adobe PageMill, Claris HomePage, Microsoft Front Page). However, you are limited to the features that each program is capable of producing. You can take advantage of the shortcuts provided by such an HTML editor, and then add the features it may not yet recognize by using the techniques described in this book. That way, you get the best of both worlds.

In this book, you'll find clear, easy-to-follow instructions that will take you through the process of creating Web pages step-by-step. It is perfect for the beginner, with no knowledge of HTML, who wants to begin to create HTML pages.

You can also use the book as a reference, looking up topics in the hefty index and consulting just those subjects that you need information on.

More information about this book and on-line examples can be found at *http://www.peachpit.com/peachpit/features/htmlvqs/htmlvqs.html*. Or write me at *lcastro@cookwood.com*.

HTML and the Web

Somehow, it shouldn't be surprising that the lingua franca of the World Wide Web was developed in Switzerland, which has four official state languages. Perhaps acutely aware of how difficult it is for people to communicate without a common language, the programmers at the CERN research lab created a kind of Esperanto for computers: the Hypertext Markup Language, or HTML.

HTML allows you to format text, add rules, graphics, sound, and video and save it all in a text-only ASCII file that any computer can read. (Of course, to project video or play sounds, the computer must have the necessary hardware.) The key to HTML is in the *tags*, keywords enclosed in less than (<) and greater than (>) signs, that indicate what kind of content is coming up.

Of course, HTML just looks like a lot of text sprinkled with greater than and less than signs until you open the file with a special program called a *browser*. A browser can interpret the HTML tags and then show the formatted document on screen. For more information on browsers, consult *HTML browsers* on page 16.

HTML is not just another way to create beautiful documents, however. Its key ingredient is in the first part of its name: *Hypertext*. HTML documents can contain links to other HTML documents or to practically anything else on the Internet. This means that you can create several Web pages and have your users jump from one to another as needed. You can also create links to other organizations' Web pages, giving your users access to information held at other sites.

Figure i.1 *It doesn't matter if the original file is from a Windows machine (above), a Macintosh (right), or any other computer, as long as it uses HTML coding and is saved as a text-only file.*

onallthree.html

Figure i.2 *Each computer (Unix, top left, Windows, above and Mac, left) shows the HTML code in its own way. The results are actually very similar; the differences are mostly cosmetic.*

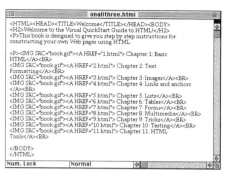

Figure i.3 *There is nothing in HTML code that cannot be expressed with simple numbers, letters, and symbols. This makes it easy for any kind of computer system to understand it.*

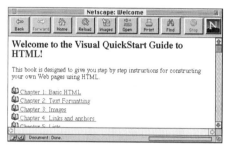

Figure i.4 *This is a browser on the Macintosh. Notice the graphic icons and different font sizes.*

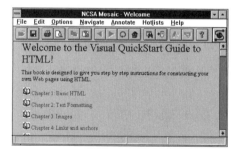

Figure i.5 *This is a browser in Windows showing the same HTML document. The differences are pretty minor.*

Users vs. Programmers

Think for a minute about the wide variety of computers that exist in the world. Each and every one of them can read HTML, but they all do it in a slightly different way—according to what is allowed in their particular operating system. For example, some computers can only display text: letters and numbers, a few symbols, but no graphics or color of any kind.

On the other hand, Windows and Macintosh systems were practically created with graphics and color in mind. Even so, Windows machines tend to be limited to displaying 256 colors while Macintoshes generally are not.

In addition, the way that your users will connect to the Internet may affect the way their computer can view Web pages. Even a Mac user won't be able to see the graphics on your pages if she is connected to the Web through a Unix shell account, or through Telnet.

Further, there is a big difference between the user who connects to the Web with a slow computer, through a slow modem, and the user who has a direct, high speed connection and a computer that can make the most of it. The first user will go crazy waiting for images to download while the second may not even notice a delay.

Finally, many browsers let the user decide how to view certain elements on a Web page. The user might be able to change the text and background colors, the text formatting, or even whether or not to show graphics.

Therefore, it is important to realize that each person who looks at your page may see it in a different way, according to the kind of computer system they have, the browser they have chosen, the graphics capacity they have, the speed of their modem and connection to the Web, and the settings they have chosen for their browser.

You, as the programmer or designer of the Web page, have *limited control* over how the page actually looks once it reaches your user, the person who is seeing your page through a browser. The primary concern of HTML is that your page be understandable by any computer, not that it be beautiful.

Many people are not satisfied with this lack of control. They add special effects to their pages with nonstandard HTML that may make the pages illegible to many browsers. Or they don't use alternative text for images, thereby restricting meaningful access to their pages to computers with graphics cards and fast Internet connections.

This one is your call. You decide how universal you want your document to be. On the continuum between plain Web pages that can be read by all and beautiful Web masterpieces that can be viewed by just a few, *you* must decide where your pages will fall.

In this book, I refer to the person who designs Web pages as *you* (or sometimes the programmer or designer). On the other hand, the *user* is the person who will look at your Web pages once you've published them.

Users vs. Programmers

Different versions of HTML

Democracy can be a great thing: many people give their input and a consensus is reached that aims to satisfy the largest group of people. The Internet is democracy in action. While the original HTML standard was developed by CERN, new versions are hashed out through a series of online meetings open to anyone on the Internet. Then they are analyzed, discussed, decided and published by the W3 Consortium, led by the Laboratory for Computer Science at the Massachusetts Institute of Technology (MIT) and INRIA, a French technology group, in collaboration with CERN.

There is one annoying thing about democracy: it's incredibly slow. At press time, although HTML 3.2 is considered the current standard, the actual guidelines had not yet been finalized. In addition, two commercial companies—Netscape Communications and Microsoft—continue to add features to their browsers without worrying much if these features will be supported by other browsers.

Although the features added by these two commercial giants may make pages more aesthetically pleasing, they also make pages less universal. Neither browser supports all the extensions of the other, thus the possibility that a page will look the same on both systems becomes more and more remote.

In this book, you will learn both standard HTML as well as the extensions developed by Netscape and Microsoft that have made these browsers so popular. Netscape extensions are marked with the Netscape Only icon while features only available for Microsoft's Internet Explorer are marked with the IE only icon **(Figure i.6)**.

Figure i.6 *HTML code that is only recognized by Netscape is marked with the N only icon (left). Code that is only recognized when viewed with Internet Explorer is marked with the IE only icon (right).*

HTML browsers

Perhaps the most important tool for creating HTML documents is the HTML browser. You might think that only your users need to have a browser, but you'd be wrong. It is absolutely vital that you have at least one, and preferably three or four of the principal browsers in use around the world. This way you can test your HTML pages and make sure that they look the way you want them to—regardless of the browser used.

Figure i.7 *This is Netscape 3 Gold for Windows showing Netscape Communications' home page.*

The two most popular browsers are Netscape Navigator (soon to be Communicator) and Microsoft Internet Explorer. Both are available on a variety of platforms.

Netscape Navigator

According to the latest statistics floating around the Net, Netscape Navigator (most often referred to simply as *Netscape*) is used by about 70% of the Web browsing public. Developed by some of the same engineers who created Mosaic, Netscape has distanced itself from the competition by offering non-standard features that make Netscape-enhanced pages much more attractive to the eye—if much more taxing on the modem. For more information, jump to *http://home.netscape.com* **(Figure i.7)**.

Figure i.8 *This is Internet Explorer 3 for Windows 95 showing Microsoft's Internet Explorer home page.*

Microsoft Internet Explorer

Thanks to Microsoft's hefty public relations team as well as to Internet Explorer's solid performance and acceptance of all of HTML 3.2's tags plus most of Netscape's proprietary extensions, Internet Explorer is quickly becoming a viable alternative to Netscape, used by some 25% of the Web public. For more information, jump to *http://www.microsoft.com/ie/* **(Figure i.8)**.

Basic HTML

Tags in this book

In this book, all tags and attributes are written in ALL CAPS, and all values are shown in lower case letters. HTML does not require this system; I use it here solely to help distinguish the tags, attributes, and values from the surrounding text in the examples.

Writing HTML

You can create an HTML document with any word processor or text editor, including the very basic TeachText or SimpleText on the Mac and Notepad or Wordpad for Windows, both of which come free with the corresponding system software.

Nevertheless, there are certain tools that may help you create HTML documents. These are discussed in Appendix A, *HTML Tools*.

HTML Tags

HTML tags are commands written between less than (<) and greater than (>) signs, also known as *angle brackets*, that indicate how the browser should display the text **(Figure 1.1)**. There are opening and closing versions for many (but not all) tags, and the affected text is *contained* within the two tags. Both the opening and closing tags use the same command word but the closing tag carries an initial extra forward slash symbol /.

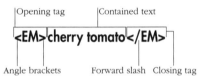

Figure 1.1 *The anatomy of an HTML tag. Notice there are no extra spaces between the contained text and the angle brackets (greater than and less than signs).*

Attributes

Many tags have special attributes that offer a variety of options for the contained text. The attribute is entered between the command word and the final greater than symbol **(Figure 1.2)**. Often, you can use a series of attributes in a single tag. Simply write one after the other, with a space between each one.

Figure 1.2 *Some tags can take optional attributes that further define the formatting desired.*

Values

Attributes in turn often have *values*. In some cases, you must pick a value from a small group of choices. For example, the CLEAR attribute for the BR tag can take values of *left, right,* or *all*. Any other value given will be ignored **(Figure 1.3)**.

Other attributes are more strict about the *type* of values they accept. For example, the HSPACE attribute of the IMG tag will accept only integers as its value, and the SRC attribute of the IMG tag will only accept URLs for its value **(Figure 1.4)**.

Quotation marks

Generally speaking, attributes that accept any value require that you enclose the value in straight quotation marks (") NOT curly ones (""). It is a good idea to use quotes around any URL to ensure that it is not misinterpreted by the server.

Nesting tags

In some cases, you may want to modify your page contents with more than one tag. For example, you may want to add italic formatting to a word inside a header. There are two things to keep in mind here. First, not all tags can contain all other kinds of tags. In this book, each tag's description details which other tags it may contain and which tags it may not.

Second, order is everything. Whenever you use a closing tag it should correspond to the last unclosed opening tag. In other words, first A then B, then /B, and then /A **(Figure 1.5)**.

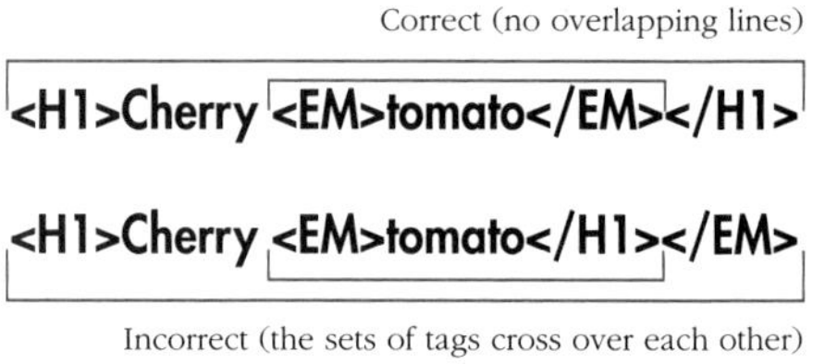

Figure 1.3 *Some tags, like BR shown here, take attributes with given values, of which you can choose only one. You don't need to enclose one word values in quotation marks.*

Figure 1.4 *Some tags, like IMG shown here, can take more than one attribute, each with its own values.*

Correct (no overlapping lines)

<H1>Cherry <EM>tomato</EM></H1>

<H1>Cherry <EM>tomato</H1></EM>

Incorrect (the sets of tags cross over each other)

Figure 1.5 *To make sure your tags are correctly nested, connect each set with a line. None of your sets of tags should overlap any other set; each interior set should be completely enclosed within the next larger set.*

Figure 1.6 *Your basic URL contains a protocol, server name, path and file name.*

Figure 1.7 *A URL with a trailing forward slash and no file name points to the default file in the last directory named (in this case the* liz *directory). The default file on many servers is* index.html.

Figure 1.8 *When the user clicks this URL, the browser will begin an FTP transfer of the file* prog.exe.

Figure 1.9 *A URL for a newsgroup looks a bit different. There are no forward slashes after the protocol and colon, and generally, there is no file name. (Although you could add the message number or ID, a message's extremely short lifespan limits its usefulness as a link.)*

"mailto:lcastro@cookwood.com"

Figure 1.10 *A URL for an e-mail address is similar in design to a newsgroup URL (Figure 1.9); it includes the mailto protocol followed by a colon but no forward slashes, and then the e-mail address itself.*

URLs

Uniform resource locator, or URL, is a fancy name for *address*. It contains information about where a file is and what a browser should do with it. Each file on the Internet has a unique URL.

The first part of the URL is called the *protocol*. It tells the browser how to deal with the file that it is about to open. One of the most common protocols you will see is HTTP, or Hypertext Transfer Protocol. It is used to access Web pages **(Figure 1.6)**.

The second part of the URL is the name of the server where the file is located, followed by the path that leads to the file and the file's name itself. Sometimes, a URL ends in a trailing forward slash with no file name given **(Figure 1.7)**. In this case the URL refers to the default file in the last directory in the path (which generally corresponds to the home page).

Other common protocols are HTTPS, for secure Web pages, FTP (File Transfer Protocol) for downloading files from the Net **(Figure 1.8)**, Gopher, for searching for information, News, for sending and reading messages posted to a Usenet newsgroup **(Figure 1.9)**, and Mailto, for sending electronic mail **(Figure 1.10)**.

A protocol is generally followed by a colon and two forward slashes. Mailto and News are the major exceptions; these take only a colon. Always type protocols in lower case letters.

Absolute URLs

URLs can be either absolute or relative. An *absolute URL* shows the entire path to the file, including the protocol, server name, the complete path and the file name itself. An absolute URL is analogous to a complete street address, including name, street and number, city, state, zip code, and country. No matter where a letter is sent from, the post office will be able to find the recipient. In terms of URLs, this means that the location of the absolute URL itself has no bearing on the location of the actual file referenced—whether it is in a Web page on your server or on mine, an absolute URL will look exactly the same.

If you're referencing a file from someone else's server, you'll have to use an absolute URL. You'll also need to use absolute URLs for FTP and Gopher sites and for Newsgroups and e-mail addresses—in short, any kind of URL that doesn't use an HTTP protocol.

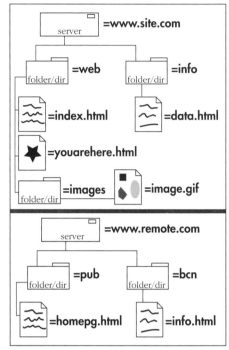

Figure 1.11 *Here is a typical, but simple representation of two servers (or hard disks), and the files that each contains. The table below shows the relative URLs for each file that you would use when writing the* youarehere.html *file. The absolute URLs shown would work in* any *file.*

File name	Absolute URL (anywhere)	Relative URL (in *youarehere.html*)
index.html	www.site.com/web/index.html	index.html
image.gif	www.site.com/web/images/image.gif	/images/image.gif
data.html	www.site.com/info/data.html	../info/data.html
homepg.html	www.remote.com/pub/homepg.html	*(none: use absolute)*
info.html	www.remote.com/bcn/info.html	*(none: use absolute)*

Absolute URLs vs. Relative URLs

URLs

File name

Figure 1.12 *The relative URL for a file in the same folder (see Figure 1.11) as the file that contains the link is just the file's name and extension.*

Inside the current folder...
...there's a folder called "images"...

"/images/image.gif"

...that contains...
...a file called "image.gif".

Figure 1.13 *For a file that is within a folder inside the current folder (see Figure 1.11), add a forward slash and the folder's name in front of the file name.*

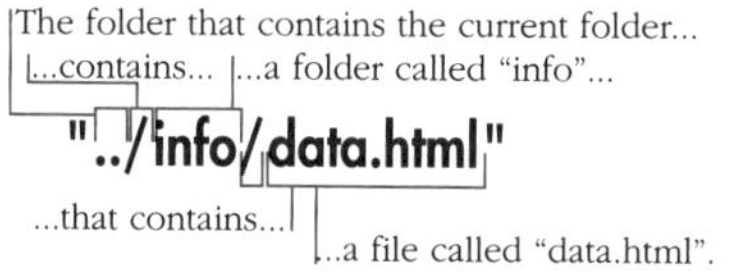

The folder that contains the current folder...
...contains... ...a folder called "info"...

"../info/data.html"

...that contains...
...a file called "data.html".

Figure 1.14 *This file, as you can see in Figure 1.11, is in a folder that is inside the folder that contains the current folder (whew!). In that case, you use two periods (..) to go up a level, and the customary forward slash to go back down.*

Relative URLs

To give you directions to my neighbor's house, instead of giving her complete address, I might just say "it's three doors down on the right". This is a *relative* address—where it points to depends on where the information is given from. With the same information in a different city, you'd never find my neighbor.

In the same way, a *relative URL* describes the location of the desired file with reference to the location of the file that contains the URL itself. So, you might have the URL say something like "show the xyz image that's in the same directory as the current file".

Thus, the relative URL for a file that is in the same directory as the current file (that is, the one containing the URL in question) is simply the file name and extension **(Figure 1.12)**. You create the URL for a file in a subdirectory of the current directory by placing a forward slash (/) before the name of the subdirectory and following it with another forward slash and then the name and extension of the desired file **(Figure 1.13)**.

To reference a file in a directory at a *higher* level of the file hierarchy, use two periods (..) **(Figure 1.14)**. You can combine and repeat the two periods and forward slash to reference any file on the same hard disk as the current file.

Generally, you should always use relative URLs. They're much easier to type and they make it easy to move your pages from a local system to a server—as long as the relative position of each file remains constant, the links will work correctly.

One added advantage of relative URLs is that you don't have to type the protocol—as long as it's HTTP.

URLs

Special symbols

The standard ASCII set contains 128 characters and can be used perfectly well for English documents. However, accents, diacritical marks, and many commonly used symbols unfortunately cannot be found in this group. Luckily, HTML can contain any character in the full ISO Latin-1 character set (also known as ISO 8859-1). In Windows and Unix systems, simply enter the character in the usual (convoluted) way and it will display properly in the browser.

Watch out! Even though you can type special characters, accents and so on in your Macintosh and DOS based PC, these systems do not use the standard ISO Latin-1 character set for the characters numbered 129-255 and will not display them correctly in the Web page. You must enter these special characters with either *name* or *number codes* **(Figure 1.15)**.

Name codes are more descriptive (and are case sensitive), like è for é and Ñ for Ñ. However, not every character has a name code. In that case, you will need to use a number code, which is composed of an ampersand, number symbol, the character number in the Latin-1 character set and a semicolon. The number code for é is é and for Ñ is Ñ. See *Special Symbols* on page 233 for a complete listing and more instructions.

There are four symbols that have special meanings in HTML documents. These are the greater than (>), less than (<), double quotation marks (") and ampersand (&). If you simply type them in your HTML document, the browser may attempt to interpret them **(Figure 1.16)**. To show the symbols themselves, use a name or number code.

Typing a ç on a Mac gets you a Ÿ. (In DOS, you'd get a ‡.)

`<H1>Visca el Barça</H1>`

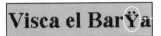

The number code for ç

`<H1>Visca el Bar&#231;a</H1>`

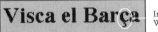

In the Web page

Figure 1.15 *To display a ç properly, you must use either its number or its name. It looks awful in your HTML document, but on the Web page, where it counts, it's beautiful.*

If you type < and > ...

Use <BR> for line breaks

...the BR tag is interpreted and creates a line break

If you use name codes for < and >...

Use <BR> for line breaks

...the symbols are shown but not interpreted

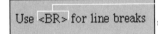

Figure 1.16 *You must use name or number codes to show the symbols <, >, " and & on your Web page. See Special Symbols on page 233 for details.*

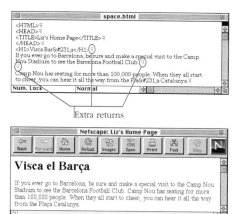

Extra returns

Figure 1.17 *Extra returns and spaces help distinguish the different parts of the HTML document in the text editor but are completely ignored by the browser.*

Paragraph tag

Figure 1.18 *I've removed all the returns from the document in Figure 1.17, but added a single <P> tag. The only difference in the final result is from the new tag.*

Spacing

HTML browsers will ignore any extra spaces that exist between the tags in your HTML document. You can use this to your advantage by adding spaces and returns to help view the elements in your HTML document more clearly while you're writing and designing your page **(Figure 1.17)**.

On the other hand, you won't be able to count on returns or spaces to format your document. A return at the end of a paragraph in your HTML document will not appear in the browsed page. Instead, use a P tag to begin each new paragraph **(Figure 1.18)**.

Further, you cannot repeat several P (or BR) tags to add space between paragraphs. The extra tags are simply ignored.

Netscape has developed an extension to help designers better control the spacing in their documents. It's not quite "basic" though and will be discussed on page 83. You might also consult the section on pixel shims, discussed on page 86.

Tags with automatic line breaks

Some tags include automatic, logical line breaks. For example, you don't need to use a new paragraph marker after a header, since a header automatically includes a line break. In fact, inserting a new paragraph marker after a header has no effect whatsoever.

Spacing

Starting and finishing an HTML document

When a user jumps to the URL that corresponds to your Web page, the browser needs information right away about what kind of document it is, and how it should be displayed. It gets this information from the !DOCTYPE and HTML tags. The !DOCTYPE tag, which is *required* for HTML 3.2 documents, identifies the version of HTML contained in the file so that browsers know what to expect. The HTML tag identifies the file as HTML code so that it can be recognized by other applications across the Internet.

To start and finish an HTML 3.2 document:

1. Type **<!DOCTYPE HTML PUBLIC "-//W3C//DTD HTML 3.2 Final//EN"> <HTML>**.

2. Create your HTML document.

3. Type **</HTML>**.

✔ Tips

■ Theoretically, the !DOCTYPE tag is required while the HTML tag is not. In fact, most browsers will recognize HTML pages correctly without either tag. It's a good idea to always include both in order to ensure that your document is correctly recognized, regardless of the browser used.

■ For writing files with HTML 2.0, use the following: **<!DOCTYPE HTML PUBLIC "-//IETF//DTD HTML 2.0//EN">**

■ Create an HTML document template with the opening and closing !DOCTYPE and HTML tags already typed in as a starting place for all your HTML documents.

Figure 1.19 *The !DOCTYPE and HTML tags identify your document so that the browser knows what to do with it.*

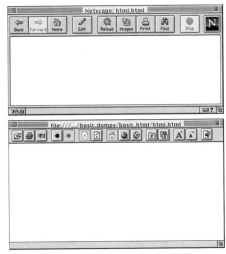

Figure 1.20 *An empty HTML document will appear empty in the browser as well (Netscape top, Internet Explorer, bottom), with the file name as the title (including the path, in IE).*

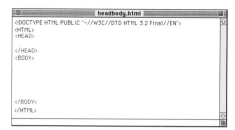

Figure 1.21 *Every HTML document should be divided into a HEAD and a BODY.*

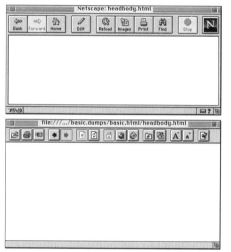

Figure 1.22 *With no title and no contents, the browsers have to scrape together a little substance (in the form of a title) from the file name of the HTML document (including the path, in IE).*

The HEAD and BODY

The HEAD section provides information about the URL of your Web page as well as its relationship with the other pages at your site. The only element in the HEAD section that is visible to the user is the title of the Web page *(see page 26).*

To create the HEAD section:

1. Directly after the initial !DOCTYPE and HTML tags *(see page 24),* type **<HEAD>**.

2. Create the HEAD section, including the TITLE *(see page 26)* and the BASE *(see page 92),* if desired.

3. Type **</HEAD>**.

The BODY of your HTML document contains the bulk of your Web page, including all the text, graphics and formatting.

To create the BODY:

1. After the final </HEAD> tag and before anything else, type **<BODY>**.

2. Create the contents of your Web page.

3. Type **</BODY>**.

✔ Tip

■ For pages with frames, the BODY section must be contained within the NOFRAMES tags. For more information, consult *Creating alternatives to frames* on page 152.

The HEAD and BODY

Creating a title

Each HTML page must have a title. A title should be short and descriptive. In some browsers, the title appears in the title bar of the window; in others, the title is centered at the top of the screen. The title is used in indexes as well as in browsers' history lists and bookmarks.

Figure 1.23 *The TITLE tag is the only element in the HEAD section that is visible to the user. It is a required element.*

To create a title:

1. Place the cursor between the opening and closing HEAD tags *(see page 25)*.

2. Type **<TITLE>**.

3. Enter the title of your web page.

4. Type **</TITLE>**.

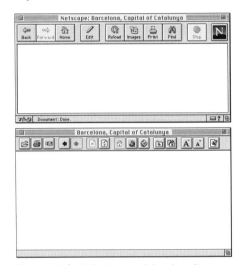

Figure 1.24 *Both Netscape (above) and Internet Explorer show the title of a Web page in the title bar of the window.*

✔ Tips

- A title cannot contain any formatting, images, or links to other pages.

- Don't use colons or backslashes in your titles. These symbols cannot be used by some operating systems for file names, and if someone tries to save your page as text (or source HTML), they will have to remove the offending character manually.

- It's a good idea to use a common element to begin each page's title. For example, you could begin each page with "XYZ Company -" followed by the specific area described on that page.

- If your title has special characters like accents or foreign letters, you'll have to format these characters with their name or number codes. Consult *Special Symbols* on page 233 for more information.

- There must be one and only one TITLE tag in each HTML 3.2 document.

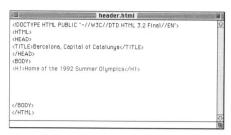

Figure 1.25 *Don't repeat the information from your title in the header. The header should help organize the information on the page in sections while the title summarizes that information.*

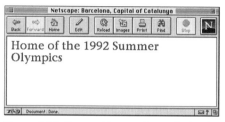

Figure 1.26 *Because Netscape has wider borders around its browser window, the header doesn't fit on one line. Of course, the size and font used depend on the user's preferences.*

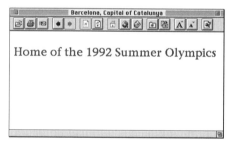

Figure 1.27 *Internet Explorer leaves a larger margin of blank space between the top of the page and the beginning of the text.*

Organizing the page

HTML provides for up to six levels of headers in your Web page. You will seldom have to use more than three. Since headers can be used to compile a table of contents of your Web pages, you should be as consistent as possible when applying them.

To use headers to organize your Web page:

1. In the BODY section of your HTML document, type **<Hn**, where *n* is a number from 1 to 6, depending on the level of header that you want to create.

2. If desired, to align the header, type **ALIGN=direction**, where *direction* is left, right, or center.

3. Type **>**.

4. Type the contents of the header.

5. Type **</Hn>** where *n* is the same number used in step 1.

✔ Tips

■ Think of your headers as chapter names—they are hierarchical dividers. Use them consistently.

■ Headers are formatted logically: the higher the level (the smaller the number), the more prominently the header will be displayed.

■ Add a named anchor to your headers so that you can create links directly to that header from a different web page *(see page 95)*.

■ Headers have an automatic line break; there is no need to add an additional one (nor any advantage in doing so).

Organizing the page

Starting a new paragraph

HTML does not recognize the returns that you enter in your text editor. To start a new paragraph in your Web page, you must use the P tag.

To begin a new paragraph:

1. Type **<P**.

2. If desired, to align the text in the paragraph, type **ALIGN=direction**, where *direction* is left, right or center.

3. Type **>**.

4. Type the contents of the new paragraph.

5. If desired, you may type **</P>** to end the paragraph, but it is not necessary.

✔ Tip

■ The header (Hn) and horizontal rule (HR) tags include automatic paragraph markers, so you don't need to add a <P> to start a new paragraph after using them **(Figure 1.28)**.

Figure 1.28 *Since headers include automatic line breaks, there is no need to include a <P> before the first paragraph. You do need to insert a <P> before the second paragraph.*

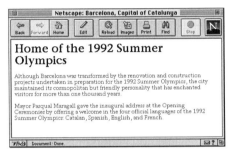

Figure 1.29 *The amount of space inserted with a <P> tag depends on the size of the text surrounding it. For more controlled spacing, see page 83.*

Figure 1.30 *Notice how the divisions from line to line are different from browser to browser (Netscape above, IE below). It is important to realize just what you can and cannot control.*

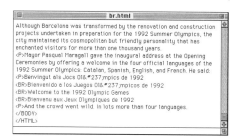

Figure 1.31 *I've used a P tag to start the first line to set the group off from the remaining text. Then, each "welcome" is separated with a line break.*

Figure 1.32 *I have to admit, I don't actually remember what Maragall said in French. Perhaps he was drowned out by the crowd and I didn't hear him...*

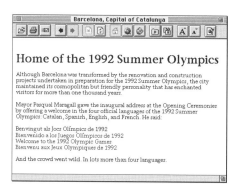

Figure 1.33 *The page looks almost identical in Internet Explorer.*

Creating a line break

When you start a new paragraph with the P tag (described on the previous page), most browsers insert a large amount of space. To begin a new line without so much space, use a line break.

The BR tag is perfect for poems or other short lines of text that should appear one after another without a lot of space in between.

To insert a line break:

Type **
** where the line break should occur. There is no closing BR tag.

✔ Tips

- You can use special values with the BR tag for creating line breaks with text that is wrapped around images. For more information, consult *Stopping text wrap* on page 63.

- Netscape has created special extensions for controlling the space between lines. For more information, consult *Creating indents* on page 83. You can also use a transparent image to create the proper amount of space between lines. For more information on this technique, consult *Using pixel shims* on page 86.

Creating a line break

Adding comments to your pages

One diagnostic tool available to every HTML author is the addition of comments to your HTML documents to remind you (or future editors) what you were trying to achieve with your HTML tags.

These comments appear only in the HTML document when opened with a text or HTML editor. They will be completely invisible to the user.

To add comments to your HTML page:

1. In your HTML document, where you wish to insert comments, type **<!--**.

2. Type the comments.

3. Type **-->** to complete the commented text.

✔ Tips

■ Comments are particularly useful for describing why you used a particular tag and what effect you were hoping to achieve.

■ Another good use for comments is to remind yourself (or future editors) to include, remove, or update certain sections.

■ View your commented page with a browser before publishing (see Chapter 14, *Publishing*) to avoid sharing your (possibly) private comments with your public.

■ Beware, however, of comments that are *too* private. While invisible in the browser, they cheerfully reappear when the user saves the page as HTML code (source).

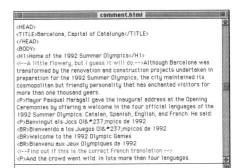

Figure 1.34 *Comments are a great way to add reminders to your text. You can also use them to keep track of revisions.*

Figure 1.35 *The comments are completely invisible to the user when the page is viewed in a browser (Netscape above, IE below)—unless she decides to download the source HTML.*

Text Formatting

Formatting text in a Web page is much different from formatting text in any kind of desktop publishing program for one simple reason: you cannot completely control how your user will view the document. Some of your users may view your Web page with Netscape on the Mac while others may see it with Internet Explorer for Windows. Still others may use a non-graphical browser like Lynx. None of these programs shows text formatting in exactly the same way.

Until recently, Web page designers were quite limited in their choices of text formatting. With HTML 3.2, however, and the advent of the FONT tag in particular—which lets you change the size, color and typeface of any number of letters on your page—Web pages have become downright attractive, at least when viewed with Netscape or Internet Explorer.

Like the popular desktop publishing programs, you can choose between character-level and paragraph-level formatting. The former affects one or more characters, the latter affects an entire paragraph.

HTML also offers *logical formatting*, which defines an area of your document according to its use. Each browser then formats the affected area as best it can, given the platform's strengths and limitations. The great advantage of logical formatting is that while the actual formatting may not be the same from browser to browser, the effect is. While one browser may show emphasis (see page 32) in italics while another shows it in bold, each browser will have emphasized the text in the most effective way it has.

Text Formatting

Emphasizing text logically

HTML provides two ways to emphasize your text: with logical markers that identify your text as "emphatic" or "strong" and with physical markers that identify the text as "bold" or "italic". Logical markers allow the *browser* (and sometimes the users) to choose how to view important text—perhaps in bold red lettering— while physical formatting appears how you, the page's *designer,* intended, as long as the browser supports your formatting choices.

To emphasize text logically:

1. Type **<EM>** or **<STRONG>**. Text formatted with EM generally appears in italics. Text formatted with STRONG most often appears in bold. In some browsers, the user can change the display of either of these two formats.

2. Type the emphatic or strong text.

3. Type **</EM>** or **</STRONG>**.

✔ Tips

■ Logical formatting ensures that the text will receive some formatting in the event that the browser does not recognize certain types of physical formatting.

■ Don't emphasize everything. If you shout everything at your viewers, you will lose their confidence and their attention.

■ You may not add emphasis to titles or form elements. In some browsers, block quotes can include the EM tag but not the STRONG tag.

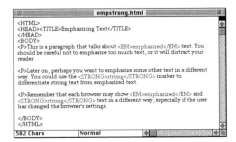

Figure 2.1 *Creating emphatic or strong text on your Web page is as simple as adding the appropriate marker before and after the text to be formatted.*

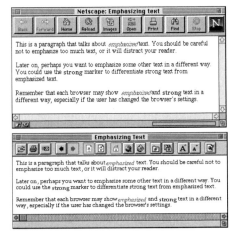

Figure 2.2 *Both Netscape (above) and Internet Explorer—and indeed most other browsers— display emphatic text in italics and strong text in bold.*

Figure 2.3 *You may use bold or italic formatting anywhere in your HTML document, except in the TITLE.*

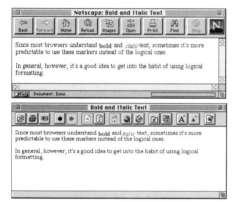

Figure 2.4 *In most browsers, including Netscape (above) and Internet Explorer, the bold and italic formatting are identical to strong and emphatic formatting, respectively.*

Making text bold or italic

There are several physical markers you can use to make your text stand out. In general, you should use logical formatting (EM and STRONG) for making text bold and italic, respectively *(see page 32)*. Use physical formatting when you don't want the user to be able to change the display of the text.

To make text bold:

1. Type **<B>**.

2. Type the text that you want to make bold.

3. Type **</B>**.

To make text italic:

1. Type **<I>**.

2. Type the text that you want to make italic.

3. Type **</I>**.

✔ Tips

■ Remember that not all browsers can display text in bold and italics. If they do not recognize the tags, the text will have no formatting at all.

■ You may use CITE (the logical tag for marking citations) to make text italic, although it is less widely recognized and less widely used than the I marker.

Making text bold or italic

Using a monospaced font

If you are displaying computer codes, URLs, or other text that you wish to offset from the main page, you can format it with a monospaced font. There are several markers that use a monospaced font as their principal attribute: CODE (computer code), KBD (keyboard input), SAMP (sample text) and TT (typewriter text), only the last of which is considered physical formatting.

To format text with a monospaced font:

1. Type **<CODE>**, **<KBD>**, **<SAMP>**, or **<TT>**.

2. Type the text that you want to display in a monospaced font.

3. Type **</CODE>**, **</KBD>**, **</SAMP>**, or **</TT>**. Use the marker that matches the code you chose in step 1.

✔ Tips

■ TT is the monospaced font marker that is used most often.

■ Remember that the monospaced font markers will not have a very dramatic effect in browsers that display all their text in monospaced fonts (like Lynx).

■ To format several lines of monospaced text, you should use the PRE marker *(see page 38)*.

■ Internet Explorer reduces the size of monospaced text by one unit, with respect to the body text. Netscape displays monospaced text according to the settings chosen in the Fonts tab of the General Preferences dialog box.

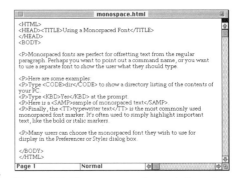

Figure 2.5 *There are several ways to format your text with a monospaced font. TT is the most common.*

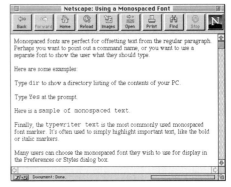

Figure 2.6 *Netscape displays monospaced text in the font and size chosen for "fixed width" text in the Fonts tab of the General Preferences dialog box.*

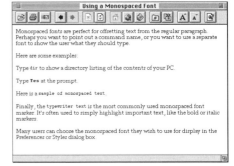

Figure 2.7 *Internet Explorer only lets its users choose the font for monospaced text (in this example, it's Courier, as in Figure 2.6 above). However, IE then reduces the size of all monospaced text by one unit. In addition, the KBD tagged text is rendered in bold.*

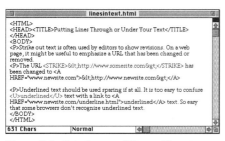

Figure 2.8 *Note the use of < and > to produce the less than and greater than symbols as shown below.*

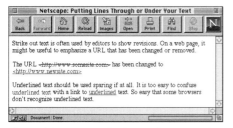

Figure 2.9 *Netscape displays strike out text, but not underlined text.*

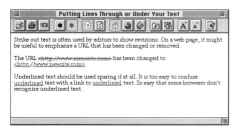

Figure 2.10 *Internet Explorer displays both strike out and underlined text. Notice, however, how confusing the underlined text can be, especially on a monochrome screen.*

Striking out or underlining text

A few browsers can display lines either through or under text. Strike out text is most useful to show revisions to text. Underlining is another way of emphasizing text.

To strike out or underline text:

1. Type **<STRIKE>** or **<U>** for strike out text and underlining, respectively.

2. Type the text that should appear with a line through or under it.

3. Type **</STRIKE>** or **</U>**.

✔ Tips

■ Netscape and Internet Explorer both understand the shorthand S tag in place of the standard STRIKE tag. It is possible that the new, shorter tag will replace the older one in future revisions of HTML.

■ Some browsers don't understand the STRIKE or U tags and will display the strike out or underlined text with no formatting at all.

■ Users with black and white or grayscale screens often use underlining to indicate links to other web pages. You may confuse them by underlining text that does not bring them to a new page.

■ Lynx displays EM and STRONG text with an underline. Users may be confused by further underlining.

Using superscripts and subscripts

Letters or numbers that are raised or lowered slightly relative to the main body text are called superscripts and subscripts, respectively. HTML 3.2 includes tags for defining both kinds of offset text.

To create superscripts or subscripts:

1. Type **<SUB>** to create a subscript or **<SUP>** to create a superscript.

2. Type the characters or symbols that you wish to offset relative to the main text.

3. Type **</SUB>** or **</SUP>**, depending on what you used in step 1, to complete the offset text.

Figure 2.11 *The opening SUP or SUB tag precedes the text to be affected.*

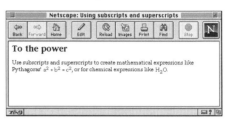

Figure 2.12 *Although earlier versions of Netscape were unable to display subscripts and superscripts, Netscape 2 and 3 have no trouble with them at all.*

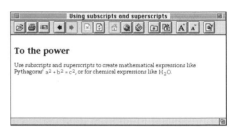

Figure 2.13 *Internet Explorer also displays superscripts and subscripts correctly.*

Using superscripts and subscripts

Figure 2.14 *A block quote can be as short or as long as you need. You can even divide it into various paragraphs by adding P tags as necessary.*

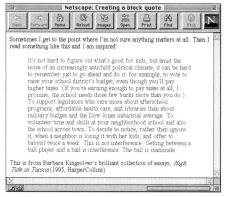

Figure 2.15 *Netscape centers a block quote, indenting it to se it off from the surrounding text.*

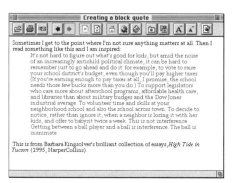

Figure 2.16 *Internet Explorer doesn't add a line break before the block quote and as a result, it gets jammed up against the preceding line.*

Using block quotes

You can use block quotes to set off a section of your text—like a quotation by a famous author—from the surrounding text. As usual, different browsers display block quotes in different ways. Some center the text in an indented paragraph in the middle of the page, while others simply italicize the special text.

To create a block quote:

1. Type **<BLOCKQUOTE>**.

2. Type the desired HTML formatting for the text, like **<P>**, for example.

3. Type the text that you wish to appear set off from the preceding and following text.

4. Complete the HTML tag begun in step 2, if necessary.

5. Type **</BLOCKQUOTE>**.

✔ Tips

■ Text should not be placed directly between the opening and closing BLOCKQUOTE tags, but rather between other HTML tags within the BLOCKQUOTE tags. (However, many browsers will display a block quote correctly even if you ignore this rule.)

■ Block quotes can contain additional text formatting like STRONG or EM.

Using preformatted text

Usually, each browser decides where to divide each line of text, depending mostly on the window size, and eliminates extra spaces and returns. Preformatted text lets you maintain the original line breaks and spacing that you've inserted in the text. It is ideal for homemade tables and ASCII art.

To use preformatted text:

1. Type **<PRE>**.

2. Type the text that you wish to preformat, with all the necessary spaces, returns and line breaks.

3. Type **</PRE>**.

✔ Tips

■ Use a monospaced font in your text or HTML editor when composing the preformatted text so that you can see what it will look like in the browser.

■ You can insert additional formatting (like STRONG or EM) within preformatted text **(Figures 2.19 and 2.20)**. However, you should do it *after* you set up your text, since the tags take up space in the HTML document, but not in the page.

■ You can make homemade tables with preformatted text just by controlling the spaces between column entries. These tables will be readable by *all* browsers, not just the ones that currently support official tables.

■ Use PRE to format an image's alternative text. This allows you to use an ASCII image as alternative text.

Figure 2.17 *By using a monospaced font in your text editor, you can see just how the preformatted text will appear.*

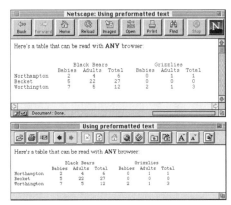

Figure 2.18 *Both Netscape (above) and Internet Explorer show preformatted text with a monospaced font (and one size smaller in IE).*

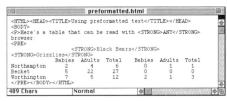

Figure 2.19 *Make sure you don't format the spaces in preformatted text. A bold space takes up more room than a regular one and may throw off your alignment.*

Figure 2.20 *Although the headers looked badly aligned in the HTML document (Figure 2.19), they look fine both in Netscape (shown) and Internet Explorer when the tags disappear.*

Figure 2.21 *Don't choose a basefont size that is too large to fit comfortably in your users' screens.*

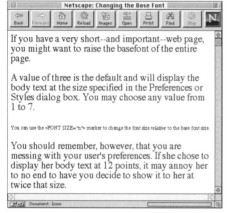

Figure 2.22 *You should have a good reason to change the base font size. Remember that your users have probably already chosen how they prefer to view text.*

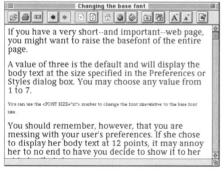

Figure 2.23 *Most browsers, including Internet Explorer, shown here, now recognize the BASE-FONT tag.*

Changing the font size of all the body text

Although your users generally will specify for themselves the size of the text on the pages they view, you can also have a hand in the process. The BASEFONT tag changes the size of all of the body text, but has no effect whatsoever on headers. The FONT, BIG, and SMALL tags, described on the following pages, can be used to change the size of individual characters.

To change the font size of all the body text:

1. Type **<BASEFONT**.

2. Type **SIZE="n">** where *n* is a number from 1 to 7. The default is 3, which displays the font at the size the user has chosen in the Preferences or Styles dialog box.

✔ Tips

■ Use a slightly larger basefont in short web pages to give more importance to the whole page. Use a smaller basefont in lengthy text-intensive pages to fit more text on a page.

■ Only use one BASEFONT tag in each HTML document. The tag affects all the succeeding text. To change the font size of individual characters, use the FONT marker *(see page 40)*.

■ The BASEFONT tag has no affect on headers. Be careful, then, not to make the body text larger than the headers, or you'll confuse your readers.

Changing the font size of a few letters

A good way to make your text stand out is to change the font size of a few characters or a few words.

To change the font size of one or more characters:

1. Type **<FONT**.

2. Type **SIZE="n">** where *n* is a number from 1 to 7. You may also use *+n* and *-n* to denote a value relative to the BASEFONT value *(see page 39)*.

3. Type the text whose font size you wish to change.

4. Type **</FONT>**.

✔ Tips

■ Use the FONT marker to change the font size of just a few characters or a few words. Use BASEFONT to change the font size of the whole document.

■ A value of 3 represents the size that the user has chosen for text in the Preferences dialog box or the default font size used by the browser.

■ You can make fisheye designs by changing the FONT size of each letter in a word in an ascending and then descending pattern.

■ The FONT tag is also used to change the color and typeface of individual letters.

Figure 2.24 *The big differences between FONT and BASEFONT, as illustrated here, are that FONT can use relative values and depend on the BASEFONT value, and that it affects individual characters, instead of the entire page.*

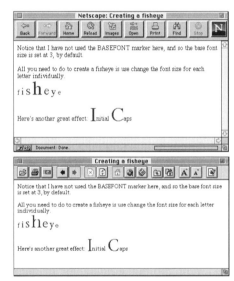

Figure 2.25 *You can create some interesting effects by raising or lowering the font size of individual characters. Both Netscape (above) and Internet Explorer understand the FONT tag.*

Figure 2.26 The BIG and SMALL tags are part of the standard version of HTML 3.2.

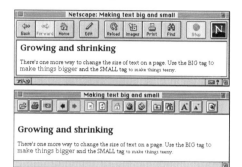

Figure 2.27 As long as the text is normal size (3), both Netscape and Internet Explorer display BIG and SMALL text in the same way.

Figure 2.28 The only difference between this HTML document and the one shown in Figure 2.26 is the addition of the BASEFONT tag.

Figure 2.29 In Netscape, with a BASEFONT of size 4, the BIG text is still bigger and the SMALL text is still smaller than the body text.

Figure 2.30 In Internet Explorer with a BASE-FONT of 4, the BIG text is not effective, since it, too, is always shown at size 4.

Using BIG and SMALL to change the size

The BIG and SMALL tags were meant to change the relative size of a given word or phrase with respect to the surrounding text. Unfortunately, not all browsers display the effect of BIG and SMALL properly, and when combined with the BASEFONT or FONT tags, the results can be unexpected.

To change font size with BIG and SMALL:

1. Type **<BIG>** or **<SMALL>** before the text that you wish to make bigger or smaller, respectively.

2. Type the text that should be bigger or smaller.

3. Type **</BIG>** or **</SMALL>** according to the tag used in step 1.

✓ Tips

■ Netscape takes an intelligent approach to BIG and SMALL. Text formatted with BIG is always one size larger than the surrounding text, unless the surrounding text is size 7, in which case BIG has no effect. Text formatted with SMALL is one size smaller, unless the surrounding text is size 2 or less, in which case SMALL has no effect **(Figure 2.29)**.

■ Internet Explorer, on the other hand, *always* shows BIG text at size 4 and SMALL text at size 2. If you've changed the size of the body text with the BASEFONT or FONT tags, the result may not be "big" or "small" text, but just the opposite, or perhaps no change at all **(Figure 2.30)**.

Changing the font

Ever since the Web was flooded with pages from the general public, designers have chafed under the restrictions imposed on font usage. In order to make Web pages more universal, early versions of HTML did not allow the designer to specify a particular font. HTML 3.2, however, pushed by Netscape and Microsoft, does let you choose exactly what fonts you'd *prefer* to have the page (or just a portion of the text) displayed in. If the user does not have the desired fonts, the text is rendered in the default font.

To change the font:

1. Before the text to be changed, type **<FONT FACE="fontname1**, where *fontname1* is your first choice of fonts. Type the complete name of the desired font, including the style.

2. If desired, type **, fontname2**, where *fontname2* is your second choice of fonts, should the user not have the first font in his system software. Each successive font should be separated from the previous one by a comma.

3. Repeat step 2 for each additional font choice.

4. Type **">** to complete the FONT tag.

5. Type the text that will be displayed in the given font.

6. Type **</FONT>**.

✔ Tip

■ The FONT tag is also used to change the size *(see page 40)* and the color *(see page 43)* of the text. You can combine all attributes in the same tag, e.g., **<FONT SIZE=10 FACE="Gara-mond Bold" COLOR="#121212">**.

Figure 2.31 *You may list as many fonts as you wish in each FONT tag in order of preference. Separate each choice with a comma and a space. Don't forget to add the desired style (Bold, Condensed, etc.)*

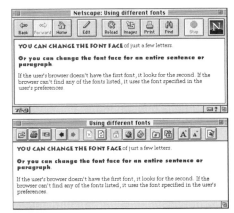

Figure 2.32 *Both Netscape (above) and Internet Explorer, show fonts almost identically. Note that only Lithos, in the first paragraph, and Futura ExtraBold—but not New Century—in the second paragraph, were available on this system. The last paragraph is displayed in the default font since neither of the special fonts chosen was available on the system.*

Figure 2.33 *Remember to select a text color that works well with your background color. (If you don't specify the background color, it will be either be gray, by default, or the color the user chooses in the Preferences dialog box.)*

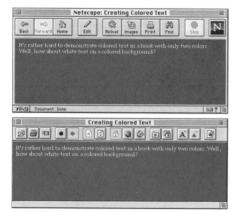

Figure 2.34 *Although this example is pretty basic, you can see that changing the color of your text can give your Web pages an immediate impact, whether it be in Netscape (above) or Internet Explorer.*

Changing the color of all of the body text

The TEXT marker gives you, the designer, the power to change the color of the text. Although most browsers have no problem with colored text, it will not be appreciated by users with black and white or grayscale monitors.

To change the color of all of the body text:

1. Inside the BODY marker, type **TEXT**.

2. Type **="#rrggbb"**, where *rrggbb* is the hexadecimal representation of the color.

   Or type **="color"**, where color is one of the 16 predefined colors.

✔ Tips

- The TEXT attribute lets you choose one color for all of the text. The FONT tag with the COLOR attribute *(see page 44)* lets you choose a color for individual letters or words and overrides the TEXT attribute.

- See Appendix C and the inside back cover for a complete listing of hexadecimal values and common color representations.

- Be sure to choose complementary colors for your background *(see page 90)* and links *(see page 45)* that work well with your body text color.

- Check your page on a monochrome monitor before distributing it. What looks good in color may be impossible to read in grays.

Changing the color of a few letters

Sometimes, instead of changing all of the text to one color, you'll prefer to change some of the text to one color and leave the rest in black. Or you can create a rainbow effect and really distract your readers.

To change the color of a few letters:

1. In front of the text whose color you wish to change, type **<FONT COLOR**.

2. Type **="#rrggbb"**, where *rrggbb* is the hexadecimal representation of the desired color.

Or type **="color"**, where color is one of the 16 predefined colors.

3. Type the final **>** of the FONT tag.

4. Type the text that you wish to color.

5. Type **</FONT>**.

✔ Tips

■ See Appendix C and the inside back cover for a complete listing of hexadecimal values and common color representations.

■ Besides color, the FONT tag is also used to change the size *(see page 40)* and font *(see page 42)* of the text. You can change all three attributes at the same time: **<FONT SIZE=5 FACE= "Garamond" COLOR="red">**.

■ To change the color of all of the body text at once, use the TEXT attribute in the BODY tag *(see page 43)*.

■ The FONT/COLOR tag overrides colors specified with BODY/TEXT.

Figure 2.35 *You can use either a named color (as in the header) or a hexadecimal color (as in the paragraph) to choose a text color.*

Figure 2.36 *Both Netscape and Internet Explorer can understand the FONT tag with the COLOR attribute. Note that the text looks like a rainbow, with the header in red, and the paragraph in orange, yellow, green, blue, and violet. Really!*

Changing the color of a few letters

Figure 2.37 *You may select a color for new links, visited links, and active links (one that is being clicked).*

Figure 2.38 *It is important to choose colors (or shades of gray, as in this example) that have enough contrast so that you can see all the items on the page, but not so much (especially with colors) as to be garish and distracting.*

Changing the color of links

The LINK markers let you change the color of links. Since certain standard link colors have already been established— like blue for links that have not yet been visited—you should try not to confuse your user with inopportune color choices.

To change the color of links:

1. Place the cursor inside the BODY marker, after BODY but before the >.

2. To change the color of links that have not yet been visited, type **LINK**.

To change the color of links that have been already been visited, type **VLINK**.

To change the color of a link when the user clicks on it, type **ALINK.**

3. Type **="#rrggbb"**, where *rrggbb* is the hexadecimal representation of the desired color.

Or type **=color**, where *color* is one of the 16 predefined colors.

4. Repeat steps 2-3 for each kind of link.

✔ Tips

■ See Appendix C and the inside back cover for a complete listing of hexadecimal values and the equivalents for many common colors.

■ Make sure you test the colors of your text, links, and background together. Also test your color page on a black and white and a grayscale monitor.

■ Don't use different colors for links from page to page. The users won't know what to click on or which pages they've already visited. Likewise, don't use the same color for both visited and new links.

Changing the color of links

Making text blink

 Another way to make text stand out is to make it blink. You can apply the BLINK tag to anchors, links, or any important text that you have on the page.

To make text blink:

1. Type **\<BLINK\>**.

2. Type the text that you want to blink.

3. Type **\</BLINK\>**.

✔ Tips

■ In this age of graphic interfaces, blinking text virtually cries out to be clicked on. If you use blinking text for anything but a link, make it large so that it is not confused with a link.

■ You can include an image in your blinking definition, but it won't blink.

■ Blinking text blinks in a slightly lighter shade of its normal color. A blinking URL that the user has not visited, for example, will blink in shades of blue, while normal text will blink in shades of gray.

■ You may not use blinking text in the TITLE.

■ Internet Explorer does not recognize the BLINK tag.

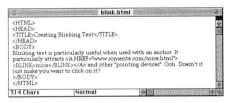

Figure 2.39 *Although you can include an image in your blinking definition, so to speak, only the text will blink.*

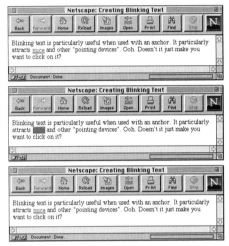

Figure 2.40 *Blinking text appears normal (top), then highlighted in a lighter shade (middle), and then normal again (bottom).*

Creating Images

Programs used in examples

In this chapter, I use Adobe Photoshop 3 to work with images. It is the best all around image editing program and is available for several operating systems, including Macintosh and Windows.

If you don't have Adobe Photoshop, I recommend the shareware program GraphicConverter for Macintosh. For Windows, try PaintShop Pro or LView Pro.

Using images on a Web page that were originally created for a printed document is something like taking someone else's prescription medicine. It might work well for you but then again it might make you really sick. Although the basic characteristics of Web images and printable images are the same, there are many factors that make some images work better for your Web pages. The most important of these factors are size, format, and color palette.

The *file size* of an image is crucial because it determines how fast the image can be loaded onto a page. In general, you should keep the entire contents of your page, including images, to 30K, which at 14.4KBps, will take some 30 seconds to load. That's about as long as you can expect anyone to wait. An image's file size is determined by its physical size, number of colors, resolution, and compression.

Since your images will be viewed on many different kinds of computers, it is important to use a widely supported *format*. The most common formats are GIF and JPEG. There is a growing movement to support PNG, although as yet, it is not widely found on the Web.

Finally, you need to be careful about the *number of colors* used in your image. Many computers are limited to 256 colors. If your image has more than 256 colors, or if you have several images that use different sets of colors, the browser may try to dither existing colors to reproduce the missing ones, or it may simply replace them with available colors. The results are not always pretty.

Image formats

The Web is accessed every day by millions of Macs, Windows-based PCs, Unix machines and other kinds of computers. The graphics you use in your Web page must be in a format that each of these operating systems can recognize. Presently, the two most widely used formats on the Web are GIF and JPEG. Most browsers can view GIF inline images; version 3 of both Netscape and Internet Explorer can also view JPEG images inline.

GIF Format

GIF, or Graphics Interchange Format, was developed by CompuServe for platform independent images on its online service. Its use of LZW compression reduces the size of images with large blocks of the same color—which are common in computer generated art. In addition, LZW is a lossless compression scheme. You can compress, uncompress and recompress the image without any loss in quality.

The latest GIF format, called GIF 89a, lets you create transparent *(see page 52)*, interlaced images *(see page 55)*, and compile animated images *(see page 59)*.

JPEG/JFIF Format

The JPEG (Joint Photographic Experts Group) compression scheme (saved in JFIF format files) is ideal for photographs and other "natural" color images. JPEG compressed images may have millions of colors, and their file size is determined primarily by their image size, not their number of colors.

However, JPEG is "lossy" compression—deciding that the eye cannot distinguish as many colors as are in your original image, it may eliminate them permanently to save space. Uncompressing the image will not

Figure 3.1 *Logotypes and other computer generated images, or images with few colors should be saved in GIF format.*

Figure 3.2 *Full-color photographs and other naturally created images, or images with more than 256 colors should be saved in JPEG format.*

restore the lost data. Most programs that let you save images with JPEG compression allow you to control the ratio between data loss and image compression.

Although there is no way to designate transparency in a JPEG image, nor any way to animate a series of JPEG images, you can create what are called *progressive JPEGs,* which act similarly to interlaced GIFs by appearing gradually when the user jumps to the corresponding page.

PNG Format

In late 1996, the World Wide Web Consortium endorsed the PNG (Portable Network Graphics) format, which it hopes will allow for faster-loading graphics of varying quality across platforms. PNG includes a compression algorithm that on average, is 30% more effective than LZW, which is used in GIF images. PNG supports transparency and has an advanced interlacing scheme that begins showing an image much faster than an interlaced GIF image. In addition, PNG images can even contain searchable keywords, making it easier for users to find particular images.

Neither Netscape nor Internet Explorer can currently view PNG images inline. However, since both Netscape Corporation and Microsoft are members of the W3C, upcoming versions of their browsers are bound to embrace the new format.

Image formats

Exporting GIF images from Photoshop

Use the GIF format for logos, banners and other computer generated images. GIF images are limited to 256 colors or less. You'll need Photoshop's GIF89a Export plug-in to follow the steps on these pages. You can find it at *http://www.adobe.com/*. It works with Photoshop 3.0.4 and later, for both Mac and Windows. (Adobe also offers a GIF Export plug-in for Illustrator.)

To export GIF images from Photoshop:

1. Create an RGB image at 72 dpi **(Figure 3.3)**.

2. Choose Gif89a Export in the Export submenu of the File menu **(Fig. 3.4)**.

3. Choose an option in the Palette submenu **(Figure 3.5)**. Exact is ideal if the image has less than 256 colors and you don't want to reduce the colors further. Otherwise, use Adaptive and enter the desired number of colors in the Color box. For details, consult *Reducing the colors* on page 56.

4. If desired, click the Preview button to see how the image will appear given the palette and number of colors chosen in the previous step.

5. If desired, click the Interlace option in the bottom left corner. For more information, consult *Interlacing GIF images* on page 55.

6. Click OK.

7. In the dialog box that appears, give the image a short name with the .gif extension **(Figure 3.6)**.

Figure 3.3 *Create an RGB image at 72 dpi. Since most monitors can't view images at higher resolutions, any higher value is just wasting bandwidth—and your users' time. And yes, that is a* quarter *moon.*

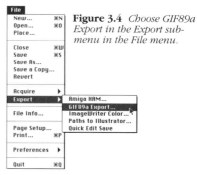

Figure 3.4 *Choose GIF89a Export in the Export submenu in the File menu.*

Figure 3.5 *If it's available, choose Exact for Palette (shown). Otherwise, choose Adaptive.*

Figure 3.6 *Once you click OK in the GIF89a Export dialog box (Figure 3.5), the Save dialog box appears. Photoshop automatically appends the .gif extension to the name. If necessary, change the name and/or folder. Then click Save.*

Figure 3.7 *If you have several layers in your document and only want to include some of them in the exported GIF, simply hide the unwanted ones before exporting. In this example, I've hidden the background to export just the main portion of the logo.*

Figure 3.8 *To export a caption with your GIF image, first choose File Info in the File menu.*

Figure 3.9 *Type a caption in the File Info dialog box. Then when you go to export the GIF, you'll be able to mark the Export Caption option.*

✔ Tips

■ If you don't have the Export plug-in and don't want to download and install it (although it's free), you can create GIF images by converting the document to Indexed color, Grayscale, or Bitmap mode, and then saving the document in CompuServe GIF format.

■ Since image previews can add to the size of your file, choose Never or Ask when saving in the More Preferences dialog box.

■ By using the Export plug-in, you maintain the original (RGB) image as well as the new GIF image. You can return to the RGB image, modify it and then export new GIFs as desired.

■ Only the visible layers are exported. You can hide any layers that you don't want to be included in the GIF image **(Figure 3.7)**.

■ If your image is on a transparent layer, the Export plug-in automatically converts the transparent areas to transparency in the GIF image. For more information, consult *Creating transparency* on page 52.

■ The fewer colors in your final image, the smaller it will be and the faster it will load. Experiment with fewer bits/ pixels in step 3 until you achieve the minimum number of colors with acceptable quality. For information, consult *Reducing the colors* on page 56.

■ Check the Export Caption option if you've added a caption to the File Info dialog box (under File) and you want to include that information with the GIF file (for use with Fetch or other image cataloguing software) **(Figures 3.8 and 3.9)**.

Exporting GIF images from Photoshop

Creating transparency

With Photoshop's Export GIF89a plug-in, you can make any part of a GIF image transparent so that it blends almost seamlessly with the page. You can create your image on a transparent layer, make one or more colors transparent, or you can create an alpha channel and make *it* transparent.

To make a layer transparent:

1. Open an RGB image in Photoshop.

2. Select the part of the image that you wish to export **(Figure 3.10)**.

3. Choose Copy in the Edit menu. Then choose Paste Layer **(Figure 3.11)**.

4. Hide or eliminate all layers except the transparent one **(Figure 3.12)**.

5. Continue from step 2 on page 50.

To make certain colors transparent:

1. Create or open an Indexed color image in Photoshop.

2. Choose GIF89a Export in the Export submenu in the File menu.

3. In the dialog box that appears, choose the eyedropper and click the color(s) in the image that you want to make transparent **(Figure 3.13)**. You can also click colors in the color table below the image. Hold down Option (Mac) or Alt (Windows) as you click to restore colors to their original state.

4. The transparent areas of the image are displayed in the color shown in the Transparency Color Index box. Click in the box to change the color.

5. Click OK and give the file a name.

Figure 3.10 *Select the part of the image that you wish to export as a GIF image.*

Figure 3.11 *Choose Copy in the Edit menu (left). Then choose Paste Layer in the Edit menu (right).*

Figure 3.12 *Hide all the layers except the transparent one by clicking on the eye icon to the left of the layer name. Note that transparency in Photoshop is displayed with a checkerboard (left).*

Figure 3.13 *If you export an Indexed Color image, you can choose which colors should be transparent by clicking them with the eyedropper. Hold down Option (Mac) or Alt (Windows) to restore colors to their original state. (Note that the moon, because it is white like the background, is also made transparent.)*

Creating transparency

Figure 3.14 *Select the part of the image that you want to make transparent. In this example, the white background is selected but the white moon is not.*

Figure 3.15 *Choose Inverse in the Select menu (left). Then choose Save Selection in the Select menu.*

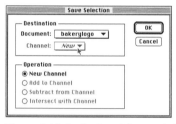

Figure 3.16 *In the Save Selection dialog box, choose New in the Channel menu and click OK.*

Figure 3.17 *Choose the desired channel in the Transparency from submenu. The transparent areas will be shown with the Transparency Index Color. Notice that the moon will not be transparent, even though it is the same color as the rest of the transparent area (the background).*

Photoshop also lets you makes certain areas transparent, regardless of their color. This is ideal for creating a transparent background without knocking out similar colors in the body of the image.

To make a selection transparent:

1. Create or open an indexed color image in Photoshop.

2. Select the part of the image that you want to be transparent **(Figure 3.14)**.

3. Choose Inverse in the Select menu **(Figure 3.15)**.

4. Choose Save Selection in the Select menu **(Figure 3.15)**.

5. In the Save Selection dialog box that appears, choose New under Channel and then click OK **(Figure 3.16)**.

6. Deselect everything.

7. Choose Export GIF89a in the Export submenu under File.

8. In the dialog box that appears, choose the channel number in the Transparency from submenu **(Figure 3.17)**. Hold down Option (Mac) or Alt (Windows) to invert the selection.

9. Click OK and give the file a name.

✔ Tips

■ For more information on changing RGB images to indexed color, consult *Reducing the colors* on page 56.

■ In browsers that can't show transparency itself, the transparent areas are shown with the color specified in the Transparency Color Index box.

Creating fake transparency

Because sharp edges next to transparent areas can sometimes look really bad, you may want to try using *fake* transparency whenever possible. Fake transparency means making the background the same color as the background of your page so that the image blends in as if the background were transparent.

Figure 3.18
Select the image itself, using the lasso or other selection tools.

To make the background a solid color:

1. Open the image in Photoshop, or another image editing program.

2. Use the Lasso and other selection tools to select everything except the background **(Figure 3.18)**.

Figure 3.19 *Use the Inverse command in the Select menu to select everything but the image, that is, the background.*

3. Select Inverse in the Selection menu to select only the background **(Figure 3.19)**.

4. Click the background color to set it to the color of your choice.

5. Press Delete to change the color of the selected area (the background) to the current background color **(Figure 3.20)**.

6. Save the image.

✔ Tips

■ You can also use this method to create fake transparency in JPEG images.

■ This is also a good way to prepare images for programs that only allow you to make one color transparent.

Background color control

Figure 3.20 *Once you've inverted the selection, click the Background color control, choose the desired background color, and then press the Delete key to change the background to one solid color, in this case, white.*

Figure 3.21 *If you are exporting a GIF image from an RGB image, the Interlace option will appear in the bottom left corner of the GIF89a Export dialog box.*

Figure 3.22 *If it was an Indexed Color image, the Interlace option appears at the center right.*

Figure 3.23 *A browser will show the interlaced image gradually, allowing the user to move around the page and read the text while the image comes into full view.*

Interlacing GIF images

Interlacing an image prepares it so that a browser can show it at gradually increasing resolutions. Although the initial image is blurry, the user does not have to wait for the finished image to appear. Instead, the user can scroll around the page and then return when the image is complete.

To interlace an image:

1. Open the image in Photoshop.

2. Choose Export GIF89a in the Export submenu under the File menu.

3. Check the Interlace option in the dialog box that appears. The box is slightly different for RGB **(Fig. 3.21)** vs. indexed color images **(Fig. 3.22)**, but the Interlace option is the same.

4. Click OK.

5. Enter a short name and extension in the dialog box that appears.

✔ Tip

■ For information on creating JPEG images that appear gradually, similar to the interlacing effect in GIF images, consult *Creating JPEG images* on page 60.

Interlacing GIF images

Reducing the colors

A GIF image's size is directly related to the number of colors it has. It can have at most 256 colors, and if you can reduce the number even further, you can save considerably on load time and user patience.

To reduce the number of colors with Photoshop:

1. Open an RGB image with Photoshop.

2. Choose Export GIF89a in the Export submenu under the File menu.

3. Choose Adaptive in the Palette pop-up menu **(Figure 3.24)**.

4. Enter the desired number of colors in the Colors box.

5. Click Preview to see how the image will look with this number of colors **(Figures 3.25 and 3.26)**. Use the magnifying glass and the hand to examine the image carefully. Click OK to return to the main dialog.

6. Repeat steps 3–5 until you find the least number of colors you can live with.

7. Click OK and save the document.

✔ Tip

■ If the image is already in Indexed Color mode and you wish to reduce the colors further, you have two choices. Either convert the document to RGB mode and then follow the steps above, or convert the image to RGB mode and then choose Indexed color mode and enter a smaller number of colors under Resolution in the dialog box that appears.

Figure 3.24 *Choose Adaptive for Palette and then enter the desired number of colors in the Colors box. Finally, click the Preview button to see how the illustration will look on the page.*

Figure 3.25 *With only eight colors, the image appears quite pixelated. Click OK to go back to the GIF89a Export dialog box and try another value.*

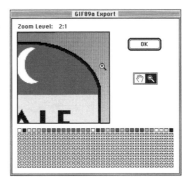

Figure 3.26 *A value of 32 considerably reduces the amount of colors—with minimal pixelation.*

Figure 3.27 *Choose Indexed Color in the Mode menu.*

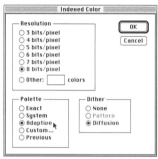

Figure 3.28 *Choose 8 bits/pixel under Resolution, Adaptive under Palette and Diffusion under Dither.*

Figure 3.29 *Choose Color Table in the Mode menu.*

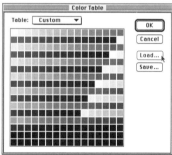

Figure 3.30 *Click the Load button in the Color Table dialog box to load the common color palette. You can also change each color individually by clicking the desired color.*

Common color tables

In order to use the maximum number of colors without fear of running over the limit of 256, use the same color table for each image.

To use the same color table for several new images:

1. Create a new document in Photoshop.

2. Select Indexed Color in the Mode menu **(Figure 3.27)**.

3. In the dialog box that appears, choose 8 bits/pixel under Resolution, Adaptive under Palette, and Diffusion under Dither **(Figure 3.28)**.

4. Choose Color Table in the Mode menu **(Figure 3.29)**.

5. In the Color Table dialog box, click the Load button to load the common color table **(Figure 3.30)**.

6. Choose the desired color table in the Open dialog box that appears.

7. Click OK to close the Color Table dialog box.

8. Create the document as usual. Only the colors that you've loaded from the common color table will be available.

✔ **Tip**

■ Netscape uses a 216 color palette that you can download from many sites on the Web. One source is Tom Venetianer's page. For Macintosh, use *ftp://ftp.mvassist.pair.com/pub/mac/NS2colors.sea.hqx*. For Windows, use *ftp://ftp.mvassist.pair.com/pub/win/NS2COLOR.ZIP.* He has a good article on Netscape's palette at *http://mvassist.pair.com/Articles/NS2colors.html.*

Common color tables

57

To use the same color table for several existing images:

1. In Photoshop, or your image editing program of choice, create one new, blank image large enough to hold each of your individual images.

2. Either create or copy the individual images into the larger one **(Figure 3.31)**.

3. Select Indexed Color in the Mode menu, and 8 bits/pixel under Resolution (or fewer) and Adaptive under Palette in the dialog box that appears.

4. Save the document with a name like "combined images".

5. With the cropping tool, cut out one of the individual images **(Figure 3.32)**.

6. Save the new reduced image with a new name **(Figure 3.33)**.

7. Open the *combined images* file and repeat steps 5 and 6 for each individual image.

✔ **Tip**

■ Although it seems like you should be able to save the Color Table (using the Save button in the Color Table dialog box) and then load it into each smaller image, the result is not quite what you'd expect. In fact, since there is no way to map which colors go to which parts of the image, the result is quite ugly. Try it.

Figure 3.31 *The only way to ensure that each image shares the same color table is to combine them in one document and then apply the Indexed Color command.*

Figure 3.32 *The crop tool (left) can cut out part of an image while retaining all of the original image's properties, including color mode and color table.*

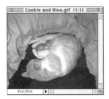

Figure 3.33 *Be sure and save the new file with a new name so that you don't replace the combined images file.*

Common color tables

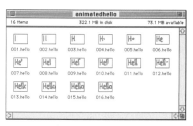

Figure 3.34 *Create the individual files in Photoshop, PICT, or GIF format. If you number them sequentially, they'll appear in order automatically in GIFBuilder.*

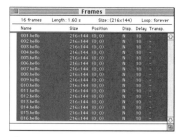

Figure 3.35 *Once you drag the files to the GIF-Builder Frames window, they'll appear in alphabetical order. Reorder them as needed.*

Figure 3.36 *You can test the animated GIF by choosing Start in the Animation menu and watching the image in the Animation window. It's kind of hard to show in a book...*

Figure 3.37 *When you're satisfied with the animated GIF, choose Save in the File menu and then give the file a name, preferably with the .gif extension in the Save dialog box. Click Save.*

Figure 3.38 *The resulting GIF image looks normal in the Finder, but it dances on any browser that recognizes the GIF89a format.*

Creating animated GIFs

The GIF89a format can contain several images at once which, when viewed with a browser that supports animated GIFs, are displayed one after another. You can use this feature to create slide shows or to approximate moving images. Perhaps the best tool for creating animated GIFs on the Macintosh is GIFBuilder, a freeware program developed by Yves Piguet.

To create an animated GIF:

1. Create the series of images that will form the animated GIF **(Figure 3.34)**. The images can be in Photoshop, PICT, or GIF format, among others.

2. Open GIFBuilder.

3. Select all the images and drag them to the GIFBuilder window. The images will appear in alphabetical order, by default **(Figure 3.35)**. You can reorder them as necessary.

4. If desired, choose Start from the Animation menu to see a preview of your animated GIF **(Figure 3.36)**.

5. If desired, choose Loop in the Options menu to determine if the animation should play once, more than once, or continuously (Forever).

6. Add new images by choosing Add image in the File menu.

7. Once you are satisfied with your animated GIF, choose Save in the File menu.

8. In the Save dialog box, give the animated GIF a name, preferably ending with the .gif extension **(Figure 3.37)**. The new conglomerated file looks just like a regular GIF **(Figure 3.38)**.

Creating animated GIFs

59

Creating JPEG images

Use JPEG compression for photographs and for images with more than 256 colors.

To save an image with JPEG compression:

1. Open the image with Photoshop, or the desired image editing program.

2. Choose RGB Color or CMYK Color in the Mode menu **(Figure 3.39)**.

3. Select Save As in the File menu.

4. Choose JPEG in the Format pop-up menu **(Figure 3.40)**.

5. Give the file a name and the .jpg or .jpeg extension, and then click OK.

6. Choose the desired quality in the JPEG Options dialog box. **(Fig. 3.41)**.

✔ Tips

■ You may want to experiment with different compression values until you get an image with sufficient quality at a file size you (and your users) can live with.

■ There are several programs (Photoshop 4, GraphicConverter 2.5, and others) that allow you to save *Progressive* JPEG images, that is images that appear gradually on the screen in the same way as interlaced GIF images. Both Netscape 3 and Internet Explorer 3 can view progressive JPEGs, though older browsers may have more trouble.

Figure 3.39 *In Photoshop, a JPEG image may be in either RGB Color or CMYK Color.*

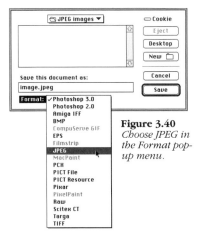

Figure 3.40 *Choose JPEG in the Format pop-up menu.*

Figure 3.41 *The higher the image quality you choose in the JPEG Options dialog box, the less compression you will achieve.*

Creating JPEG images

Figure 3.42 *Choose Image Size in the Image menu.*

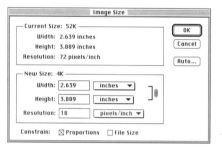

Figure 3.43 *With Proportions checked and File Size unchecked, change the value in the Resolution box, preferably to a number that divides evenly into 72 (like 36, 18, or even 9).*

Creating low resolution images

If you have a lot of large images on your page, you can make life more pleasant for your user by creating a low resolution image that Netscape can show immediately while it takes its time loading the higher resolution image.

To create a low resolution version of your image:

1. Open your image in Photoshop, or other image editing program.

2. Select Image Size in the Image menu **(Figure 3.42)**.

3. Check File Size and Proportions in the Image Size dialog box. **(Figure 3.43)**.

4. Change the value of Resolution to 72 dpi or lower and click OK **(Figure 3.43)**.

5. Choose Save As in the File menu and save the low resolution image with a new name.

Creating low resolution images

Creating miniatures of large images

Another way to give your users access to large images without compelling them to wait for them to load is by creating small icons that are linked to the larger images. This way, the user can choose to see the larger images or just to continue with your Web page.

To create a miniature version of a large image:

1. Open the large image in Photoshop, or other image editing program.

2. Select Image Size in the Image menu.

3. Check the Proportions option and make sure the File Size option is unchecked **(Figure 3.44)**.

4. Select inches in the pop-up menu to the right of Width.

5. Type **.5** in the Width box (or whatever smaller size you wish). The Height will be adjusted automatically.

6. Select Save As in the File menu.

7. Type a new name for the icon, so you don't replace the full size image.

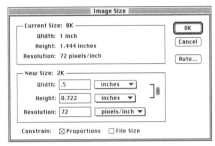

Figure 3.44 *Check the Proportions and uncheck the File Size options in the Image Size dialog box. Then, with inches selected, type the new width in the Width box.*

Figure 3.45 *The original image (shown above at 91% of its normal size so I could fit it on the page) and the corresponding miniature version (at left at full size).*

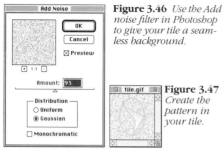

Figure 3.46 *Use the Add noise filter in Photoshop to give your tile a seamless background.*

Figure 3.47 *Create the pattern in your tile.*

Figure 3.48 *Use the Offset filter to convert the tile into a repeatable pattern.*

```
                   backtile.html
<HTML><HEAD>
<TITLE>Using an image as a background</TITLE></HEAD>
<BODY BACKGROUND="tile.gif">
You can also use an image for the background. Make sure the images are as
small as possible. Your users won't wait forever. <P>
<FONT SIZE=+3>
<UL><STRONG>Starsearch Enterprises Web page</STRONG><P>
<LI>New products<P>
<LI>Press Releases<P>
<LI>PSO Scheduled<P>
<LI>Job Opportunities at SE<P>
</UL>
</FONT>
</BODY>
</HTML>
Num. Lock          Normal
```

Figure 3.49 *There is no difference in the HTML code between using one image for the background and tiling an image several times for the background. Netscape decides how to treat an image based on its size.*

Figure 3.50 *Netscape tiles your image as many times as necessary to fill the background.*

Creating tiled images for the background

If the image you select for your background is smaller than the user's window, it will automatically be tiled to fill the background. You can tweak the image so that it tiles seamlessly.

To create images for a tiled background:

1. Create a new image of about 100 x 100 pixels in Photoshop.

2. Choose the Add Noise filter in the Noise submenu in the Filters menu to create a textured background **(Figure 3.46)**.

3. Create the desired pattern **(Fig. 3.47)**.

4. Select the Offset filter under Others in the Filters menu **(Figure 3.48)** to create a repeatable pattern.

5. In the Offset filter dialog box, type **10** in the Horizontal and Vertical fields and click Wrap Around.

6. Click OK.

7. Adjust the interior of the image to make the seams disappear. Do not change the borders once you have used the Offset filter.

8. Use the Hue/Saturation and Brightness/Contrast options to reduce the Contrast and make the image lighter. Make it twice as light as you can stand. It is background, after all.

9. Save the image and define it as a background image **(Figures 3.49 and 3.50)**. For more information on background images, see page 77.

Creating tiled images for the background

Using Images

Perhaps the greatest appeal of the World Wide Web is that pages can contain colorful images. You can insert a photo of your cat on your personal home page, or your company's logo on your business page. You can add images to link definitions, making buttons that take your reader to their next destination. You can use custom icons in lists or use miniature images to point to larger ones. And perhaps most exciting of all, you can create images with more than one hot spot, so that a click in one area brings the user to point A while a click in a different area brings the user to point B.

Inserting images on a page

You can place all kinds of images on your Web page, from logos to photographs. Images placed as described here appear automatically when the user jumps to your page, as long as his browser is set up to view them.

To insert an image on a page:

1. Place the cursor where you want the image to appear.

2. Type **<IMG SRC="image.location"** where *image.location* shows the location of the image file on the server.

3. Type the final **>**.

✔ Tips

■ For information on creating images especially for Web pages, consult Chapter 3, *Creating Images*.

■ The general technique for placing images described here works for any kind of image that the browser recognizes, including GIF, JPEG, and PNG, or even animated GIFs *(see page 59)*.

■ Don't expect your users to wait more than 30 seconds to load and view your page (about 30K total with a 14.4 Kbps modem connection). To get by this limit, create miniatures *(see page 62)* of large images and let users choose to view the larger images *(see page 69)* only if desired.

■ Use alternative text for browsers, like Lynx, that don't support images *(see page 67)*, or for users who turn off image viewing to make pages load faster.

Figure 4.1 *Use a <P> or <BR> before an image definition to start it on its own line.*

Figure 4.2 *Images are aligned to the left side of the page, by default. Unless you use the align attributes (see pages 71 and 72), you can't wrap the text around the image.*

Inserting images on a page

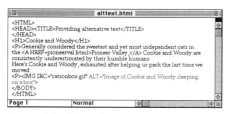

Figure 4.3 *If your alternative text contains one or more spaces, you must enclose it in quotation marks.*

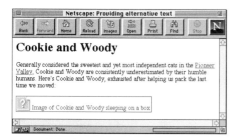

Figure 4.4 *The alternative text will appear if the image cannot be found, if the user has deselected Autoload images, or if the browser does not support images.*

Alternative text

Some browsers do not support images at all. Other browsers support them but the user may have such a slow connection that they choose not to view the images, or to load them in manually. You can create text that will appear if the image, for whatever reason, does not.

To provide alternative text when images don't appear:

1. Place the cursor where you want the image (or alternative text) to appear.

2. Type **<IMG SRC="image.gif"** where *image.gif* is the location of the image on the server.

3. Type **ALT="**.

4. Type the text that should appear if, for some reason, the image itself does not.

5. Type **">**.

✔ Tip

■ Some browsers, like Lynx, that do not support images, are used by the blind because they can speak the contents to the user. This is just one more reason to add alternative text to your images.

Alternative text

Specifying size for speedier viewing

When a browser gets to the HTML code for an image, it must load the image to see how big it is and how much space must be reserved for it. If you specify the image's dimensions, the browser can fill in the text around the image as the image loads, so that your users can read the page without having to wait for the images.

To specify the size of your image:

1. Open the image in Photoshop, or other image editing program.

2. Select Image Size in the Image menu.

3. Choose pixels for the Unit of measure in both the Width and Height text boxes **(Figure 4.5)**.

4. Write down the values shown in the Width and Height text boxes.

5. In your HTML document where you wish the image to appear, type **<IMG SRC="image.location"**, where *image.location* is the location of the image on the server.

6. Type **WIDTH=x HEIGHT=y>**, using the values you jotted down in step 4 to specify the values for *x* and *y* (the width and height of your image) in pixels. For more information on using WIDTH and HEIGHT to scale images consult *Scaling an image* on page 75.

7. Add other image attributes as desired and then type the final **>**.

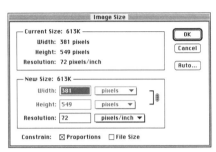

Figure 4.5 *Select pixels in the Width and Height pop-up menus and write down the values shown (in this example, 381 and 549).*

Figure 4.6 *If you specify the exact height and width values in pixels, Netscape won't have to spend time doing it and will display the image more quickly.*

Figure 4.7 *The image at its original size.*

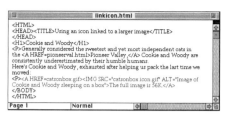

Figure 4.8 *Remember to use the full size image in the link and the icon in the image definition.*

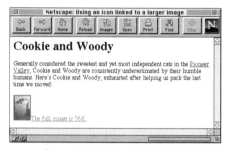

Figure 4.9 *In this example, the icon is 2K and takes 2 seconds to load. The user can choose to view the larger image (by clicking the icon) or to continue reading the page.*

Figure 4.10 *If the user clicks the icon, Netscape opens a new window with the full size image.*

Linking icons to external images

If you have a particularly large image, you can create a miniature version or icon of it *(see page 62)* that displays quickly on the page and then add a link to the miniature that takes the user to the full size image, if he wishes.

To link a small icon to your larger image:

1. Place the cursor in your HTML page where you wish the icon to be placed.

2. Type **<A HREF="image.location">**, where *image.location* is the location of the full sized image on your server.

3. Type **<IMG SRC="icon.location"**, where *icon.location* is the location of your icon on the server.

4. If desired, type **ALT="alternative text"**, where *alternative text* is the text that should appear if, for some reason, the icon does not.

5. Type the final **>** of the icon definition.

6. Type the clickable text that you wish to accompany the icon. It's a good idea to include the actual size in K of the full sized image so the user knows what they're getting into by clicking it.

7. Type **</A>** to complete the link to the full sized image.

✔ **Tip**

■ Using miniatures is an ideal way to get a lot of graphic information on a page without making your users wait too long to see it. Then they can view the images that they are most interested in at their leisure.

Using low resolution images

You can reference both high and low resolution versions of your image so that the low resolution loads quickly and keeps the user's interest while the high resolution version wows your users, once it loads in.

Figure 4.11 *The HEIGHT and WIDTH attributes are discussed on page 53. They are necessary here to show both images at the proper size.*

To use a low resolution version of an image:

1. Create a low resolution version of your image *(see page 61)*.

2. Place the cursor where you want the full resolution image to appear.

3. Type **<IMG SRC="image.gif"** where *image.gif* is the location on the server of the high resolution image.

4. Type **LOWSRC="imagelow.gif"** where *imagelow.gif* is the location on the server of the low resolution image.

5. Type **HEIGHT=x WIDTH=y**, where *x* and *y* are the height and width in pixels, respectively. If you do not specify these values, Netscape uses the size of the smaller (low resolution) image for both images.

6. If desired, type **ALT="substitute text"** where *substitute text* is the text that will appear if the user can't view images with their browser.

7. Type the final **>**.

✔ Tip

■ To speed things up and keep them simple at the same time, create a single, low resolution, placeholder image and use it in the LOWSRC tag for all of the images on the page.

Figure 4.12 *The low resolution image is replaced gradually by the higher resolution image. The call out line marks the division between the two. The status information in the lower left corner shows how much more time it will take to finish loading the high resolution image. Without the lower resolution image, the user would have to wait all that time before seeing anything.*

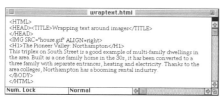

Figure 4.13 *When you align an image to the right, you are actually wrapping text to the left (and vice versa).*

Figure 4.14 *Netscape leaves a little space between images and the text wrapped around them.*

Figure 4.15 *To make the image appear on the left with the text wrapped around the right side, use ALIGN=left.*

Figure 4.16 *Internet Explorer leaves no space between images and wrapped text. You can add space manually with the HSPACE and VSPACE attributes (see page 74).*

Wrapping text around images

You can use the ALIGN attribute (with the *left* and *right* variables only) to wrap text around an image. (Yes, these really should have their own attribute, like WRAP, instead of ALIGN which seems like it should do something rather different—which it does on page 76.)

To wrap text around one side of an image:

1. Type **<IMG SRC="image.location"** where *image.location* indicates the location of the image on the server.

2. *Either* type **ALIGN=left** to align the image to the left of the screen while the text flows to the right *or* type **ALIGN=right** to align the image to the right edge of the screen while the text flows on the left side of the image.

3. Add other image attributes, as described in other parts of this chapter, if desired.

4. Type the final **>**.

5. Type the text that should flow next to the image.

✔ Tip

■ Don't get confused about right and left. When you choose **ALIGN=right**, it's the *image* that goes to the right (while the text goes to the left). When you choose **ALIGN=left**, again, the image will be on the left side with the text flowing around the right side.

Wrapping text around images

To wrap text between two images:

1. Type **<IMG SRC="right.image" ALIGN=right>** where *right.image* indicates the location on the server of the image that should appear on the right side of the screen.

2. Type the text that should flow around the first image.

3. Type **<IMG SRC="left.image" ALIGN=left>** where *left.image* indicates the location on the server of the image that should appear on the left side of the screen.

4. If desired, type **<P>** to begin a new paragraph, that will be aligned with the image placed in step 3.

5. Type the text that should flow around the second image.

✔ Tips

■ The key is to place each image *directly before* the text it should "disrupt."

■ Each image will continue to push the text to one side until it either encounters a break *(see page 73)* or until there is no more text.

■ Notice that in this example one of the images has a transparent background and one doesn't. You can mix all types of images on a page. For more information on creating transparency, see page 52.

Figure 4.17 *The image always precedes the text that should flow around it.*

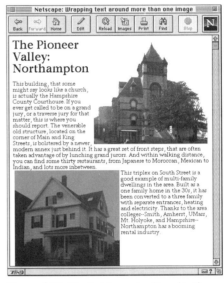

Figure 4.18 *The first image is aligned to the right and the text flows to its left. The next image appears after the last line of text in the preceding paragraph and pushes the following paragraph to the right.*

Figure 4.19 *Notice the order: first comes the image of the house, then the header, then the logo, then the paragraph.*

Figure 4.20 *The Clear=left attribute makes the text stop flowing until it reaches an empty left margin (that is, below the bottom of the left-aligned image).*

Figure 4.21 *The order is the same as in the last example; only the CLEAR attribute has changed.*

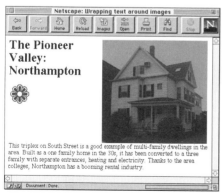

Figure 4.22 *The CLEAR=all code stops the flow of text until all images have been passed.*

Stopping text wrap

A wrapped image affects all the text that follows it, unless you insert a special line break. The CLEAR attribute added to the regular BR tag indicates that the text should not begin until the specified margin is clear (that is, at the end of the image or images).

To stop the text from wrapping:

1. Create your image and the text *(see pages 71 and 72).*

2. Place the cursor where you want to stop wrapping text to the side of the image.

3. *Either* type **<BR CLEAR=left>** to stop flowing text until there are no more images aligned to the left margin, *or* type **<BR CLEAR=right>** to stop flowing text until there are no more images aligned to the right margin, *or* type **<BR CLEAR=all>** to stop flowing text until there are no more images on either margin.

Stopping text wrap

Adding space around an image

Look carefully at the image in Figure 4.23. If you don't want your text butting right up to the image, you can use the Netscape extensions VSPACE and HSPACE to add a buffer around your image.

To add space around an image:

1. Type **<IMG SRC="image.location"** where *image.location* indicates the location on the server of your image.

2. Type **HSPACE=x** where *x* is the number of pixels of space to add on *both* the right and left sides of the image.

3. Type **VSPACE=x** where *x* is the number of pixels of space to add on *both* the top and bottom of the image.

4. Add other image attributes as desired and type the final **>**.

✔ Tips

■ You don't have to add both HSPACE and VSPACE at the same time.

■ If you just want to add space to one side of the image, use Photoshop to add blank space to that side, and skip HSPACE and VSPACE altogether. Then, make the blank space transparent *(see page 52)*.

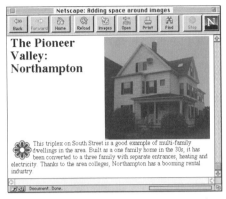

Figure 4.23 *Both Netscape and Internet Explorer have the bad habit of cramming text right up next to images. Netscape (shown) leaves no space above or below an image. Internet Explorer leaves hardly any space to either side of the image.*

Figure 4.24 *You can add either HSPACE or VSPACE, or both, to your images.*

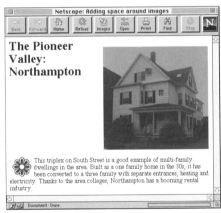

Figure 4.25 *One of the unfortunate side effects of VSPACE is that it adds space both to the top and to the bottom of an image. Although the lower paragraph is no longer jammed against the house, the words* The Pioneer *are no longer aligned with the top of the image.*

Figure 4.26 *The image's original size is revealed in Photoshop by holding down the Option key and clicking in the lower left corner of the window.*

Figure 4.27 *Use dimensions that are multiples of the original size to keep the image in proportion.*

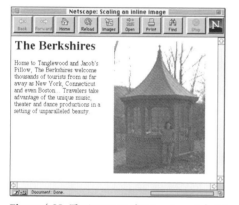

Figure 4.28 *The image quality is not great, but it loads twice as fast as a regular sized image.*

Figure 4.29 *(Above and right.) You can distort an image to fit nicely with the text as I've done here, but beware: other browsers with other settings may quickly undo your adjustments.*

Scaling an image

Netscape lets you change the size of an image just by specifying a new height and width in pixels. This is a great way to have large images on your page without long loading times. Beware, though, if you enlarge your pictures too much, they'll be grainy and ugly.

To scale an image:

1. Type **<IMG SRC="image.location"**, where *image.location* is the location on the server of the image.

2. Type **WIDTH=x HEIGHT=y** where *x* and *y* are the desired width and height, respectively, in pixels, of your image.

3. Add any other image attributes as desired and then type the final **>**.

✔ Tips

■ Don't use the WIDTH and HEIGHT extensions to *reduce* the image size. Instead, create a smaller image. It will load faster and look better.

■ The WIDTH and HEIGHT values don't have to be proportional—you can stretch or elongate an image for a "special" effect **(Figure 4.29)**.

Aligning images

Perhaps, the more expected use of the ALIGN attribute is for aligning images with text. You can align an image in various ways to a single line in a paragraph. However, be careful with multiple images on the same line—different ALIGN options have different effects depending on which image is taller and which appears first.

To align an image with text:

1. Type **<IMG SRC="image.location"** where *image.location* indicates the location on the server of the image.

2. Type **ALIGN=direction** where *direction* is one of the attributes described in Figure 4.31: *texttop, top, middle, absmiddle, bottom,* or *absbottom.*

3. Add other attributes as desired and then type the final **>**.

4. Type the text with which you wish to align the image. (This text may also precede the image.)

✔ Tips

■ You may not align an image and wrap text around it at the same time.

■ Internet Explorer has trouble with aligning more than one image on a line. The results are erratic. In addition, it treats *texttop* as *top, absmiddle* as *middle* and *absbottom* as *bottom.*

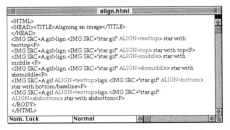

Figure 4.30 *It's important to note that the letter A is an image, not an actual letter. It is aligned (by default) with the bottom of the text in the top four examples, and with the top of the text in the last two examples.*

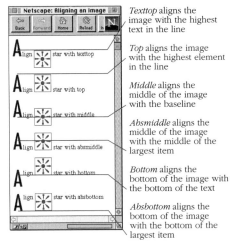

Texttop aligns the image with the highest text in the line

Top aligns the image with the highest element in the line

Middle aligns the middle of the image with the baseline

Absmiddle aligns the middle of the image with the middle of the largest item

Bottom aligns the bottom of the image with the bottom of the text

Absbottom aligns the bottom of the image with the bottom of the largest item

Figure 4.31 *There are four elements on each line: an image of the letter A, some text, a star, and some more text. The six possible alignment positions are illustrated with the star.*

```
backimage.html
<HTML><HEAD>
<TITLE>Using an image as a background</TITLE></HEAD>
<BODY BACKGROUND="backimage.gif">
You can also use an image for the background. Make sure the images are as
small as possible. Your users won't wait forever. <P>
<FONT SIZE=+3>
<UL><STRONG>Starsearch Enterprises Web page</STRONG><P>
<LI>New products<P>
<LI>Press Releases<P>
<LI>PSO Scheduled<P>
<LI>Job Opportunities at SE<P>
</UL>
</FONT>
</BODY>
</HTML>
Num. Lock          Normal
```

Figure 4.32 *You can't add extra image attributes (like LOWSRC) to the BODY tag.*

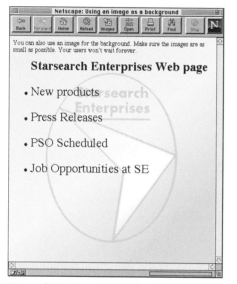

Figure 4.33 *You probably shouldn't put text on a background image. It's apt to be covered by your page text.*

Using background images

You can use one image as the backdrop for your entire page. *Backdrop* is the operative word here. A background image should not detract from the readability of your page, but instead make it more attractive.

To use a background image:

1. In the BODY tag at the beginning of your HTML document, after the word BODY but before the final >, type **BACKGROUND=**.

2. Type **"bgimage.gif"**, where *bgimage.gif* is the location on the server of the image you want to use for the background of your page.

3. 🄸 If desired, type **BGPROPERTIES= fixed** to make the image a stationary watermark.

4. Add other body attributes—like link and text color *(see pages 43 and 45).*

✔ Tips

■ With an image editing program, try increasing the brightness and lowering the contrast to soften the background image so it doesn't distract from your page's content.

■ Save your user loading time by using the same background image on a series of pages. After the image has been loaded for the first page, each subsequent page uses a cached version which loads much more quickly.

■ Small images are automatically tiled to fill the background. For more information, consult *Creating tiled images for the background* on page 63.

Using a banner

Having a newspaper-like banner at the top of every Web page is a good way to link your pages together visually.

To place a banner at the top of each page:

1. Create an image that measures approximately 450 x 100 pixels. You can make it narrower and shorter, but you shouldn't make it much wider. Otherwise it won't fit easily on most screens **(Figure 4.34)**.

2. After converting it to Indexed color, using the smallest bits/pixel ratio you can stand, save it as a GIF image.

3. Use this exact same image at the top of each of your Web pages, by typing **<IMG SRC="image.name">**, where *image.name* is the location on the server of the banner.

4. By using the same image on each Web page, you create the illusion of a static banner. At the same time, since the image is saved in the cache after it is loaded the first time, it will load almost immediately onto each new page your user jumps to.

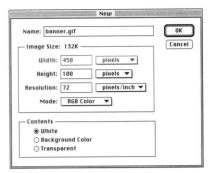

Figure 4.34 *When you create your image (here in Photoshop) make sure it is 450 pixels wide, or less.*

Figure 4.35 *The only thing special about a banner is that it is the first element in the BODY section.*

Figure 4.36 *Banners appear similarly in Netscape (above) and Internet Explorer.*

```
                  rule.html
<HTML><HEAD>
<TITLE>Using horizontal rules</TITLE></HEAD>
<BODY>
<IMG SRC="banner.gif" ALT="SE banner">
<H1>New products</H1>
<UL>
<LI>AstroFinder 3
<LI>Pleiades Expander
<LI>Southern Cross
</UL>
<HR SIZE=10 WIDTH=80% ALIGN=center NOSHADE>
</BODY>
</HTML>
Num. Lock          Normal
```

Figure 4.37 *The HR tag includes an automatic line break both before and after the rule.*

Figure 4.38 *Netscape and Internet Explorer understand all the HR attributes, which are actually Netscape extensions.*

Adding horizontal rules

One graphic element that is completely supported by the majority of the browsers is the horizontal rule. Although Netscape introduced extensions to jazz up the horizontal rule, those extensions are now part of the HTML 3.2 standard.

To insert a horizontal rule:

1. Type **<HR** where you want the rule to appear. The text that follows will appear in a new paragraph below the new rule.

2. If desired, type **SIZE=n**, where *n* is the rule's height in pixels.

3. If desired, type **WIDTH=w**, where *w* is the width of the rule in pixels, or as a percentage of the document's width.

4. If desired, type **ALIGN=direction**, where *direction* refers to the way a rule should be aligned on the page; either *left, right* or *center.* The ALIGN attribute is only effective if you have made the rule narrower than the document.

5. If desired, type **NOSHADE** to create a solid bar, with no shading.

6. Type the final **>** to complete the horizontal rule definition.

Adding horizontal rules

Page Layout

5

HTML 3.2 has a number of features that apply to an entire page, instead of being limited to just a few words or paragraphs. I call these elements *page layout* features and restrict them to this chapter.

Included among these features are setting margins and columns, controlling the spacing between the elements on a page, changing the background color for the entire page, dividing a page into logical sections, and determining when line breaks should, and shouldn't, occur.

Page layout

Specifying the margins

Both Netscape and Internet Explorer add a certain amount of space, by default, between the content of a page and the edges of the window. You can use the LEFTMARGIN and TOPMARGIN tags to specify just how much space you'd like there to be—but only IE understands it.

To specify the margins:

1. Inside the BODY tag, after the word BODY but before the final >, type **LEFTMARGIN=x**, where x is the width in pixels of the space between the left border of the window and the contents of the page.

2. Type **TOPMARGIN=y**, where y is the height in pixels of the space between the top border of the window and the contents of the page.

✓ Tips

■ Netscape always uses a value of 8 pixels for both the top and left margins. It ignores any instructions given in the LEFTMARGIN and TOPMARGIN tags.

■ You can use either the LEFTMARGIN or the TOPMARGIN tag, or both.

Figure 5.1 *Inside the BODY tag, type the values for LEFTMARGIN and TOPMARGIN.*

Figure 5.2 *Netscape doesn't understand the LEFTMARGIN and TOPMARGIN tags and thus, always leaves 8 pixels at the top and left side of the page.*

Figure 5.3 *With a value of 0 for both LEFTMARGIN and TOPMARGIN, the text in Internet Explorer is jammed right up next to the top left corner of the page.*

Figure 5.4 *Although I've chosen to use the same value for the left and top margins in both examples, you can use different values if you prefer.*

Figure 5.5 *Extra space in the margins can be handy, depending on the design of the page.*

Specifying the margins

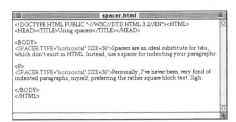

Figure 5.6 *Use horizontal spacers for indenting paragraphs, or any place you need to add an invisible, horizontal block of space.*

Figure 5.7 *Horizontal spacers are effective when viewed with Netscape.*

Figure 5.8 *Internet Explorer ignores horizontal spacers completely, aligning all text to the left.*

Creating indents

You can't type a tab, or specify a tab stop in HTML documents. However, there are a number of ways to create indents for your paragraphs.

To create indents:

1. Place the cursor where you want the space to appear.

2. Type **<SPACER**.

3. Type **TYPE=horizontal**.

4. Type **SIZE=n**, where *n* is the desired indent size, in pixels.

5. Type the final **>** tag.

6. Type the text of the indented paragraph.

✔ Tips

- You can use horizontal spaces anywhere you want, not just at the beginning of a text paragraph.

- How much is a pixel? It all depends on the resolution of your users' screens, which is typically, but not always, 72 dpi. In this case, 36 pixels is 1/2 inch, 18 pixels is 1/4 inch. Your best bet is to be consistent on your page and/or test the result on more than one screen.

- You can also use pixel shims *(see page 86)* to create indented paragraphs.

- Internet Explorer does not yet understand the SPACER tag.

- For information on controlling vertical spacing, consult *Specifying the space between paragraphs* on page 84.

Creating indents

Specifying the space between paragraphs

 The amount of space between paragraphs, when you use the P or BR tags, is determined by the size of the surrounding text. Larger text has larger spaces. Smaller text has smaller spaces. Netscape's SPACER tag lets you specify exactly how much space should appear between one line and another.

To specify the space between paragraphs:

1. Place the cursor between the two lines to be separated.

2. Type **<SPACER**.

3. Type **TYPE=vertical**.

4. Type **SIZE=n**, where *n* is the amount of space, in pixels, that should appear between the two lines.

5. Type the final **>**.

✔ Tips

■ The space between lines is usually specified in points, not pixels. Thanks to Steve Jobs, on most Macintosh monitors one point is almost exactly equal to one pixel. So if you want 10 points of space, use a value of 10 in step 4. Windows monitors tend to have a slightly lower resolution, and thus slightly bigger pixels. For 10 points, use 8 or 9 pixels.

■ The SPACER tag with the a value of vertical for the TYPE attribute creates an automatic line break. You do not need to use the P tag—it will create the same amount of space it always has, in addition to the SPACER's space.

Figure 5.9 *Make sure you take out any P tags when using vertical spacers. Otherwise, you the paragraphs will have extra space between them.*

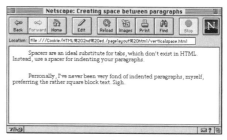

Figure 5.10 *On a 72 dpi screen, there will be exactly 1/3 inch of white space between the two paragraphs—as long as they're viewed in Netscape.*

Figure 5.11 *Since we haven't used a P tag, the two paragraphs run together in Internet Explorer, which doesn't understand the SPACER tag.*

Specifying the space between paragraphs

```
block.html
<!DOCTYPE HTML PUBLIC "-//W3C//DTD HTML 3.2//EN"><HTML>
<HEAD><TITLE>Creating blocks of space</TITLE></HEAD>

<BODY>
<SPACER TYPE="block" WIDTH=100 HEIGHT=100 ALIGN=left>If you like to
create big margins around your text, spacers are ideal for the job.
<P>Just use the spacer tag as if it were an invisible image. And wrap the text
right around it as usual.

</BODY>
</HTML>
```

Figure 5.12 *When creating a block-shaped space, you have to specify the width and the height, along with an alignment to determine where the space will appear.*

Figure 5.13 *Block shaped spaces are ideal for setting large, invisible margins—in Netscape.*

Figure 5.14 *Again, the spacer tag has no effect in Internet Explorer.*

```
block+horiz.html
<!DOCTYPE HTML PUBLIC "-//W3C//DTD HTML 3.2//EN"><HTML>
<HEAD><TITLE>Using blocks and horizontal space</TITLE></HEAD>

<BODY>
<SPACER TYPE="block" WIDTH=100 HEIGHT=100 ALIGN=left><SPACER
TYPE="horizontal" SIZE=36>If you like to create big margins around your text,
spacers are ideal for the job.
<P><SPACER TYPE="horizontal" SIZE=36>Just use the spacer tag as if it were an
invisible image. And wrap the text right around it as usual.
</BODY>
```

Figure 5.15 *Use horizontal and block spacers to create both effects at the same time.*

Figure 5.16 *Here the entire text is offset with a block spacer while each paragraph is indented with a horizontal spacer.*

Creating blocks of space

 The SPACER tag is also useful for creating blocks of space that you can wrap text around.

To create blocks of space:

1. Place the cursor where the space should appear, before any text that will wrap around it.

2. Type **<SPACER**.

3. Type **TYPE=block**.

4. Type **WIDTH=w HEIGHT=h**, where w and h are the width and height, respectively, of the block, in pixels.

5. To wrap text around the block, type **ALIGN=left** or **ALIGN=right**, depending on which side of the image you want the text.

To align the image next to the text, without wrapping the text around it, type **ALIGN=direction**, where *direction* is top, middle, or bottom.

6. Type the final **>**.

✔ Tips

■ For more information on wrapping text, consult *Wrapping text around images* on page 71. For more information on the alignment options, consult *Aligning images* on page 76.

■ Internet Explorer does not understand the SPACER tag.

■ To create a *colored* block of space, use a pixel shim *(see page 86)*.

Creating blocks of space

Using pixel shims

A shim in the physical world is a little piece of wood (or sometimes paper) that you stick under one of the legs of your table (for example) to make it stop wobbling. A *pixel shim* is a wedge of pixels, sometimes in color, that you insert between elements on a page to shore up the balance and alignment.

To use a pixel shim:

1. In Photoshop or other image editing program, create a 1 pixel by 1 pixel GIF image in the desired color.

2. In your HTML document, type **<IMG SRC=pixelshim.gif**, where *pixelshim .gif* is the name of the image created in step 1.

3. Type **WIDTH=w HEIGHT=h**, where w and h are the desired (not the actual) width and height, in pixels, of the desired space.

4. To wrap text around the shim, type **ALIGN=left** or **ALIGN=right**, depending on which side of the image you want the text.

To align the image next to the text, without wrapping the text around it, type **ALIGN=direction**, where *direction* is top, middle, or bottom.

5. Add other image attributes, as desired.

6. Type the final **>**.

✔ Tips

■ Pixel shims are recognized by most browsers since they're just images, forced to work in a new way.

■ In addition, pixel shims are tiny (and thus, load quickly) and can be made any color you want—or transparent.

Figure 5.17 *A pixel shim is nothing more than a one pixel by one pixel image, of any color you like, amplified to the desired size, and aligned as necessary.*

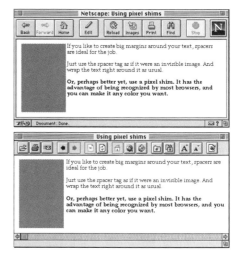

Figure 5.18 *The principal advantage of pixel shims is that they work in almost any browser. In addition, however, they are small and load quickly and they can be made any color you need.*

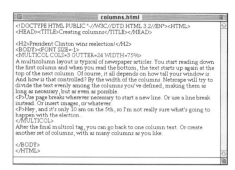

```
columns.html
<!DOCTYPE HTML PUBLIC "-//W3C//DTD HTML 3.2//EN"><HTML>
<HEAD><TITLE>Creating columns</TITLE></HEAD>

<H2>President Clinton wins reelection!</H2>
<BODY><FONT SIZE=-1>
<MULTICOL COLS=3 GUTTER=24 WIDTH=75%>
A multicolumn layout is typical of newspaper articles. You start reading down
the first column and when you read the bottom, the text starts up again at the
top of the next column. Of course, it all depends on how tall your window is.
And how is that controlled? By the width of the columns. Netscape will try to
divide the text evenly among the columns you've defined, making them as
long as necessary, but as even as possible.
<P>Use page breaks wherever necessary to start a new line. Or use a line break
instead. Or insert images, or whatever.
<P>Hey, and it's only 10 am on the 5th, so I'm not really sure what's going to
happen with the election.
</MULTICOL>
After the final multicol tag, you can go back to one column text. Or create
another set of columns, with as many columns as you like.

</BODY>
</HTML>
```

Figure 5.19 *The only required attribute in the MULTICOL tag is COLS: you must determine how many columns you want. If you choose to, you can set both the Gutter and Width size, either in pixels or as a percentage of window size.*

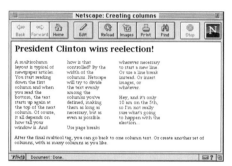

Figure 5.20 *Columns are perfect for newspaper style articles. Notice that the columns (and gutters) take up 75% of the screen, as defined in the HTML document, while the last paragraph, outside of the MULTICOL definition, spans the entire width of the window. In addition, I've made the text one size smaller so as to better fit in the columns.*

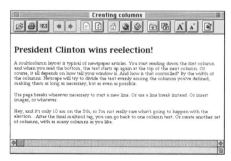

Figure 5.21 *Internet Explorer does not recognize the MULTICOL tag. Notice that the last paragraph runs into the column text, since there was no P tag.*

Creating columns

 You can divide your page into columns with a special extension that only Netscape recognizes. The extension is still pretty limited, however. First, all columns must be the same width. Second, if you make the columns too narrow, they will overlap and look horrible.

To create columns:

1. In your HTML document, type **<MULTICOL**.

2. Type **COLS=n**, where *n* is the number of columns desired. Each column will be the same size.

3. If desired, type **GUTTER=n**, where *n* is the width of the space between the columns, in pixels or as a percentage.

4. If desired, type **WIDTH=n**, where *n* is the width of the entire column set, including the gutter, in pixels or as a percentage of window size.

5. Type the final **>** to finish the column definition.

6. Create the elements (text or images) that will go into the columns.

7. Type **</MULTICOL>**.

✔ Tips

■ If you omit the WIDTH attribute, the columns will expand to fit whatever size window the user has created.

■ You can nest one set of columns with another. Simply repeat steps 1-7 when you reach step 6 of the outer set.

■ If you don't use the GUTTER attribute, Netscape automatically leaves 10 pixels between columns.

Centering elements on a page

In Chapter 1, *Basic HTML*, you learned how to align paragraphs and headers. There is, however, a more general centering tag that can be used with virtually any element on your page: the CENTER tag.

To center elements on a page:

1. Type **<CENTER>**.

2. Create the element that you wish to center.

3. Type **</CENTER>**.

✔ Tips

■ You can use the CENTER tag with almost every kind of HTML element, including paragraphs, headers, images, and forms, even if there is another method for centering that element.

■ For more information on aligning paragraphs, consult *Starting a new paragraph* on page 28. For more information on aligning headers, consult *Organizing the page* on page 27.

■ For information on aligning images with text, consult *Aligning images* on page 66.

■ For details on dividing your document into sections that you can then align, consult *Special tags for styles* on page 188.

```
center.html
<HTML><HEAD><TITLE>Centering text</TITLE></HEAD>
<BODY>
<H2 ALIGN=CENTER>The Earth's Core</H2>
<CENTER>At the center of the earth, more than 6000 kilometers from the
surface, the temperature is a toasty 6500 degrees Kelvin </CENTER>
<P>Not bad for a little planet.
</BODY>
<HTML>
Num. Lock          Normal
```

Figure 5.22 *Note that the header, The Earth's Core is centered by the method described on page 27.*

Figure 5.23 *The display of centered text is virtually indistinguishable in Netscape (top) and Internet Explorer (bottom).*

Centering elements on a page

Figure 5.24 *Here is the HTML document with no control over line breaks.*

Figure 5.25 *In both Netscape and Internet Explorer (not just Netscape, shown here), the lines are divided according to the width of the window.*

Figure 5.26 *The NOBR tag keeps all the enclosed elements on the same line. The WBR tag allows a line break—if necessary—depending on window size.*

Figure 5.27 *Both browsers interpret the NOBR and WBR tags correctly. Notice how the header extends beyond the width of the window, while the first line break comes before the word* met *which is just where the WBR was. The second line again extends beyond the width of the window, and breaks where the WBR tag is.*

Controlling line breaks

You may have certain phrases in your document that you don't want separated. Or you may want to keep a word and an image together, no matter what. There are a couple special tags for this purpose.

To keep elements on one line:

1. Type **<NOBR>**.

2. Create the text or elements that should appear all on one line.

3. Type **</NOBR>**.

To insert soft line breaks in a nonbreakable line:

In a block of nonbreakable text, as that created above, type **<WBR>** where you would allow a line break, if, and only if, the size of the user's window required it.

✔ Tips

- Line breaks created with WBR only appear if the window is small enough to warrant them. Otherwise, the elements will not be separated.

- Elements within NOBR tags will not be separated, unless there is a WBR tag, even if the size of the window causes them to be displayed off screen, and thus invisible to the user.

- Unlike the NOWRAP attribute used in tables *(see page 133)* to keep a cell's contents on a single line, the NOBR tag must have an opening and closing tag and only affects the text contained within the two.

Controlling line breaks

Using background color

Tired of basic gray? The BGCOLOR tag lets you set the background color of each Web page you create.

To set the background color:

1. In the BODY tag, after the word BODY but before the final >, type **BGCOLOR="#rrggbb"**, where *rrggbb* is the hexadecimal representation of the desired color.

Or type **BGCOLOR=color**, where *color* is one of the 16 predefined colors.

2. Add other attributes to the BODY (like link and text colors) as desired.

✔ Tips

■ See Appendix C and the inside back cover for a complete listing of hexadecimal values and common color representations. Appendix C also includes a list of the 16 predefined colors.

■ For more information on setting the link colors, consult *Changing the color of links* on page 45. For more information on setting the text color, consult *Changing the font size of all the body text* on page 39 or *Changing the font size of a few letters* on page 40.

■ To use an image for the background, consult *Using background images* on page 77.

■ Most browsers let the user override any background color set by you, the page designer.

Figure 5.28 *Add the BGCOLOR attribute to the BODY tag to set the background color for the page.*

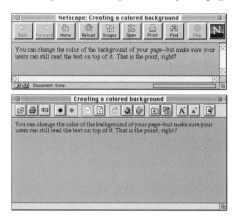

Figure 5.29 *Most browsers, including Netscape (above) and Internet Explorer, can interpret the BGCOLOR attribute correctly. Most also, however, allow the user to override such settings.*

Links and Anchors

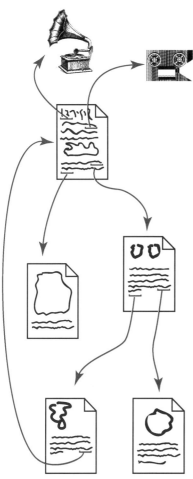

Figure 6.1 *Some of your pages may have links to many other pages. Other pages may have only one link. And still others may have no links at all.*

Creating links

Links are the distinguishing feature of the World Wide Web. They let you skip from one page to another, call up a movie or a recording of Bill playing his sax, and download files with FTP.

To create a link:

1. Type **<A HREF="url.address">**, where *url.address* is the URL of the destination file to be viewed.

2. Type the clickable text, that is, the text that will be underlined or highlighted in blue, and that when clicked upon will take the user to the URL referenced in step 1.

3. Type **</A>** to complete the definition of the link.

✔ Tips

- Don't use excessive amounts of clickable text. If the clickable text is part of a longer sentence, keep only the key words within the link definition, with the rest of the sentence before and after the less than and greater signs.

- Don't use "Click here" as clickable text. Instead use the key words that already exist in your text to identify the link.

- You may apply text formatting to the clickable text.

- For more information on constructing URLs, consult *URLs* on page 19.

Creating links

Using the BASE tag

Generally, relative URLs are constructed according to the current location of the HTML document that contains the URL. If you use relative URLs in your HTML documents *(see page 21)*, you can use the BASE tag to define the URL of the current HTML document—regardless of its actual location on the server.

To create a base URL:

1. In the HEAD section of your HTML document (after <HEAD> but before </HEAD>), type **<BASE HREF="**.

2. Type **http://www.site.com/path/filename.html** where *http://www.site.com/path/filename.html* indicates the desired URL for the HTML file. All relative URLs contained in the HTML document will be built using this URL as a reference.

3. Type **">** to complete the BASE tag.

✔ Tip

■ The BASE tag is optional. If you do not use it, relative URLs will be constructed from the actual location of the file, instead of from the URL given in the BASE tag.

Figure 6.2 *The BASE tag, which goes in the HEAD section of the HTML document, gives the URL of the current file, in this case that of basetag.html.*

Figure 6.3 *The relative URL, ../index.html, combined with the base URL results in the file that is in the directory that is one level higher than the base URL's directory.*

Figure 6.4 *The relative URL,* createanchors.html, *combined with the base URL indicates the file will be in the current directory.*

Figure 6.5 *The relative URL, ../images/* index.html, *combined with the base URL indicates the file that is inside the directory* images *which is at the same level as the current directory.*

Figure 6.6 *Only the text within the link definition (in this case the words* Pioneer Valley*) will be clickable.*

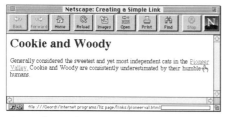

Figure 6.7 *A click on a link (generally shown with underlined or blue text or both)...*

Figure 6.8 *...brings you to the associated URL (below).*

Creating a link to another Web page

If you have more than one Web page, you will probably want to create links from one page to the next (and back again). You can also create connections to Web pages designed by other people on other computers. Whenever you create a link to another Web page, you must use the HTTP protocol.

To create a link to another Web page using HTTP:

1. Type **<A HREF="http://www.site.com/homepage.html">** where *www.site.com/homepage.html* is the URL of the Web page. *www.site.com* is the name of the server and *home page.html* is the file name of the destination page.

2. Type the clickable text, that is, the text that will be underlined or highlighted in blue, and that when clicked upon will take the user to the URL referenced in step 1.

3. Type **</A>** to complete the definition of the link.

✔ Tips

■ When creating links, make them as specific as possible. If you just create a link to a huge site, the user might not be able to find the specific page you had in mind.

■ You can often create a link to a site's home page by using *http://www.site.com/directory/*. The trailing forward slash tells the browser to search for the default file, usually called *index.html*, in the last directory mentioned.

Targeting links to specific windows

One of the most useful additions to HTML 3.2 is the ability to open a link in a particular window, or even in a new window created especially for that link. This way, the page that creates the link stays open, enabling the user to go back and forth between the page of links and the information from each of those links.

To target links to specific windows:

Within the link definition, type **TARGET=**
title, where *title* is the name of the window where the corresponding page should be displayed.

✔ Tips

■ If you target several links to the same window (e.g., using the same name), in Netscape, the links will all open in that same window. In Internet Explorer, each link will open in a separate, new window.

■ You can target a link to another page on your site or to a page at another site. You can even target an FTP link *(see page 97)* to a new window.

■ It doesn't make sense, however, to target e-mail or news links, since these open in different kinds of windows.

■ For more information on targeting frames, consult *Targeting links to particular frames* on page 149.

■ In fact, you can use targeted windows as a substitute for frames, which may not be supported by some browsers.

Figure 6.9 *Add the TARGET attribute to a link to open the corresponding page in a new window.*

Figure 6.10 *When the user clicks a targeted link...*

Figure 6.11 *...the corresponding page is shown in a new window.*

Targeting links to specific windows

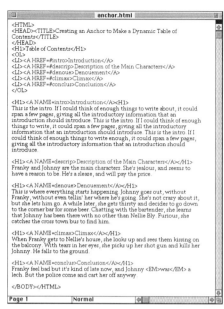

```
                  anchor.html
<HTML>
<HEAD><TITLE>Creating an Anchor to Make a Dynamic Table of
Contents</TITLE>
</HEAD>
<H1>Table of Contents</H1>
<OL>
<LI><A HREF=#intro>Introduction</A>
<LI><A HREF=#descrip> Description of the Main Characters</A>
<LI><A HREF=#denoue> Denouement</A>
<LI><A HREF=#climax>Climax</A>
<LI><A HREF=#conclus>Conclusion</A>
</OL>

<H1><A NAME=intro>Introduction</A></H1>
This is the intro. If I could think of enough things to write about, it could
span a few pages, giving all the introductory information that an
introduction should introduce. This is the intro. If I could think of enough
things to write, it could span a few pages, giving all the introductory
information that an introduction should introduce. This is the intro. If I
could think of enough things to write enough, it could span a few pages,
giving all the introductory information that an introduction should
introduce.

<H1><A NAME=descrip> Description of the Main Characters</A></H1>
Franky and Johnny are the main characters. She's jealous, and seems to
have a reason to be. He's a sleaze, and will pay the price.

<H1><A NAME=denoue>Denouement</A></H1>
This is where everything starts happening. Johnny goes out, without
Franky, without even tellin' her where he's going. She's not crazy about it,
but she lets him go. A while later, she gets thirsty and decides to go down
to the corner bar for some beer. Chatting with the bartender, she learns
that Johnny has been there with no other than Nellie Bly. Furious, she
catches the cross town bus to find him.

<H1><A NAME=climax>Climax</A></H1>
When Franky gets to Nellie's house, she looks up and sees them kissing on
the balcony. With tears in her eyes, she picks up her shot gun and kills her
Johnny. He falls to the ground.

<H1><A NAME=conclus>Conclusion</A></H1>
Franky feel bad but it's kind of late now, and Johnny <EM>was</EM> a
lech. But the police come and cart her off anyway.

</BODY></HTML>
```
Page 1   Normal

Figure 6.12 *A long document like this one can be greatly helped by a dynamic table of contents. In this example, each section has its own anchor name so that a click on the corresponding item in the table of contents brings the user directly to the section they're interested in. (See Figure 6.13 and Figure 6.14 on page 96).*

Creating anchors

Generally, a click on a link brings the user to the *top* of the appropriate Web page. If you want to have the user jump to a specific section of the Web page, you have to create an *anchor* and then reference that anchor in the link.

To create an anchor:

1. Place the cursor in the part of the Web page that you wish the user to jump to.

2. Type **<A NAME="anchor name">**, where *anchor name* is the text you will use internally to identify that section of the Web page.

3. Add the words or images that you wish to be referenced.

4. Type **</A>** to complete the definition of the anchor.

✔ Tips

■ You only need to add quotation marks around the anchor name if it is more than one word.

■ In a long document, create an anchor for each section and link it to the corresponding item in the table of contents.

■ Be aware that Netscape uses the term *targets* or *named anchors* when they mean anchors, although targets are something completely different *(see page 94).*

Creating anchors

Linking to a specific anchor

Once you have created an anchor you can define a link so that a user's click will bring her directly to the section of the document that contains the anchor, not just the top of that document.

To create a link to an anchor:

1. Type **<A HREF="#**.

2. Type **anchor name"** where *anchor name* is the NAME of the destination section *(see page 95)*.

3. Type the clickable text, that is, the text that will be underlined or highlighted in blue, and that when clicked upon will take the user to the section referenced in step 1.

4. Type **</A>** to complete the definition of the link.

✔ Tips

■ If the anchor is in a separate document, use *<A HREF="url.address #anchor name">* to reference the section. (There should be no space between *url.address* and the # symbol.)

■ Although you obviously can't add anchors to other people's pages, you can take advantage of the ones that they have already created. Save their documents in HTML format to see which anchor names correspond to which sections. (For more information on saving HTML code, consult *The inspiration of others* on page 208.)

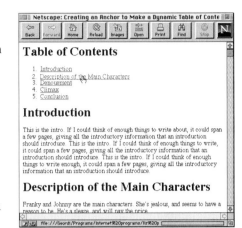

Figure 6.13 *A click in the referenced link brings the user...*

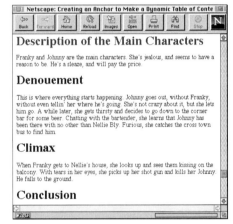

Figure 6.14 *...to the corresponding anchor farther down in the same document (as in this example) or to a specific position in a separate document.*

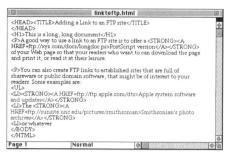

Figure 6.15 *Creating a link to an FTP site is very similar to creating a link to a Web page; just substitute the FTP site address in the link definition.*

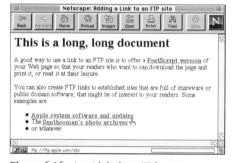

Figure 6.16 *As with links to Web pages, you should incorporate your links to FTP sites right into your text. Here I've used strong formatting to help the links stand out better.*

Linking to an anonymous FTP site

You can create links to FTP servers directly from your Web page. Many browsers can complete non-Web type connections, while others automatically open an appropriate helper program (like Fetch) if they can't handle the connection directly.

To create a link to an FTP site:

1. Type **<A HREF="ftp://ftp.site.com/ directory/filename">** where *ftp.site.com/directory/filename* is the URL of the destination file available through FTP.

2. Type the clickable text, that is, the text that will be underlined or highlighted in blue, and that when clicked upon will take the user to the URL referenced in step 1.

3. Type **</A>** to complete the definition of the link.

✔ Tips

■ If you don't want to create the link to a specific file, but instead to a particular directory on the FTP site, simply use *ftp://ftp.site.com/directory*. You don't need to use the trailing forward slash. When you don't specify a particular file to download, FTP automatically displays the last directory's contents.

■ A user may have trouble connecting to an anonymous FTP site if they have not filled in their e-mail address in the browser's preferences or settings dialog box.

Linking to an anonymous FTP site

Linking to an FTP site with a user name and password

Not all FTP sites accept anonymous connections. You may include a link to an FTP site using your user name and password, but since there is no way to hide your password, you should not use this kind of link in a page that is published on the Web for all to see.

To create a link to an FTP site with a user name and password:

1. Type **<A HREF="ftp://yourname: password@ftp.site.com/directory/">** where *yourname* is your user name, *password* is your password and *ftp.site.com/directory/* is the URL of the destination directory available through FTP.

2. Type the clickable text, that is, the text that will be underlined or highlighted in blue, and that when clicked upon will take the user to the URL referenced in step 1.

3. Type **</A>** to complete the definition of the link.

✔ Tips

■ Add your favorite FTP sites, complete with passwords, to a personal bookmarks or hotlist page that you keep on your local computer.

■ If your browser keeps a record of your trips around the Web, it may keep a record of your password as well. In Netscape, type **about=global** in the location box to see what it remembers.

Figure 6.17 *Add the user name and password before the site name in the URL address.*

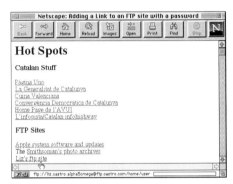

Figure 6.18 *Since you don't want to share the password to your (or anyone else's) account with the rest of the world, only include the user name and password to FTP sites in personal pages on a local computer.*

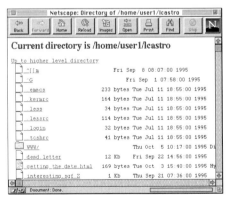

Figure 6.19 *Once you connect to the FTP site, it works the same way as anonymous FTP connections. (Pardon the mess!)*

Linking to an FTP site with a user name

Figure 6.20 *Don't forget to type the word "gopher" twice, once as the protocol and once as part of the domain name.*

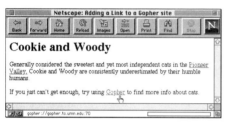

Figure 6.21 *OK, the text here is not particularly brilliant, but the idea is clear: make the link part of your text.*

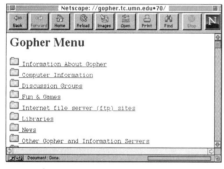

Figure 6.22 *Once the user clicks on your Gopher link they are directly connected to the Gopher site and can perform their search as usual. Other browsers may choose to open a Gopher helper program (like TurboGopher) instead.*

Linking to Gopher servers

Creating a link to a Gopher server is very similar to creating a link to an FTP site.

To create a link to a Gopher server:

1. Type **<A HREF="gopher://site.edu">** where *site.edu* is the URL of the Gopher server.

2. Type the clickable text, that is, the text that will be underlined or highlighted in blue, and that when clicked upon will take the user to the URL referenced in step 1.

3. Type **</A>** to complete the definition of the link.

Linking to e-mail

Although not all browsers currently support e-mail links, the ones that do make it quite easy for your users to contact you. A link to e-mail is called a *mailto* and is a special link that pops up an automatically addressed e-mail form.

To create a mailto link:

1. Type **<A HREF="mailto:name@ site.com">**, where *name@site.com* is the electronic mail address of the person who should receive the mail.

2. Type the clickable text, that is, the text that will be underlined or highlighted, and that when clicked upon will open an e-mail form addressed to the person in step 1.

3. Type **</A>** to complete the definition of the link.

✔ Tip

■ Mailto links are ideal for eliciting comments about your Web page. They ensure that the comments will go to the proper person.

Figure 6.23 *A mailto URL does not use forward slashes; a colon divides the protocol (mailto) from the recipient's e-mail address.*

Figure 6.24 *Placing the cursor over the mailto link shows the recipient's e-mail address in the destination area of the browser (below left in the Netscape window as shown here).*

Figure 6.25 *Once the user clicks the mailto link, an e-mail form pops up with the From: and To: boxes automatically filled in. If you respond to your own Web pages, you, too, can write schizophrenic notes like this one.*

Linking to e-mail

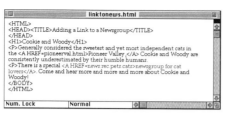

Figure 6.26 *The newsgroup protocol is format-ted differently than most others, with a colon and no forward slashes.*

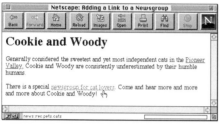

Figure 6.27 *This particular newsgroup is remarkably active, with three hundred messages daily. It's a bit of a struggle to keep up with, even for a cat lover.*

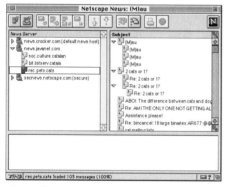

Figure 6.28 *Netscape has a special window for displaying Usenet newsgroups.*

Linking to a newsgroup

You can create a link from your page to an entire newsgroup or to just one article in the newsgroup.

To create a link to a newsgroup:

1. Type **<A HREF="news:newsgroup">** where *newsgroup* is the name of the newsgroup (like *bit.listserv.catala* or *rec.pets.cats*).

2. Type the clickable text, that is, the text that will be underlined or high-lighted in blue, and that when clicked upon will take the user to the URL ref-erenced in step 1.

3. Type **</A>** to complete the definition of the link.

To create a link to a single article:

1. Type **<A HREF="news:articlenumb">** where *articlenumb* is the number (as shown in the header) of the individ-ual article.

2. Type the clickable text, that is, the text that will be underlined or high-lighted in blue, and that when clicked upon will take the user to the URL ref-erenced in step 1.

3. Type **</A>** to complete the definition of the link.

Linking to a newsgroup

Creating navigational buttons

In this age of graphical interfaces, people are used to clicking on images and icons to make things happen. Adding an image to a link allows the user to click the image to access the referenced URL. (For more information about how to create and use images, see Chapter 3, *Creating Images* and Chapter 4, *Using Images*.)

To create links with buttons:

1. Type **<A HREF="url.address">**, where *url.address* identifies the page that the user will jump to when they click the button.

2. Type **<IMG SRC="image.location"** where *image.location* gives the location of the image file on the server.

3. If desired, type **BORDER=n**, where *n* is the width in pixels of the border. Use a value of 0 for no border.

4. Add other image attributes as desired and then type the final **>**.

5. Type the clickable text, that is, the text that will be underlined or highlighted in blue, that when clicked upon will take the user to the URL referenced in step 1.

6. Type **</A>** to complete the link.

✔ Tips

■ If you invert steps 5 and 6, only a click on the *image* will produce the desired jump. A click on the text has no effect.

■ Use small images.

■ Clickable images are surrounded by a border with the same color as the active links (generally blue). For no border, use a value of 0 in step 3.

Figure 6.29 *There is no text in the first two button links. The final </A> comes right after the image source information.*

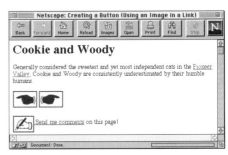

Figure 6.30 *If you do add text to the link, make sure you insert a space between the text and the image (or use Netscape's extensions to space the text, see page 74).*

Figure 6.31 *This is the original pointright.gif image. It does not have a border. Borders are automatically added to all clickable images in the browser. You can adjust the border with the BORDER attribute in the IMG tag.*

Figure 6.32 *In Photoshop, choose Show Info in the Palettes submenu in the Window menu.*

Figure 6.33 *Place the cursor in the left hand corner of the rectangle and jot down the x and y coordinates shown in Photoshop's Info palette. (In this example x=395 and y=18.)*

Dividing an image into clickable regions

A clickable image is like a collection of buttons combined together in one image. A click in one part of the image brings the user to one destination. A click in another area brings the user to a different destination.

There are two important steps to implementing a clickable image: First you must map out the different regions of your image, and second you must create a script that defines which destinations correspond to which areas of the image.

To divide an image into regions:

1. Create a GIF image, consulting Chapter 3, *Creating Images* as necessary.

2. Open the GIF image in Photoshop, or other image editing program.

3. Choose Show Info in the Palettes submenu in the Window menu.

4. Point the cursor over the region you wish to define. Using the Info window, jot down the *x* and *y* coordinates, **(Figure 6.33)**.

5. Repeat step 4 for each corner of a rectangle, or each point of a polygon.

✔ Tip

■ For more information on a few tools that can help you divide your image into clickable regions, consult *Image Map Tools* on page 232.

Dividing an image into clickable regions

Creating a client-side image map

Image maps link the areas of an image with a series of URLs. A click in each area brings the user to a different page. There are two kinds of image maps, *client-side* and *server side (see page 106)*. Client-side image maps run more quickly because they are interpreted in your users' browsers and don't have to consult the server for each click. In addition since they do not require a CGI script, they are simpler to create and you don't need to consult your Internet service provider, nor get their permission. But, older browsers may not understand them.

To create a client-side image map:

1. In the HTML document that contains the image, type **<MAP**.

2. Type **NAME="label">**, where *label* is the name of the map.

3. Type **<AREA** to define the first clickable area.

4. Type **SHAPE="type"**, where *type* represents the area's shape. Use *rect* for a rectangle, *circle* for a circle, and *poly* for an irregular shape.

5. For a rectangle, type **COORDS="x1,y1, x2, y2"**, where *x1, y1, x2,* and *y2* represent the corners of the rectangle, as obtained on page 103, (Figure 6.33).

For a circle, type **COORDS="x, y, r"** where *x* and *y* represent the center of the circle and *r* is the radius.

For a polygon, type **COORDS="x1,y1 x2, y2 x3, y3"** (and so on), giving the x and y coordinates of each point on the polygon.

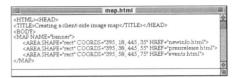

Figure 6.34 *You can place the map anywhere in your HTML document. Each clickable area is defined by its own set of coordinates, and has an individual URL.*

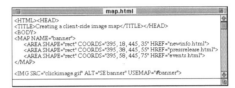

Figure 6.35 *Type the image definition in the desired place in your HTML document. The most important piece is the USEMAP=#label attribute. Don't forget the number sign (#).*

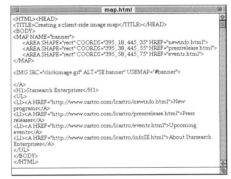

Figure 6.36 *Below the image it's a good idea to repeat the links in text form for those users who can't or don't want to view images. Otherwise, those users won't be able to get to your other pages.*

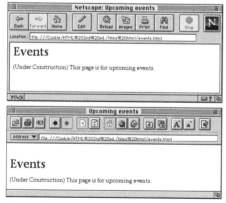

Figure 6.37 *When your users point at one of the defined areas, the destination URL appears in the status bar at the bottom of the window (Netscape is above, Internet Explorer, below).*

Figure 6.38 *And if a user clicks the link, the browser (Netscape above, IE below) will immediately display the corresponding page.*

6. Type **HREF="url.html"**, where *url.html* is the address of the page that should appear when the user clicks in this area.

Or type **NOHREF** if a click in this area should have no result.

7. Type **TARGET=windowname**, where *windowname* is the name of the window where the page should appear. For more information, see page 94.

8. Type **>** to complete the definition of the clickable area.

9. Repeat steps 3-8 for each area.

10. Type **</MAP>** to complete the map.

11. Type **<IMG SRC="image.gif"**, where *image.gif* is the name of the image to be used as an image map.

12. Add any other image attributes.

13. Type **USEMAP="#label"**, where *label* is the map name defined in step 2.

14. Type the final **>** for the image.

15. Continue creating the page as usual.

✔ Tips

■ Internet Explorer can use maps that are in a different HTML file. Simply add the URL in front of the label name: **USEMAP="map.html#label"**.

■ For information on using server-side image maps, see page 106.

■ With overlapping areas, most browsers use the URL of the first one defined.

Creating a client-side image map

Using a server-side image map

To use a server-side image map, you have to have the *imagemap* program on your NCSA HTTPd server or *htimage* on your CERN server. The program should be located in the cgi-bin directory. Ask your server administrator for help, if necessary.

To use a server-side image map:

1. In your HTML document type **<A HREF="http://www.yoursite.com/cgi-bin/imagemap**, where *imagemap* is the name of the program that interprets your set of coordinates.

2. Type **/path/coords"** (adding no spaces after step 1) indicating the path to the text file that contains the coordinates (the map) for the image.

3. Type the final **>** of the link definition.

4. Type **<IMG SRC="clickimage.gif"** where *clickimage.gif* is the image that you want your readers to click.

5. Type **ISMAP** to indicate a clickable image for a server-side map.

6. Add any other image attributes as desired and then type the final **>**.

7. Type the clickable text that should appear next to the image, if any.

8. Type **</A>** to complete the link.

✔ Tip

■ For information on creating sets of coordinates for server-side image maps, consult your Internet service provider. They'll be able to tell you what kind of server they have and in what format the coordinates should be.

Figure 6.39 *Notice how the text-based alternative pointers below the image point to the same URLs as the buttons in the clickable image. This gives equal opportunity to your users who can't see the images.*

Figure 6.40 *In Netscape, when your user points at a part of a clickable image, the cursor changes into a hand and the corresponding URL shows in the bottom part of the window.*

Figure 6.41 *In Internet Explorer, the cursor changes to a hand when placed over a clickable image, but the status line does not show the particular coordinates.*

Lists

The HTML specifications contain special codes for creating lists of items. You can create plain, numbered, or bulleted lists, as well as lists of definitions. You can also nest one kind of list inside another. In the sometimes sketchy shorthand of the Internet, lists come in very handy.

All lists are formed by a principal code to specify what sort of list you want to create (DL for definition list, OL for ordered list, etc.) and a secondary code to specify what sort of items you want to create (DT for definition term, LI for list item, etc.).

Lists

Creating ordered lists

The ordered list is perfect for explaining step-by-step instructions for how to complete a particular task or for creating an outline (complete with links to corresponding sections, if desired) of a larger document. You may create an ordered list anywhere in the BODY section of your HTML document.

To create ordered lists:

1. Type the title of the ordered list.

2. Type **<OL**.

3. If desired, type **TYPE=X**, where *X* represents the symbols that should be used in the ordered list: *A* for capital letters, *a* for small letters, *I* for capital roman numerals, *i* for small roman numerals, and *1* for numbers, which is the default.

4. If desired, type **START=n**, where *n* represents the initial value for this list item. The START value is always numeric and is converted automatically, according to the TYPE value.

5. Type **>** to finish the ordered list definition. Any text entered after the OL marker and before the first LI marker will appear with the same indentation as the first item in the list, but without a number.

6. Type **<LI**.

7. If desired, type **TYPE=X**, where *X* represents the symbols that should be used for this and subsequent line items. Changing the TYPE here overrides the value chosen in step 3.

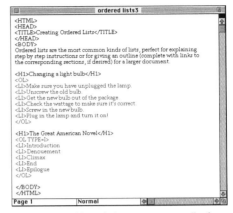

Figure 7.1 *Although there was some talk of creating a special header for lists in HTML 3, it never materialized. Instead, use a regular header.*

Figure 7.2 *The first list uses the default TYPE=1 attribute to create a numbered list. The second list uses the TYPE=I to create a list headed by capital roman numerals.*

Figure 7.3 *Internet Explorer displays the numbered lists types as well as Netscape.*

8. If desired, type **VALUE=n**, where *n* represents the initial value for this line item. The VALUE is always specified numerically and is converted automatically to the type of symbol specified by the TYPE value. The VALUE attribute overrides the START value chosen in step 4.

9. Type the final **>** to complete the list item definition.

10. Type the text to be included in the line item.

11. Repeat steps 6-10 for each new line item.

12. Type **</OL>** to complete the ordered list.

✔ Tips

■ Keep the text in your list items short. If you have more than a few lines of text in each item, you may have better luck using headers (H1, H2, etc.) and paragraphs (P).

■ Inserting a line break (BR) in a list item breaks the text to the next line, but maintains the same indenting.

■ Text placed after the OL marker appears indented by the same amount as the following line item, but without a number or letter.

■ You may create one type of list inside another. For more information, consult *Creating nested lists* on page 113.

■ HTML 3.2 also includes the COMPACT attribute, which theoretically can be added to the OL tag to make entries appear with less space between each one. However, neither Netscape nor Internet Explorer recognize it.

Creating unordered lists

Unordered lists are probably the most widely used lists on the Web. Use them to list any series of items that have no particular order, such as hot web sites or names.

To create unordered lists:

1. Type the introductory text for the unordered list, if desired.

2. Type **<UL**.

3. If desired, type **TYPE=shape**, where *shape* represents the kind of bullet that should be used with each list item. You may choose *disc* for a solid round bullet (the default for first level lists), *circle* for an empty round bullet (the default for second level lists), or *square* for square bullets (the default for third level lists).

4. Type **>** to finish the unordered list definition. Any text entered after the UL marker and before the first LI marker will appear with the same indentation as the first item in the list, but without a bullet.

5. Type **<LI**.

6. Type **TYPE=shape**, where *shape* represents the kind of bullet (*disc, circle,* or *square*) that should be used in this line item. You only need to specify the shape here if it differs from the one you've chosen in step 3.

7. Type **>** to finish the list item definition.

8. Type the text to be included in the line item.

9. Repeat steps 5-7 for each line item.

10. Type **</UL>** to complete the unordered list.

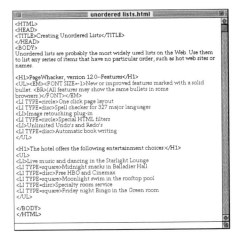

Figure 7.4 *The bullets on the first level are round and solid (disc), by default, so it's not necessary to specify the TYPE unless you wish to select a different shape.*

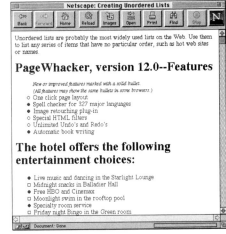

Figure 7.5 *You can use different bullet styles to distinguish among the entries as in the first example, or to add visual interest as in the second example.*

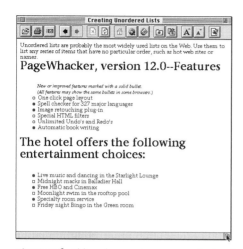

Figure 7.6 *Although many browsers understand the special bullet styles, including Internet Explorer, shown here, not all do. Either avoid giving special meaning to shaped bullets or add a text clarification.*

✔ **Tips**

■ Keep the text in your list items short. If you have more than a couple of lines of text in each item, you may have better luck using headers (H1, H2, etc.) and paragraphs (P).

■ Inserting a line break (BR) in a line item breaks the text to the next line, but maintains the same indenting.

■ Text placed after the UL marker appears indented by the same amount as the following line item, but without a bullet.

■ The TYPE marker in a list item overrides the TYPE marker used in the unordered list definition and affects the current list item as well as any subsequent list items.

■ You may create one type of list inside another. For more information, consult *Creating nested lists* on page 113.

■ HTML 3.2 also includes the COMPACT attribute, which theoretically can be added to the OL tag to make entries appear with less space between each one. However, neither Netscape nor Internet Explorer recognize it.

■ The TYPE attribute used to be a Netscape extension, with values of *disc, square,* and *round.* The *round* value is still recognized by both Netscape and Internet Explorer. However, Netscape shows it as an empty circle (equivalent to *circle*) whereas Internet Explorer fills it in (equivalent to *disc*).

Creating unordered lists

Creating definition lists

HTML provides a special marker for creating definition lists. This type of list is particularly suited to glossaries but works well with any list that pairs a word or phrase with a longer description. Imagine, for example, a list of Ancient Greek verb tenses, each followed an explanation of proper usage.

To create definition lists:

1. Type the introductory text for the definition list.

2. Type **<DL>**. You may enter text after the DL marker. It will appear on its own line, aligned to the left margin.

3. Type **<DT>**.

4. Type the word or short phrase that will be defined or explained, including any logical or physical formatting desired.

5. Type **<DD>**.

6. Type the definition of the term entered in step 4. Browsers generally indent definitions on a new line below your definition term.

7. Repeat steps 3-6 for each pair of terms and definitions.

8. Type **</DL>** to complete the list of definitions.

Figure 7.7 *You may want to add formatting to your definition term to help it stand out.*

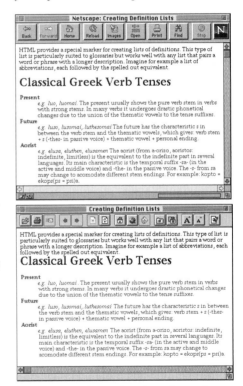

Figure 7.8 *Definition lists don't change their appearance much from browser to browser (Netscape above, Internet Explorer below).*

```
[ nested lists ]
<HTML>
<HEAD>
<TITLE>Creating Nested Lists</TITLE>
</HEAD>
<BODY>
Nested lists are ideal for outlines, but don't feel limited. You can nest any
list inside any other list. Just make sure each list has its own beginning and
ending markers.

<H1>The Great American Novel</H1>
<OL TYPE=I>
<LI>Introduction
        <OL TYPE=A>
        <LI>Boy's childhood
        <LI>Girl's childhood
        </OL>
<LI>Denouement
        <OL TYPE=A>
        <LI>Boy meets Girl
        <LI>Boy and Girl fall in love
        <LI>Boy and Girl have fight
        </OL>
<LI>Climax
        <OL TYPE=A>
        <LI>Boy gives Girl ultimatum
                <OL TYPE=1>
                <LI>Girl can't believe her ears
                <LI>Boy is indignant at Girl's indignance
                </OL>
        <LI>Girl tells Boy to get lost
        </OL>
<LI>End
<LI>Epilogue
</OL>

</BODY>
</HTML>

Page 1              Normal
```

Figure 7.9 *Browsers automatically indent nested lists, but if you use tabs to indent them in your HTML document, it will be much easier to organize and set up.*

```
[ Netscape: Creating Nested Lists ]
Back  Forward  Home  Reload  Images  Open  Print  Find  Stop    N
What's New?  What's Cool?  Handbook  Net Search  Net Directory  Newsgroups

Nested lists are ideal for outlines, but don't feel limited. You can nest any list
inside any other list. Just make sure each list has its own beginning and ending
markers.
```

The Great American Novel

```
   I. Introduction
         A. Boy's childhood
         B. Girl's childhood
  II. Denouement
         A. Boy meets Girl
         B. Boy and Girl fall in love
         C. Boy and Girl have fight
 III. Climax
         A. Boy gives Girl ultimatum
                 1. Girl can't believe her ears
                 2. Boy is indignant at Girl's indignance
         B. Girl tells Boy to get lost
  IV. End
   V. Epilogue
```

```
Document : Done.
```

Figure 7.10 *Netscape allows you, the programmer, to choose the type of numbering for each level of your outline.*

Creating nested lists

You may insert one type of list into another. This is particularly useful with an outline rendered with ordered lists, where you may want several levels of items.

To create nested lists:

1. Create your first list.

2. Place the cursor inside your first list where you want your nested list to appear.

3. Create your nested list in the same way you created the regular list.

4. Continue with the principal list.

✔ Tips

■ Use tabs to indent the nested list in your HTML document so that it is easier to see what you're doing. Nested lists are automatically indented by browsers.

■ The numbering for nested ordered lists automatically starts at one unless you specify a new value with the START marker.

■ The correct nesting order for TYPE markers, according to *The Chicago Manual of Style* is I, A, 1, a, 1.

■ By default, the first level of an unordered list will have solid round bullets, the next will have empty round bullets and the last will have square bullets. Use the TYPE tag to specify the type of bullet you want *(see page 110).*

Creating nested lists

Tables

There is nothing like a table for presenting complicated information in a simple way. Your user sees what you're getting at right away and everyone goes home happy. Too bad tables are so hard to set up. Don't be scared off, though; the result is well worth the effort.

If tables really make you miserable, of course, you can cheat. Try the shortcut described on page 214 if you use Microsoft Word.

If you are worried about users who use a browser that doesn't understand tables, you might consider creating hand-spaced tables with preformatted text *(see page 38)*. Tables made with preformatted text can be read with *any* browser.

Finally, don't limit your use of tables to rows and columns of numbers. Tables are a great way to divide your entire page into manageable sections that are easy to align and space. And consult Chapter 13, *Extras* for more tips on using tables in unconventional ways.

A simple table

There are many kinds of tables, and even many kinds of simple tables. Here we will create a table with two columns and three rows, using the first column to contain the headers and the second column to contain the data.

To create a simple table:

1. Type **<TABLE>**.

2. Type **<TR>** to define the beginning of the first row. We will add two elements to the first row: a header cell and a regular cell. If desired, press Return and Tab to visually distinguish the row elements.

3. Create a header cell in the first row by typing **<TH>**.

4. Type the contents of the first header cell.

5. Type **</TH>** to complete the definition of the first cell header.

6. Create a regular cell after the header cell in the first row by typing **<TD>**.

7. Type the contents of the regular cell.

8. Complete the definition of the regular cell by typing **</TD>**.

9. Complete the definition of the row by typing **</TR>**.

10. Repeat steps 3–9 for each row. In this example, there are two more rows, each containing a header cell and a regular cell.

11. To finish the table, type **</TABLE>**.

Figure 8.1 *The only difference between the two HTML documents above is the addition of returns and tabs to visually separate the rows and row elements to help keep things straight while constructing the table. Since browsers ignore all extra spacing, both documents create the exact same Web page. (See Figure 8.2 and Figure 8.3 below.).*

Figure 8.2 *It seems rather a lot of work for a simple table like this. Notice how Netscape formats the header cells in boldface and centers them while it leaves regular cells in plain text and left aligned.*

Figure 8.3 *Internet Explorer formats the header cells in boldface and centers them. Regular cells are in plain text and left aligned, by default.*

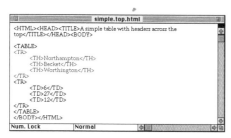

```
┌──────────── simple.top.html ────────────┐
<HTML><HEAD><TITLE>A simple table with headers across the
top</TITLE></HEAD><BODY>

<TABLE>
<TR>
    <TH>Northampton</TH>
    <TH>Becket</TH>
    <TH>Worthington</TH>
</TR>
<TR>
    <TD>6</TD>
    <TD>27</TD>
    <TD>12</TD>
</TR>
</TABLE>
</BODY></HTML>
┌── Num. Lock ──┬── Normal ──┐
```

Figure 8.4 *In the first row, you define all the headers. In the second row, you define all the regular cells.*

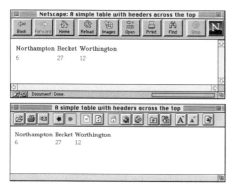

Figure 8.5 *Clearly, very simple tables like these may be better off expressed in lists. However, as you will see in the following pages, there are many ways to tweak your tables to make them beautiful—and more effective.*

Putting headers across the top of the table

On the previous page, in our simple table, we placed the headers along one side of the table. To have the headers appear along the top of the table, you have to define the cells in a slightly different order.

To create a table with headers across the top:

1. Type **<TABLE>**.

2. Type **<TR>** to define the beginning of the first row. If desired, press Return and Tab to visually distinguish the table elements.

3. Create the first header cell in the first row by typing **<TH>**.

4. Type the contents of the first header cell.

5. Type **</TH>** to complete the definition of the cell header.

6. Repeat steps 3–5 for each header cell.

7. Type **</TR>** to complete the row.

8. Type **<TR>** to begin the second row.

9. Type **<TD>** to define the first regular cell in the second row.

10. Type the cell data.

11. Type **</TD>** to complete the definition of the regular cell.

12. Repeat steps 9–11 for each regular cell.

13. Type **</TR>** to finish the row.

14. To finish the table, type **</TABLE>**.

Putting headers on top *and* left

The objective of a table is to present complicated data in a clear way. Often you will need headers across the top of the table *and* down the left side to identify the data being discussed.

To create a table with headers on top and down the left side:

1. Type **<TABLE>**.

2. Type **<TR>** to define the beginning of the first row. If desired, press Return and Tab to visually distinguish the table elements.

3. Create the empty cell in the top left corner by typing **<TD>
</TD>**.

4. Create a header cell by typing **<TH>cell contents</TH>**, where *cell contents* is the data that the cell should contain.

5. Repeat step 4 for each header cell in the first row.

6. Type **</TR>** to finish the row.

7. Type **<TR>** to begin the second row.

8. To define the first header on the left side, type **<TH>cell contents</TH>**.

9. Type **<TD>cell contents</TD>** to create a regular cell after the header cell in the second row.

10. Repeat step 9 for each remaining regular cell in the row.

11. Type **</TR>** to finish the row.

12. Repeat steps 7–11 for each remaining row.

13. To finish the table, type **</TABLE>**.

Figure 8.6 *For a four row by four column table, notice that there are four sets of TR tags with four elements in each set. Once you have defined the first set, copy and paste (and edit) to create the rest.*

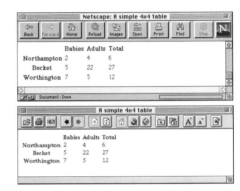

Figure 8.7 *Tables can look impressively bad without borders—both in Netscape and in Internet Explorer. (You'll add a border on page 121.)*

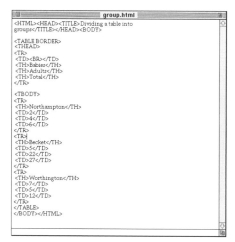

```
                    group.html
<HTML><HEAD><TITLE>Dividing a table into
groups</TITLE></HEAD><BODY>

<TABLE BORDER>
<THEAD>
<TR>
<TD><BR></TD>
<TH>Babies</TH>
<TH>Adults</TH>
<TH>Total</TH>
</TR>

<TBODY>
<TR>
<TH>Northampton</TH>
<TD>2</TD>
<TD>4</TD>
<TD>6</TD>
</TR>
<TR>
<TH>Becket</TH>
<TD>5</TD>
<TD>22</TD>
<TD>27</TD>
</TR>
<TR>
<TH>Worthington</TH>
<TD>7</TD>
<TD>5</TD>
<TD>12</TD>
</TR>
</TABLE>
</BODY></HTML>
```

Figure 8.8 *In this example, the header section is marked with the THEAD tag while the body is marked with the TBODY tag.*

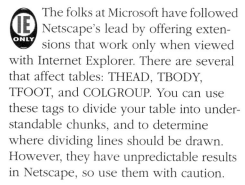

Figure 8.9 *Generally, the THEAD, TBODY, and TFOOT tags have no effect at all in Netscape. Sometimes, however, they make the table impossible to view.*

Figure 8.10 *There is no outward effect of the THEAD, TBODY, or TFOOT tags in Internet Explorer, unless you use rules. Even without rules, however, they are very helpful for organizing your tables.*

Dividing a table into sections

The folks at Microsoft have followed Netscape's lead by offering extensions that work only when viewed with Internet Explorer. There are several that affect tables: THEAD, TBODY, TFOOT, and COLGROUP. You can use these tags to divide your table into understandable chunks, and to determine where dividing lines should be drawn. However, they have unpredictable results in Netscape, so use them with caution.

To divide a table into sections:

1. Before the first <TR> tag that defines the head, body or foot section, type **<THEAD>**, **<TBODY>**, or **<TFOOT>**.

2. After the last </TR> tag that defines the section, type the corresponding closing tag, **</THEAD>**, **</TBODY>**, or **</TFOOT>**, that matches the tag you used in step 1.

✔ Tips

■ Although the THEAD, TBODY and TFOOT tags are helpful for organizing, they are especially useful for determining where internal dividers, or rules, should be drawn *(see page 123)*.

■ You can only use the THEAD, TBODY, and TFOOT sections within a table.

■ You can create as many TBODY sections as you wish, but only one THEAD and only one TFOOT. None of the sections is required.

■ You don't have to type the end tag. A section is automatically ended when a new section is begun, or when you type the closing TABLE tag.

Dividing a table into sections

Another useful way to divide your tables—at least when viewed with Internet Explorer—is into column groups. In this way, you can set the alignment for several columns at a time, in addition to determining the position of the rules.

To divide a table into column groups:

1. After the initial <TABLE> tag, type **<COLGROUP**.

2. If the column group has more than one column, type **SPAN=n**, where n is the number of columns in the group.

3. If desired, type **ALIGN=direction**, where *direction* is left, right or center.

4. Type the final **>**.

5. Repeat steps 1–4 for each column group that you wish to define.

✔ Tips

■ There is no closing tag for COLGROUP.

■ If the column group only contains one column, you don't need to use the SPAN attribute. Its default is 1.

■ Column group definitions are particularly useful for determining where dividing lines should go. For more information on inserting rules, consult Figure 8.25 on page 123.

■ Column group definitions are completely ignored by Netscape.

■ Header cells—those marked with the TH tag—are not affected by the alignment specified in a column group **(Figure 8.13)**. For more information on aligning cells, consult *Aligning a cell's contents* on page 130.

Figure 8.11 *This table has four columns, divided into two column groups, with one column in the first group and three columns in the second group.*

Figure 8.12 *Again, the COLGROUP tag has little effect in Netscape.*

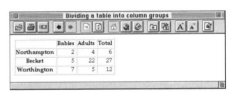

Figure 8.13 *The first column group (with the town names) looks pretty much the same. Table headers are not affected by column group alignment. You can see, however, that the regular cells in the second column group (the right three columns) are all correctly aligned to the right.*

Dividing a table into sections

Figure 8.14 *The BORDER attribute is added to the initial TABLE tag.*

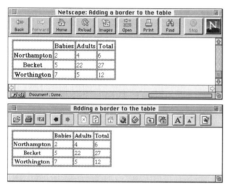

Figure 8.15 *Both Netscape and Internet Explorer create a shaded border (using the background color, by default) around each individual cell and around the table itself.*

Figure 8.16 *When you set the BORDER to 10, the external frame becomes particularly pronounced.*

Figure 8.17 *Create a shaded border in the color of your choice—at least in Internet Explorer—with the BORDERCOLORLIGHT and BORDERCOLOR-DARK tags. Unfortunately, the result is hard to show here. Try it: It looks great.*

Adding a border

Giving your table a border helps separate it from the rest of the text.

To create a border:

1. Inside the initial TABLE tag, type **BORDER**.

2. If desired, type **=n**, where *n* is the thickness in pixels of the border.

3. If desired, type **BORDERCOLOR= "#rrggbb"**, where *rrggbb* is the hexadecimal representation of the desired color for the border.

4. If desired, type **BORDERCOLOR-DARK ="#rrggbb"**, where *rrggbb* is the hexadecimal representation of the color that you want to use for the darker parts of the border (top and left borders of cells, right and bottom borders of the table itself).

5. If desired, type **BORDERCOLOR-LIGHT ="#rrggbb"**, where *rrggbb* is the hexadecimal representation of the color that you want to use for the lighter parts of the border (bottom and right borders of cells, top and left borders of the table itself)

✓ Tips

■ With no BORDERCOLOR tags, most browsers shade the border based on the background color. With just the BORDERCOLOR tag the table will have no shading, and be a solid color.

■ The BORDERCOLORLIGHT and BOR-DERCOLORDARK tags let you create a shaded border of any color you wish. Use dark and light versions of the same color for best results.

Adding a border

121

Choosing which borders to display

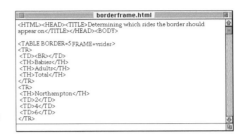

Figure 8.18 *Add the FRAME attribute just after the BORDER attribute.*

When you use the BORDER tag, described on page 121, a border appears both between each cell and around the table itself. Internet Explorer lets you choose which external sides of the table should have a border as well as which internal borders should be displayed.

To choose which external sides should have a border:

In the TABLE tag, after the required BORDER attribute, type **FRAME=location**, where location is one of the values listed below:

- *void*, for no external borders

- *above*, for a single border on top

- *below*, for a single border on bottom

- *hsides*, for a border on both the top and bottom sides

- *vsides*, for a border on both the right and left sides

- *rhs*, for a single border on the right side

- *lhs*, for a single border on the left side

- *box* or *border*, for a border on all sides (default)

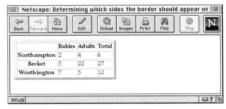

Figure 8.19 *The FRAME attribute has no effect in Netscape; the table appears with the complete border as usual.*

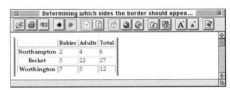

Figure 8.20 *In Internet Explorer, with a FRAME value of* vsides, *the external border appears only on the right and left sides of the table. The internal border appears as usual (and if you ask me, it looks kind of funny). To control the internal borders, use the RULES attribute described on page 123.*

Choosing which borders to display

Figure 8.21 *The RULES attribute goes in the TABLE tag, after the BORDER attribute, which is required for the RULES attribute to have an effect.*

Figure 8.22 *The RULES attribute has no effect in Netscape.*

Figure 8.23 *With RULES=cols, only the vertical rules are displayed. Notice that the thin lines at the top and bottom of the table are part of the external border and are not affected by RULES.*

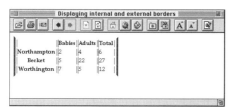

Figure 8.24 *Combining the FRAME and RULES attributes has the best effect. With FRAME=vsides and RULES=cols, only vertical borders are displayed.*

Figure 8.25 *The attribute RULES=groups is particularly useful when you've divided the table into column groups (see page 120). Instead of rules between each column, rules are only displayed between column groups.*

To choose which internal borders should be displayed:

In the TABLE tag, after the required BORDER attribute, type **RULES=area**, where *area* is one of the following values:

- *none*, for no internal rules

- *groups*, for horizontal rules between groups as defined by the tags described on page 120 **(Figure 8.25)**

- *rows*, for horizontal rules between each row in the table

- *cols*, for vertical rules between each column in the table

- *all*, for rules between each row and column in the table

✔ Tips

- You must use the BORDER tag for any of the FRAME or RULES attributes to take effect.

- *Void* seems rather pointless (you could just skip the BORDER attribute if you didn't want a border) until you pair it up with a value for RULES. The same goes for the *None* value for RULES, which makes most sense when you pair it with a positive value for FRAME.

- The default values, *box* and *border* for FRAME and *all* for RULES, are pretty superfluous. If you want all the external borders, skip the FRAME attribute altogether. If you want all the internal borders, skip the RULES attribute. Don't forget to use the BORDER tag, of course.

Choosing which borders to display

123

Adding a caption

The CAPTION tag lets you attach a descriptive title to your table.

To create a caption:

1. After the initial <TABLE> tag, but not inside any row or cell tags, type **<CAPTION**.

2. By default, the caption will appear above the table. However, if desired, type **ALIGN=bottom** to place the caption below the table **(Figures 8.28 and 8.29)**.

3. Type the final **>**.

4. Type the caption for the table (in the example shown in Figure 8.27, *Bear Sightings in Western Massachusetts*).

5. Type **</CAPTION>**.

✔ Tip

■ The ALIGN option *top* also exists, but there isn't much point in using it, since the default already places the caption at the top of the table.

Figure 8.26 *A good place to put your caption is right under the TABLE tag.*

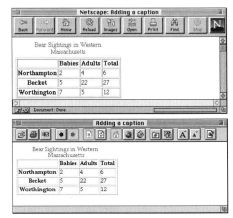

Figure 8.27 *Both Netscape and Internet Explorer center captions automatically and divide the lines to fit the table width.*

Figure 8.28 *Add the ALIGN=bottom attribute inside your CAPTION tag to place the caption below your table.*

Figure 8.29 *Captions below tables are formatted similarly to captions above tables.*

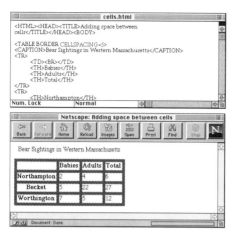

```
cells.html
<HTML><HEAD><TITLE>Adding space between
cells</TITLE></HEAD><BODY>

<TABLE BORDER CELLSPACING=5>
<CAPTION>Bear Sightings in Western Massachusetts</CAPTION>
<TR>
    <TD><BR></TD>
    <TH>Babies</TH>
    <TH>Adults</TH>
    <TH>Total</TH>
</TR>
<TR>
    <TH>Northampton</TH>
Num. Lock          Normal
```

```
Netscape: Adding space between cells
Back  Forward  Home  Reload  Images  Open  Print  Find  Stop  N

Bear Sightings in Western Massachusetts
```

	Babies	Adults	Total
Northampton	2	4	6
Becket	5	22	27
Worthington	7	5	12

```
Document: Done.
```

Figure 8.30 *Adding cell spacing increases the distance between each cell, without making the individual cells bigger.*

```
cellpad.html
<HTML><HEAD><TITLE>Adding space inside
cells</TITLE></HEAD><BODY>

<TABLE BORDER CELLPADDING=5>
<CAPTION>Bear Sightings in Western Massachusetts</CAPTION>
<TR>
    <TD><BR></TD>
    <TH>Babies</TH>
    <TH>Adults</TH>
    <TH>Total</TH>
</TR>
<TR>
    <TH>Northampton</TH>
Num. Lock          Normal
```

```
Netscape: Adding space inside cells
Back  Forward  Home  Reload  Images  Open  Print  Find  Stop  N

Bear Sightings in Western Massachusetts
```

	Babies	Adults	Total
Northampton	2	4	6
Becket	5	22	27
Worthington	7	5	12

```
Document: Done.
```

Figure 8.31 *Adding cell padding makes the cells larger, with more space around the contents.*

Spacing and padding the cells

Our table is a little squished, to be frank. Making the cells a bit larger helps make the information easier to read.

Cell spacing adds space between cells, making the table bigger without changing the size of individual cells.

To add cell spacing:

1. Within the initial TABLE tag, type **CELLSPACING=n**, where *n* is the number of pixels desired between each cell. (The attribute *cellspacing* is one word.)

2. The default value for cell spacing is 2 pixels.

Cell padding adds space around the contents of a cell, in effect, pushing the walls of the cell outward.

To add cell padding:

Within the initial TABLE tag, type **CELLPADDING=n**, where *n* is the number of pixels desired between the contents and the walls of the cell. (The attribute *cellpadding* is one word.) The default value for cell padding is 1 pixel.

✔ Tips

■ The alignment options *(see page 130)* consider the cell padding as the actual cell limits, and thus, may give unexpected results.

■ Both Netscape and Internet Explorer understand the CELLSPACING and CELLPADDING tags. There just isn't enough room to display both here.

Changing a table's width and height

You can use the WIDTH and HEIGHT attributes to resize the whole table, or to define the dimensions of particular cells.

To set the table size:

Within the initial TABLE tag, type **WIDTH=x HEIGHT=y**, where x and y are either absolute values in pixels for the height and width of the table or percentages that indicate how big the table should be with respect to the full window size.

Figure 8.32 *Add the WIDTH and HEIGHT tags to your initial TABLE marker.*

✔ Tips

- Most browsers, including Netscape and Internet Explorer, now recognize the WIDTH and HEIGHT tags. They are a standard part of HTML 3.2.

- You can center a table that is smaller than the total width of the window with the CENTER tag *(see page 88).*

Both tables are generated from identical HTML

Figure 8.33 *If you use a percentage for HEIGHT and WIDTH, the size of the table changes as your user adjusts the size of the window— although it will never get too small to hold the table's contents.*

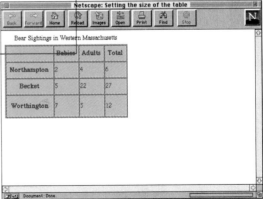

Figure 8.34 *Specify the dimensions of your cell by using the HEIGHT and WIDTH tags inside the cell definition tag (in this case, TH).*

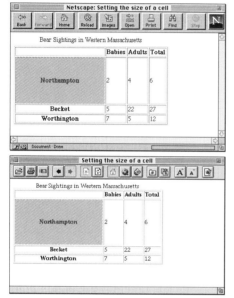

Figure 8.35 *I have had varying results—though consistent from browser to browser (Netscape above, IE below)—with WIDTH and HEIGHT when used on cells. To tell the truth, I think they are usually more trouble than they are worth.*

Changing a cell's size

You can change the width and height of individual cells to emphasize important information.

To change the size of individual cells:

1. Place the cursor inside the cell tag (either TH or TD).

2. Type **WIDTH=x HEIGHT=y**, where x and y are either absolute values in pixels for the width and height of the cell or percentages that indicate how big the cell should be with respect to the full table size.

✔ Tip

■ Changing one cell's size can affect the size of the entire row or column. You can use this fact to your advantage: you only need to adjust the width of the cells in the first row and the height of the cells in the first column (which is the first cell in each row definition).

Changing a cell's size

127

Spanning a cell across two or more columns

If you have a lot of information you wish to convey with a table, you can divide a table header into several categories by having it span several columns, and adding more specific headers in the row below.

To span a cell across two columns:

1. When you get to the point in which you need to define the cell that spans more than one column, *either* type **<TH** *or* type **<TD**, depending on whether the cell should be a header cell or a regular cell, respectively.

2. Type **COLSPAN=n>**, where *n* equals the number of columns the cell should span.

3. Type the cell's contents.

4. Type **</TH>** or **</TD>**, to match the tag you used in step 2.

5. Complete the rest of the table. If you create a cell that spans 2 columns, you will need to define one less cell in that row. If you create a cell that spans 3 columns, you will define two less cells for the row.

✔ Tip

■ Writing a table's HTML from scratch is, shall we say, challenging. Try sketching it out on paper first, as described on page 134, to get a handle on which information goes in which row and column. Or you can cheat and use the tip on page 214.

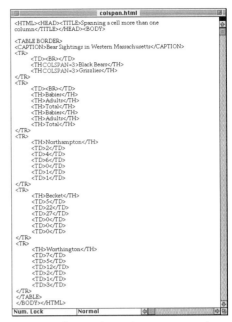

```
                      colspan.html
<HTML><HEAD><TITLE>Spanning a cell more than one
column</TITLE></HEAD><BODY>

<TABLE BORDER>
<CAPTION>Bear Sightings in Western Massachusetts</CAPTION>
<TR>
    <TD><BR></TD>
    <TH COLSPAN=3>Black Bears</TH>
    <TH COLSPAN=3>Grizzlies</TH>
</TR>
<TR>
    <TD><BR></TD>
    <TH>Babies</TH>
    <TH>Adults</TH>
    <TH>Total</TH>
    <TH>Babies</TH>
    <TH>Adults</TH>
    <TH>Total</TH>
</TR>
<TR>
    <TH>Northampton</TH>
    <TD>2</TD>
    <TD>4</TD>
    <TD>6</TD>
    <TD>0</TD>
    <TD>1</TD>
    <TD>1</TD>
</TR>
<TR>
    <TH>Becket</TH>
    <TD>5</TD>
    <TD>22</TD>
    <TD>27</TD>
    <TD>0</TD>
    <TD>0</TD>
    <TD>0</TD>
</TR>
<TR>
    <TH>Worthington</TH>
    <TD>7</TD>
    <TD>5</TD>
    <TD>12</TD>
    <TD>2</TD>
    <TD>1</TD>
    <TD>3</TD>
</TR>
</TABLE>
</BODY></HTML>
Num. Lock            Normal
```

Figure 8.36 *In each row there are seven column positions defined. In the first row there is 1 empty cell and two headers of 3 columns each (1+3+3=7). In the following rows, there is one empty or header cell and six individual cells (1+6=7).*

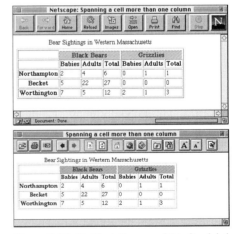

Figure 8.37 *The* Black Bears *and* Grizzlies *labels now span 3 columns each, both in Netscape (above) and Internet Explorer. (No, there aren't really Grizzly Bears in Western Massachusetts.)*

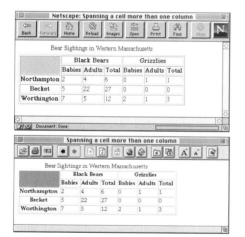

```
                  rowspan.html
<HTML><HEAD><TITLE>Spanning a cell more than one
row</TITLE></HEAD><BODY>

<TABLE BORDER>
<CAPTION>Bear Sightings in Western Massachusetts</CAPTION>
<TR>
        <TD ROWSPAN=2><BR></TD>
        <TH COLSPAN=3>Black Bears</TH>
        <TH COLSPAN=3>Grizzlies</TH>
</TR>
<TR>
        <TH>Babies</TH>
        <TH>Adults</TH>
        <TH>Total</TH>
        <TH>Babies</TH>
        <TH>Adults</TH>
        <TH>Total</TH>
</TR>
<TR>
        <TH>Northampton</TH>
        <TD>2</TD>
        <TD>4</TD>
        <TD>6</TD>
        <TD>0</TD>
        <TD>1</TD>
        <TD>1</TD>
</TR>
Num. Lock          Normal
```

Figure 8.38 *There are just two differences between this document and the one on the preceding page (Figure 8.36)—besides the fact that I haven't shown the end of the HTML document here. First, the blank cell in the first row now spans two rows. Second, because the blank cell spans two rows, the first cell in the second row is already defined, and the original code is thus eliminated from the HTML.*

Bear Sightings in Western Massachusetts

	Black Bears			Grizzlies		
	Babies	Adults	Total	Babies	Adults	Total
Northampton	2	4	6	0	1	1
Becket	5	22	27	0	0	0
Worthington	7	5	12	2	1	3

Figure 8.39 *Now that the empty cell spans two rows, the ugly line that separated the two rows disappears and the table looks much better.*

Spanning a cell across two or more rows

Creating a cell that spans more than one row is essentially identical to spanning more than one column—just from another angle. It is ideal for dividing the headers on the left side of the table into subcategories.

To span a cell across two or more rows:

1. When you get to the point in which you need to define the cell that spans more than one row, *either* type **<TH** *or* type **<TD**, depending on whether the cell should be a header cell or a regular cell, respectively.

2. Type **ROWSPAN=n>**, where *n* equals the number of rows the cell should span.

3. Type the cell's contents.

4. Type **</TH>** or **</TD>**, to match the tag you used in step 2.

5. Complete the rest of the table. If you define a cell with a rowspan of 2, you will not need to define the corresponding cell in the next row. If you define a cell with a rowspan of 3, you will not need to define the corresponding cells in the next two rows.

Spanning a cell across two or more rows

Aligning a cell's contents

Each browser shows the contents of the different cells in a table in its own way, by default, which may or may not be how you think the data looks best. To gain a little more control over the alignment of a cell's contents, use the ALIGN and VALIGN tags.

To align a cell's contents horizontally:

1. Place the cursor in the initial tag for the cell, after <TD or <TH but before the final >.

2. Type **ALIGN=direction**, where *direction* is either left, center, or right.

✔ Tips

■ The default value for ALIGN in TD tags is *left*. In TH tags it's *center*.

■ Browsers have special algorithms to decide how to view your tables, according to the amount of data in the cell and the size of the window. You may need to use the WIDTH and HEIGHT tags to adjust the cell size manually to get the full affect of cell alignment. For more details, consult *Changing a cell's size* on page 127.

■ If you have added cell padding to a cell's definition, the contents will be aligned *inside* the cell padding, as if the cell padding defined the actual limits of the cell *(see page 125)*.

■ Align an entire row by inserting the ALIGN attribute in the TR tag, as in **<TR ALIGN=left VALIGN=bottom>**.

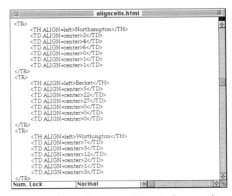

Figure 8.40 *In the same table we've been working with for the last few pages, I've aligned the left hand headers (the city names) to the left, and centered the numerical data.*

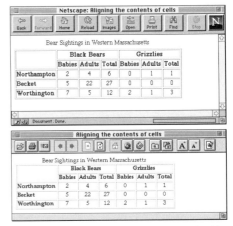

Figure 8.41 *The result is a clearer, more legible table, both in Netscape (above) and Internet Explorer.*

```
                alignall.html
<HTML><HEAD><TITLE>All the Alignment
Options</TITLE></HEAD><BODY>

<TABLE BORDER>
<CAPTION>Aligning every which way</CAPTION>
<TR>
     <TD COLSPAN=2 ROWSPAN=2><BR></TD>
     <TH COLSPAN=3>HORIZONTAL</TH>
</TR>
<TR>
     <TH>Left</TH>
     <TH>Center</TH>
     <TH>Right</TH>
</TR>
<TR>
     <TH ROWSPAN=4><IMG SRC="vertical.gif"</TH>
     <TH>Top</TH>
     <TD VALIGN=top ALIGN=left WIDTH=110 HEIGHT=80><IMG
SRC="arrows.gif" ALIGN=bottom>Top Left</TD>
     <TD VALIGN=top ALIGN=center WIDTH=110 HEIGHT=80>Top
Center</TD>
     <TD VALIGN=top ALIGN=right WIDTH=110 HEIGHT=80>Top
Right</TD>
</TR>
<TR>
     <TH>Middle</TH>
     <TD VALIGN=middle ALIGN=left WIDTH=110 HEIGHT=80>Middle
Left</TD>
     <TD VALIGN=middle ALIGN=center>Middle Center</TD>
     <TD VALIGN=middle ALIGN=right>Middle Right</TD>
</TR>
<TR>
     <TH>Bottom</TH>
     <TD VALIGN=bottom ALIGN=left WIDTH=110 HEIGHT=80>Bottom
Left</TD>
     <TD VALIGN=bottom ALIGN=center>Bottom Center</TD>
     <TD VALIGN=bottom ALIGN=right>Bottom Right</TD>
</TR>
<TR>
     <TH>Baseline</TH>
     <TD VALIGN=baseline ALIGN=left WIDTH=110 HEIGHT=80><IMG
SRC="arrows.gif" ALIGN=bottom>Baseline Left</TD>
     <TD VALIGN=baseline ALIGN=center>Baseline Center</TD>
     <TD VALIGN=baseline ALIGN=right>Baseline Right</TD>
</TR>
</TABLE>
</BODY></HTML>
Num. Lock        Normal
```

Figure 8.42 *I had to add the WIDTH and HEIGHT tags to make the cells big enough to show the difference between the alignments. If there is no extra space, there is not much difference between left and right aligned, for example.*

You can use the VALIGN attribute to align the cell's contents vertically.

To align a cell's contents vertically:

1. Place the cursor in the initial tag for the cell, after <TD or <TH but before the final >.

2. Type **VALIGN=direction**, where *direction* is either top, middle, or bottom.

✔ Tips

■ The default value for VALIGN is *middle*.

■ Netscape 2 recognized a *baseline* value for VALIGN, but version 3 doesn't.

■ Use the VALIGN attribute in a TR tag to align an entire row, as in **<TR ALIGN=left VALIGN=bottom>**.

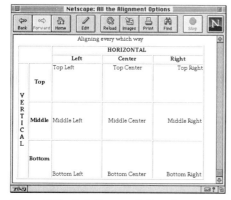
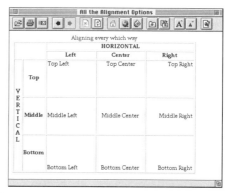

Figure 8.43 *Both Netscape (left) and Internet Explorer can align the contents of cells in each of the nine possible positions.*

Changing a cell's color

Changing the color of one or more cells is a great way to set off important information, like for example, the column of totals in a table.

To change a cell's color:

1. Within the TH or TD cell, type **BGCOLOR=**.

2. Type **"#rrggbb"**, where *rrggbb* is the hexadecimal representation of the desired color.

Or type **color**, where *color* is one of the sixteen predefined color names.

✔ Tips

■ Change the color of an entire row of cells by adding the BGCOLOR=color attribute to the TR tag.

■ Change the background of all of the cells in the table by adding the BGCOLOR attribute to the TABLE tag.

■ The BGCOLOR in an individual cell (TH or TD) overrides the color specified in a row (in a TR tag), which in turn overrides the color specified for the entire table (in the TABLE tag).

■ Consult Appendix C and the inside back cover for a complete listing of hexadecimal values and common color representations. Appendix C also includes a list of the 16 predefined colors.

Figure 8.44 *You can add the BGCOLOR attribute to TD or TH tags as shown here to modify individual cells, or to TR tags or to the TABLE tag for changing rows and the entire table, respectively.*

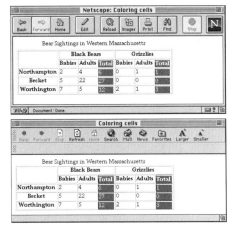

Figure 8.45 *Add the BGCOLOR attribute to all of the TD or TH cells in a particular column or columns (here, I've colored the Total columns) to make certain data stand out.*

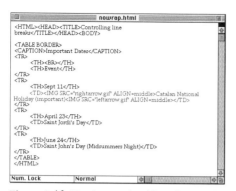

```
nowrap.html
<HTML><HEAD><TITLE>Controlling line
breaks</TITLE></HEAD><BODY>

<TABLE BORDER>
<CAPTION>Important Dates</CAPTION>
<TR>
    <TH><BR></TH>
    <TH>Event</TH>
</TR>
<TR>
    <TH>Sept 11</TH>
    <TD><IMG SRC="rightarrow.gif" ALIGN=middle>Catalan National
Holiday (important)<IMG SRC="leftarrow.gif" ALIGN=middle></TD>
</TR>
<TR>
    <TH>April 23</TH>
    <TD>Saint Jordi's Day</TD>
</TR>
<TR>
    <TH>June 24</TH>
    <TD>Saint John's Day (Midsummers Night)</TD>
</TR>
</TABLE>
</HTML>
Num. Lock          Normal
```

Figure 8.46 *Here's a simple table with two columns and four rows.*

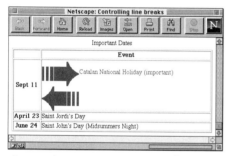

Figure 8.47 *Besides the fact that these arrows are a little strident for this small table, the arrows should be on the same line, aligned with the text.*

```
nowrap.after.html
    <TH>Sept 11</TH>
    <TD NOWRAP><IMG SRC="rightarrow.gif" ALIGN=middle>Catalan
National Holiday (important)<IMG SRC="leftarrow.gif"
ALIGN=middle></TD>
</TR>
<TR>
    <TH>April 23</TH>
    <TD>Saint Jordi's Day</TD>
Num. Lock          Normal
```

Figure 8.48 *The NOWRAP attribute has been added to the first regular cell on the second row.*

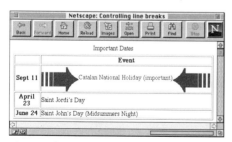

Figure 8.49 *As the arrows were shoehorned into the right column, the left column was compacted just enough to force "April 23" onto two lines. An additional NOWRAP in the corresponding cell definition will solve the problem.*

Controlling line breaks in a cell

Unless you specify otherwise, browsers will divide the lines of text in a cell as it decides on the height and width of each column and row. The NOWRAP attribute keeps all the text in a cell on one line.

To keep text in a cell on one single line:

1. Place the cursor in the initial tag for the cell, after <TD or <TH but before the final >.

2. Type **NOWRAP**.

✔ Tips

- Netscape will make the cell—and the table that contains it—as wide as it needs to accommodate the single line of text. Even if it looks really ugly.

- You can use regular line breaks (BR) between words to mark where you *do* want the text to break.

- You can also type ** ** instead of a regular space to connect pairs of words or other elements with non-breaking spaces.

- For more information on line breaks, consult *Controlling line breaks* on page 89.

Mapping out a table

Setting up complicated tables in HTML can be really confusing. All you need are a couple of column spans to throw the whole thing off. The trick is to draw a map of your table before you start.

To map out your table:

1. Sketch your table quickly on a piece of paper (yes, with a pen) **(Fig. 8.51)**.

2. Divide the table into rows and columns. Number each row and column **(Figure 8.52)**.

3. Mark the cells that will span more than one column or row **(Fig. 8.53)**.

4. Count the number of cells in each row (1 point for single cells, 2 points for cells that span two columns, 3 for cells that span three columns, etc.). There should be as many cell definitions in each row as there are columns in the table. (See step 2.)

5. Once you have your table straight on paper, write the HTML code, row by row.

Figure 8.51 *First, draw out your table as simply as possible, including all your headers, but no data.*

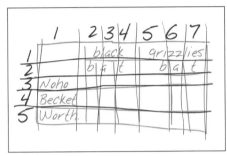

Figure 8.52 *To separate the table into rows and columns, draw a line from one end to another (either top to bottom or right to left) everywhere there is a division in the table. In this table, we find five rows and seven columns.*

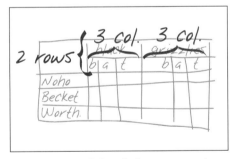

Figure 8.53 *Mark the cells that span more than one column or row. In this example, there is the top left blank row that spans 2 rows (but just 1 column), and the "black" and "grizzlies" headers that span 3 columns each (but just one row). Every other cell spans exactly one column and one row.*

Mapping out a table

Frames

One of the trickier parts of creating a Web site is giving your users an idea of the scope of information contained in your site and then making that information easily accessible without confusing or overwhelming the user. Frames can be the key to organizing your site and making it easy to navigate.

By dividing a page, called a *frameset*, into frames, you can allow the user to see more than one page at a time, without completely cluttering up her screen. Each frame contains its own Web page, and theoretically could be viewed independently in a separate window.

The beauty of having several Web pages open on a screen at a time, however, lies in the ability to interrelate the information in each of the pages. For example, you can have a stationary banner frame across the top of the window that includes your company name and logo. Meanwhile, a dynamic frame occupying the left area of the window can include a table of contents. Finally, the main area of the window will be devoted to the *contents frame*, whose data changes each time a user clicks on a new topic in the table of contents.

Although frames are not yet part of standard HTML, versions 2 and 3 of both Netscape and Internet Explorer are perfectly capable of displaying these useful elements of Web page design.

Frames

Creating a simple frameset

Think of a frameset as a window with individual panes. Each pane shows different information. You decide how many panes your window will have, what size each pane will be, how its borders should look and if it should have scroll bars or not. Once you've built the window, you create the landscape behind the window by assigning individual URLs to each pane, that is, frame.

First, you'll learn to create a simple frameset with three horizontal rows, but only one column.

To create a simple frameset:

1. Type **<FRAMESET** after the </HEAD> tag on the frameset page **(Figure 9.1)**.

2. Type **ROWS="a** where *a* is the height of the first row. The value may either be a percentage (40%), an exact number of pixels (35), or completely variable, depending on the size of the other rows (with an asterisk: *).

3. Type **, b** where *b* is the height of the second row, again expressed as a percentage, an absolute value in pixels, or a variable (with an asterisk: *).

4. Repeat step 3 for each additional row.

5. Type **">** to complete the row definition.

6. Type **<FRAME** to assign a URL and other attributes to the top row/pane.

7. Type **NAME="name"** where *name* is a reference for the frame. You can use the name to target the display of a URL in a particular frame. For more information on targeting frames, consult *Targeting links to particular frames* on page 149.

Figure 9.1 *The frameset page has no actual content. Instead, it defines the frames and links them with the pages that hold the content.*

Figure 9.2 *Once you've created a frameset, the next step is to create the pages that will appear within the frames.*

Figure 9.3 *Viewed individually, the pages shown in Figure 9.2 appear just as any other Web page.*

Creating a simple frameset

Figure 9.4 *By default, Netscape displays the frames with rather thick borders and scroll bars.*

Figure 9.5 *Internet Explorer's frames have thinner default borders, but also include scroll bars.*

8. Type **SRC="content.html">** where *content.html* is the URL for the page that you want to be displayed in this frame when the user initially navigates to this frameset.

9. Repeat steps 6–8 for each frame.

10. Type **</FRAMESET>** to finish the frameset and the construction of your "window".

11. Create the pages that will be displayed initially in the frames, that is, those referenced by the SRC tag in step 8 **(Figures 9.2 and 9.3)**. This is the "landscape" behind the window.

✔ **Tips**

■ Use the asterisk (*) to allocate to a frame whatever leftover space there is available in the window. That is, if the first two frames occupy 40 and 60 pixels respectively, and the window size is 250 pixels, the frame with the asterisk will occupy 150 pixels.

■ You can use more than one asterisk at a time. The remaining space will be divided equally among the frames marked with an asterisk. To divide the remaining space unequally, add a number to the asterisk, e.g., **2***. In this case, two thirds of the remaining space will go to the frame marked 2* and the last third will go to the frame marked with just a plain asterisk.

■ Don't insert a BODY tag before the FRAMESET tag in your HTML document. For the frames to display correctly, a BODY tag must only be included in a NOFRAMES section *(see page 152)*, if at all.

Creating frames in columns

Another simple way to divide a frameset is into columns instead of rows.

To create frames in columns:

1. Type **<FRAMESET** after the </HEAD> tag in the frameset page **(Figure 9.6)**.

2. Type **COLS="a,b">** where *a* and *b* (and any others) represent the width of the corresponding column, as a percentage, number of pixels, or variable (*).

3. Type **<FRAME** to define the leftmost frame/column.

4. Type **NAME="name"** where *name* is a reference for the frame. You can use the name to target the display of a URL in a particular frame. For more information on targeting frames, consult *Targeting links to particular frames* on page 149.

5. Type **SRC="content.html">** where *content.html* is the URL of the page that you want to be displayed in this frame when the user initially navigates to this frameset. This is the *landscape* for the frame.

6. Repeat steps 3–5 for each frame/column.

7. Type **</FRAMESET>**.

8. Create the Web pages that will be shown initially in the frameset page **(Figure 9.7)**.

✔ Tip

■ See page 137 for tips on allocating the space among frames and the use of variables (*).

Figure 9.6 *To create a page with frames in columns, use the COLS attribute instead of ROWS.*

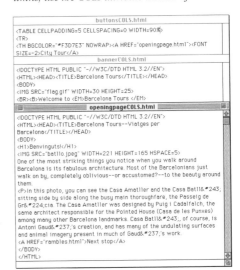

Figure 9.7 *As always, the first step is to create the content for the frames. Although these pages are very similar to the ones shown in Figure 9.2, they have been adjusted slightly to fit better vertically.*

Figure 9.8 *Both Netscape (shown here) and Internet Explorer show the columns of frames in very much the same way as they show frames in rows.*

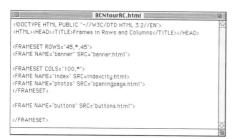

Figure 9.9 *To create a page with rows and columns, you create one frameset inside the other.*

Figure 9.10 *In this example, the first and third rows are simple frames while the second row is a frameset divided into two columns.*

Creating frames in rows *and* columns

Some information is best displayed horizontally while some looks better vertically. Meanwhile, a large, relatively square frame is often ideal for displaying your page's main data. You can create both rows and columns in the same frameset to accommodate different kinds of information.

To create a frameset with both rows *and* columns:

1. Make a sketch of your frameset and determine how many rows and columns you will need.

2. Type **<FRAMESET** to begin **(Fig. 9.9)**.

3. Type **ROWS="a,b">** where *a* and *b* (and any others) represent the height of the corresponding rows. For more information on creating rows, consult *Creating a simple frameset* on page 136.

4. In the example shown in Figure 9.9, the first and third rows are a single frame while the second row is divided into columns. For a row with just a single frame, type **<FRAME NAME= "name" SRC="contents.html">** in the usual way.

5. For the second row, which is divided into columns in this example, type **<FRAMESET COLS="a,b">** where *a* and *b* (and any others) represent the width of each column in the row.

6. Type **<FRAME NAME="name" SRC="contents.html">** where *name* is the reference for the frame and *contents.html* is the page that will be initially shown in that frame.

Creating frames in rows and columns

139

7. Repeat step 6 for each frame in the column. (In this example, there are two columns, so you'll have to define two frames in the inner frameset.)

8. When you've finished defining the frames/columns in the divided row, type **</FRAMESET>**.

9. Continue defining each row individually. For a row with just one frame (i.e., just one column), just use a FRAME tag. For rows divided into multiple columns, repeat steps 5–8.

10. Type **</FRAMESET>** to complete the frameset definition.

Figure 9.11 *By using rows and columns, you have more flexibility when placing information vertically or horizontally.*

✔ Tips

■ Although I've defined the rows first and then the columns in this example, there is no reason why you cannot do it the opposite way. In fact, when adjusting the borders, both methods have distinct advantages (see the tips on page 146). The only thing to be careful of is that each frameset have a beginning <FRAMESET> and an ending </FRAMESET> tag, and that each frameset is nested properly with no overlapping.

■ It is important to stress that not every row need be divided into columns. For rows with a single frame (i.e. that span the entire window from left to right), just use a FRAME tag. For rows divided into columns, use an inner frameset.

```
                BCNtourFLOAT.html
<!DOCTYPE HTML PUBLIC "-//W3C/DTD HTML 3.2//EN">
<HTML><HEAD><TITLE>Floating Frames</TITLE></HEAD>
<BODY BGCOLOR="#FFFFFF">

<IMG SRC="flag.gif" WIDTH=30 HEIGHT=25 ALIGN=LEFT>
<B>Welcome to <EM>Barcelona Tours </EM>
<BR>Benvinguts a <EM>Viatges per Barcelona</EM></B>

<P><CENTER>
<IFRAME WIDTH=70% HEIGHT=70% SRC="openingpage.html">
<FRAME WIDTH=70% HEIGHT=70% SRC="openingpage.html">
</IFRAME>
<CENTER>

<P>
<TABLE CELLPADDING=5 CELLSPACING=0 WIDTH=100%>
<TR>
<TH BGCOLOR="#F3D7E3" NOWRAP><A HREF="openingpage.html">City
Tour</A>
<TH BGCOLOR="#F6D5C3" NOWRAP><A HREF="market1.html">Market</A>
<TH BGCOLOR="#D8E9D6" NOWRAP><A
HREF="arch1.html">Architecture</A>
<TH BGCOLOR="#D1C9DF" NOWRAP><A HREF="sports1.html">Sports</A>
<TH BGCOLOR="#D4EBF9" NOWRAP><A
HREF="natlism1.html">Nationalism</A>
<TH BGCOLOR="#CECDB4" NOWRAP><A
HREF="language1.html">Language</A>
</TR>
</TABLE>
```

Figure 9.12 *A floating frame appears on the same page as the rest of the content material. It can contain whatever page that's referenced.*

Figure 9.13 *Floating frames simply don't appear in Netscape.*

Figure 9.14 *Only Internet Explorer (so far) can display floating frames, which appear together with the rest of the information on the main page.*

Creating a floating frame

 If you want to mix text, graphics and a frame all on one page, you'll need to create a floating frame—and hope that your users view the page with Internet Explorer.

To create a floating frame:

1. In the container page, type **<IFRAME SRC=frame.url**, where *frame.url* is the first page that should be displayed in the floating frame.

2. Type **WIDTH=x HEIGHT=y** where x and y represent the width and height, respectively, of the floating frame as a percentage or as an absolute value in pixels.

3. If desired, type **HSPACE=h** and/or **VSPACE=v** where h and v determine the amount of space, in pixels, that will surround the floating frame.

4. If desired, type **ALIGN=LEFT** or **ALIGN=RIGHT** to wrap the text that comes after the frame around the frame.

5. Type **>**.

6. Type **<FRAME**.

7. Copy each of the attributes used in steps 2–4.

8. Type **>**.

9. Type **</IFRAME>** to complete the floating frame.

✔ Tip

■ You can also use the FRAMEBORDER *(see page 146)* and SCROLLING *(see page 143)* tags with floating frames.

Adjusting a frame's margins

By default, both Netscape and Internet Explorer display a frame's contents with a margin of 8 pixels on each side **(Fig. 9.15)**. You can adjust the margin so that there is more space, or, if you prefer, so that the frame's contents start right in the top left corner.

To adjust a frame's margins:

1. In the desired FRAME tag, before the final >, type **MARGINWIDTH=w** where *w* is the desired amount of space, in pixels, between the left and right edges of the frame and the frame's contents **(Figure 9.16)**.

2. Type **MARGINHEIGHT=h** where *h* is the desired amount of space, in pixels, between the top and bottom edges of the frame and the frame's contents.

✔ Tip

■ The margin is always the same color as the background color of the page displayed in the frame.

Figure 9.15 *In this illustration you can see the default margins. Note how the contents of each frame begins slightly down and to the right.*

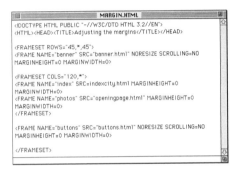

Figure 9.16 *You adjust the margins of each frame individually by adding a MARGINWIDTH and/or MARGINHEIGHT tag to the desired FRAME tags. In this case, all the margins have been set to 0.*

Figure 9.17 *With the margins set at 0, each frame's contents start right up in the top left corner of each frame.*

Adjusting a frame's margins

```
            NoScrolls.html
<!DOCTYPE HTML PUBLIC "-//W3C/DTD HTML 3.2//EN">
<HTML><HEAD><TITLE>Frames without Scroll bars</TITLE></HEAD>

<FRAMESET ROWS="45,*,45">
<FRAME NAME="banner" SRC="banner.html" SCROLLING=NO>

<FRAMESET COLS="120,*">
<FRAME NAME="index" SRC="indexcity.html">
<FRAME NAME="photos" SRC="openingpage.html">
</FRAMESET>

<FRAME NAME="buttons" SRC="buttons.html" SCROLLING=NO>

</FRAMESET>
```

Figure 9.18 *So that the top and bottom frames never display scroll bars, add SCROLLING=NO to their FRAME tag.*

Figure 9.19 *Eliminating scroll bars from certain areas makes the information much clearer and more attractive. But be careful not to take away scroll bars from areas that need them. Remember, you can't control the size of your user's window.*

Figure 9.20 *Internet Explorer can also show frames without scroll bars.*

Showing or hiding scroll bars

You can decide whether each individual frame should have a scroll bar all the time, never, or only when needed. *Only when needed* means that the scroll bars will appear only when there is more information than can be shown at one time in the frame. If the user makes the window big enough, all the scroll bars will eventually disappear.

To show scroll bars all the time:

In the FRAME tag of the particular frame for which you wish to show the scroll bar, type **SCROLLING=YES**.

To hide scroll bars all the time:

In the FRAME tag of the particular frame for which you wish to hide the scroll bar, type **SCROLLING=NO**.

✔ Tips

- The default is for scroll bars to appear only when necessary, that is, when there is more information than can fit in the frame. To use the default, type **SCROLLING=AUTO** or, more simply, don't type any SCROLLING tag at all.

- There is nothing more frustrating than jumping to a frameset page with tiny little frames that make it impossible to view the entire contents. Even worse is when you cannot scroll around (or make the frame bigger—see page page 147) to make the hidden information visible. To avoid frustrating *your* users, make sure you test your frameset page in a small window and ensure that all the frames without scroll bars are big enough to display their entire contents.

Adjusting the color of the borders

In theory, you can change the color of each frame (viewed with Netscape) individually. In practice, however, since the borders are shared between frames, the possibilities are more limited.

To adjust the color of all the borders in the frameset:

Inside the topmost FRAMESET tag before the final >, type **BORDERCOLOR= "#rrggbb"** where *rr* is the hexadecimal equivalent of the Red component, *gg* is the hexadecimal equivalent of the Green component and *bb* is the hexadecimal equivalent of the blue component **(Figure 9.21)**.

To change the color of rows, columns, or individual frames:

In the appropriate FRAMESET or FRAME tag, type **BORDERCOLOR="#rrggbb"**.

✔ Tips

■ You can also type **BORDER-COLOR=color** where color is the name of one of the sixteen standard colors. For a listing, consult xxx.

■ A BORDERCOLOR tag in an individual frame overrides a BORDER-COLOR tag in a row or column, which in turn overrides the tag defined in the topmost FRAMESET.

■ If two BORDERCOLOR tags at the same level conflict, the one that comes first in your HTML file takes precedence.

■ When you change the border of an individual frame, other frames that share its borders are also affected.

Figure 9.21 *You can add the BORDERCOLOR tag to any frameset or frame tag. Here it's been added to the topmost frameset tag so that it will affect all the frames contained within.*

Figure 9.22 *Only Netscape can show colored borders.*

Figure 9.23 *Internet Explorer keeps on displaying the same, boring, gray frame borders.*

```
BorderThickness.html
<!DOCTYPE HTML PUBLIC "-//W3C/DTD HTML 3.2//EN">
<HTML><HEAD><TITLE>Adjusting Border Thickness</TITLE></HEAD>

<FRAMESET BORDERCOLOR="#000000" BORDER=10 ROWS="45,*,45">
<FRAME NAME="banner" SRC="banner.html" SCROLLING=NO>

<FRAMESET COLS="120,*">
<FRAME NAME="index" SRC="indexcity.html>
<FRAME NAME="photos" SRC="openingpage.html">
</FRAMESET>

<FRAME NAME="buttons" SRC="buttons.html" SCROLLING=NO>

</FRAMESET>
```

Figure 9.24 *Add the BORDER tag to any frameset or frame tag to adjust the borders' thickness. In this example, I've added the tag to the topmost frameset tag so that all the frames are affected.*

Figure 9.25 *Thick, colored borders can help to divide the information on your page into understandable chunks.*

Figure 9.26 *A value of 1 for BORDER produces thinner, more discreet borders.*

Adjusting the borders' thickness

You can change the thickness of the frames' borders to suit your design—as long as your public uses Netscape, and not Internet Explorer, to view them.

To make the borders thicker or thinner:

Inside the topmost FRAMESET tag, before the final >, type **BORDER=n** where *n* is the desired width of the border in pixels **(Figure 9.24)**.

✔ Tips

■ You can set the width to 0 (BORDER=0) to make the borders disappear, but only Netscape will get it. IE will continue to display the borders.

■ In fact, if you want the frames to jut right up next to each other, you should use the BORDER tag, set to 0, (for viewing in Netscape) *as well as* the FRAMEBORDER tag described on page 146 (for viewing with Internet Explorer and Netscape).

■ The default border width is 5 pixels.

■ You cannot set the thickness for individual frames.

Hiding or showing the borders

Depending on the content of your frames, you may not want to have any visible division between them at all. In that case, you can make the borders disappear.

To make all the borders disappear:

Type **FRAMEBORDER=0** inside the topmost FRAMESET tag, before the final >.

To make *only* the vertical borders disappear:

Within each FRAME tag in the desired row, type **FRAMEBORDER=0**.

✓ Tips

■ Both Netscape and IE understand a value of 0 for the FRAMEBORDER tag. Netscape also understands "No".

■ To view *some* borders when the topmost frameset is set for none, type **FRAMEBORDER=1** (or for Netscape only, use **FRAMEBORDER=Yes**) in the desired FRAME or FRAMESET tag.

■ To make the horizontal borders disappear, define the columns in the outer frameset and the rows in the inner frameset and then type **FRAMEBORDER=0** within each of the FRAME tags in the desired column.

■ You can use the FRAMEBORDER tag with individual frames but since each frame shares its borders with other frames, the results can be unexpected.

■ FRAMEBORDER makes the borders blend with the background in Netscape, but to make adjacent frames actually touch, see page 145.

Figure 9.27 *If you want to be sure that your page has no borders, whether it is viewed in Netscape or with Internet Explorer, use both the BORDER and FRAMEBORDER tags with a value of 0 for each.*

Figure 9.28 *Netscape will only show the frames right next to each other if you use both the BORDER and FRAMEBORDER tags. FRAMEBORDER by itself merely makes the border the same color as the background. BORDER (=0) makes it invisible.*

Figure 9.29 *Internet Explorer's borders don't completely disappear if your individual frames have background colors. The only solution is to use the same background color for each frame, as well as for the frameset itself.*

146

Figure 9.30 *Normally when the user places the pointer over a border, it changes into a double-headed arrow with which she can change the size of the frame. Also notice the hash mark which indicates the frame can be resized.*

```
                    NORESIZE.HTML
<!DOCTYPE HTML PUBLIC "-//W3C/DTD HTML 3.2//EN">
<HTML><HEAD><TITLE>Keeping users from resizing</TITLE></HEAD>

<FRAMESET BORDERCOLOR="#D4D4D4" BORDER=3 ROWS="45,*,45">
<FRAME NAME="banner" SRC="banner.html" SCROLLING=NO NORESIZE>

<FRAMESET COLS="120,*">
<FRAME NAME="index" SRC="indexcity.html">
<FRAME NAME="photos" SRC="openingpage.html">
</FRAMESET>

<FRAME NAME="buttons" SRC="buttons.html" SCROLLING=NO NORESIZE>

</FRAMESET>
```

Figure 9.31 *Add the NORESIZE tag to any frames that you don't want the user to be able to resize. In this example, we've modified the top and bottom frames and left the middle frames flexible.*

Figure 9.32 *Once you've restricted the resizability, the pointer will not turn into a double-pointed arrow and the user will not be able to change the size of the frame. (In Netscape, the hash mark disappears as well.)*

Keeping users from resizing frames

Frames are always resized when the user changes the size of the browser window. However, you can also choose whether to let the user resize individual frames.

To keep users from resizing your frames:

Type **NORESIZE** in the FRAME tag for the desired frame **(Figure 9.31)**.

✔ Tips

■ In Netscape, a particular frame can be resized if it has a small hash mark in the middle of the border. If there is no hash mark, the frame cannot be resized.

■ If you use very small pixel values for your frames and the user views the frameset page in a very large window, the width of the frames will probably not be quite as you wished. The entire frameset is always stretched to fill the window.

■ If you set the border width at 0 with the BORDER tag *(see page 145)*, users who view the page in Netscape won't be able to resize the frames at all. The borders will remain flexible in Internet Explorer, since IE doesn't recognize the BORDER tag.

Keeping users from resizing frames

Adjusting the spacing between frames

 Adding spacing between frames is very similar to adding space between cells, rows and columns in a table *(see page 125)*. The major difference is that only Internet Explorer recognizes the FRAMESPACING tag, thereby limiting its usefulness.

Figure 9.33 *To add spacing between the frames, use the FRAMESPACING tag and a value in pixels.*

To adjust the spacing of all the frames at the same time:

Within the topmost FRAMESET tag, type **FRAMESPACING=n** where *n* is the width in pixels of the desired spacing **(Figure 9.33)**.

To adjust the spacing of the vertical borders between frames:

Within the FRAME tag of the desired row, type **FRAMESPACING=n** where *n* is the width in pixels of the desired spacing.

Figure 9.34 *The FRAMESPACING tag has no effect on frames viewed with Netscape.*

✔ Tips

■ You can use different FRAMESPAC-ING values for each frameset on your page. The innermost tags override the outer ones.

■ You can adjust the spacing of the horizontal borders between frames by defining first the columns and then the rows, and then setting the FRAMESPACING tag for the desired column.

Figure 9.35 *In Internet Explorer, however, the spacing is very effective and is somewhat similar to colored borders with Netscape. However, the color used is the background color (or image) specified on the frameset page.*

■ You can use the FRAMESPACING tag to create colored borders for Internet Explorer users. Simply give the frame-set page a background color (or image) and set the spacing so that the color (or image) shows through.

Adjusting the spacing between frames

Figure 9.36 *Targets will only work if the frame where you want the page to appear has a name.*

Figure 9.37 *Within the link, type* **TARGET=name** *where name is the reference to the frame where the link should appear.*

Figure 9.38 *When the user clicks the link...*

Figure 9.39 *...the corresponding page appears in the specified frame.*

Targeting links to particular frames

The initial contents of a frame is specified in the frameset with the SRC tag. However, the idea of a frame is that the user be able to view additional information in it by clicking a link in another frame, which remains constant. The trick is to target the desired frame within the link.

To target a link to a particular frame:

1. Make sure the frame on the frameset page has a name **(Figure 9.36)**. For more information, consult *Creating a simple frameset* on page 136.

2. On the page where the link should appear, type **<A HREF=contents.html** where *contents.html* is the file that should be displayed in the desired frame **(Figure 9.37)**.

3. Type **TARGET=name** where *name* is the reference given to the frame within the FRAME tag.

4. Add any other attributes as desired to the link and then type the final **>**. For more information on creating links, see Chapter 6, *Links and Anchors*.

✔ Tips

■ Obviously, the frame must have a name to be targeted. For more information on naming frames, consult *Creating a simple frameset* on page 136.

■ Frame names must begin with an alphanumeric character (except the special names described on page 150).

Targeting links to particular frames

Targeting links to special spots

Although many times you'll be happy with targeting a link to a particular frame, as described on page 149, other times you will want to make more general instructions, like having the link open in a new window, or opening the link in the same window that contained the link.

To target a link to a special spot:

1. Type **<A HREF="contents.html"** where *contents.html* is the page that you wish to be displayed in the special spot **(Figure 9.40)**.

2. Type **TARGET=_blank** to have the link open in a new, blank window. This is the ideal targeting for external links which may not fit very well inside your frames.

   Or type **TARGET=_self** to open the link in the same frame that contains the link **(Figure 9.40)**. The information in the frame (including the link itself) will be replaced by the *contents.html* file specified in step 1 **(Figures 9.41 and 9.42)**.

   Or type **TARGET=_top** to open the link in the current browser window but independently of the rest of the frameset to which it currently belongs.

   Or type **TARGET=_parent** to open the link in the frame that contains the current frameset. This will only be different from _top when you are using nested framesets. For more information on nested framesets, consult *Nesting framesets* on page 151.

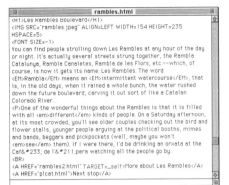

Figure 9.40 *In this example, the link accesses a second page of information. It makes sense to display this second page in the same frame.*

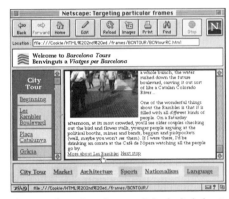

Figure 9.41 *When the user clicks the link that is targeted to the same frame that contains the link...*

Figure 9.42 *...the frame's contents are replaced with the new contents from the link.*

```
NEST.HTML
<!DOCTYPE HTML PUBLIC "-//W3C/DTD HTML 3.2//EN">
<HTML><HEAD><TITLE>Nesting Frames</TITLE></HEAD>

<FRAMESET COLS="*,4*">
<FRAME SRC="bigindex.html">
<FRAME NAME="main" SRC="BCNtourRC.html">

</FRAMESET>

</HTML>
```

Figure 9.43 *The frameset shown has two columns. The first column will contain a simple index page, while the second column will contain a distinct frameset (in fact, the one used in most of the previous examples in this chapter).*

Figure 9.44 *In this example, the Barcelona tour is easily integrated into a larger group of topics just by nesting its frameset into the larger one.*

Figure 9.45 *Nested frames can be viewed just as well in Netscape (Figure 9.44) as in Internet Explorer (shown here).*

Nesting framesets

As if frames and framesets weren't complicated enough, you can put framesets inside of frames in a different frameset to achieve special effects.

To nest framesets:

1. Build the child, or inner, frameset as described on page 136.

2. Build the parent, or outer, frameset as described on page 136 **(Figure 9.43)**. When you reach the frame in which you wish to nest the child frameset, type **SRC=childframes.html** within the FRAME tag, where *childframes.html* is the file that you built in step 1.

✔ Tip

■ You can target a link to open in the parent frame of a frameset (in this example, the right column is the parent frame of the Barcelona tour frameset). For more information, see the tips on page 150.

Nesting framesets

Creating alternatives to frames

Although Netscape and Internet Explorer have been able to display frames since version 2, frames are still not a standard part of HTML 3.2. You can add information to your page that will appear if your user's browser doesn't support frames.

To create alternatives to frames:

1. Type **<NOFRAMES>** after the last </FRAMESET> tag **(Figure 9.46)**.

2. Create the BODY section and continue writing your page as usual, as described in the rest of this book.

3. When you've finished creating the alternative to frames, type **</NOFRAMES>**.

✔ Tips

■ The information found within the NOFRAMES tags will not be shown in browsers that can interpret frames, like Netscape **(Figure 9.47)** and Internet Explorer. Instead, the frames will be shown.

■ You can set up Internet Explorer so that it displays the information in the NOFRAMES section. Choose Options in the Edit menu and then click Web Content. Finally, uncheck the Show Frames option.

■ If you don't create a NOFRAMES section, beware! When users jump to your page with a browser that can't read frames, instead of an error message, they simply won't see anything! If nothing else, the NOFRAMES section can be used to explain what the problem is **(Figure 9.48)**.

Figure 9.46 *The NOFRAMES tags come after all of the framesets and frames have been defined.*

Figure 9.47 *Netscape always displays frames, and therefore* never *displays the information between the NOFRAMES tags.*

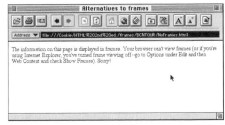

Figure 9.48 *When you turn frames off in Internet Explorer, you can see the alternate information. This is a good way to test how this information will appear. Although this example is rather simple, don't be misled: you can put practically anything in the NOFRAMES section.*

Forms

One of the most powerful parts of the Web page is the form. In conjunction with *CGI scripts,* forms let you collect information from the user and store it for later use.

In this chapter, you will first learn how to construct forms with regular HTML tags. It is extremely straightforward and is analogous to creating any other part of the Web page.

The most unusual part of a form element is the concept of name/value pairs. Basically, when the information is sent to the server, it is sent in two parts: first an identifier, or name, and then the actual data. For example, in a text box with a name like *Lastname* where the user has typed *Castro*, the data will be sent to the server as *Lastname=Castro*.

To divide the data stream into something you can use, you need a CGI script, which is a small computer program, either written by you or copied from another source, that can be activated by clicking a URL.

Unless you know how to program in C or Perl, you may have a hard time using CGI scripts. At the end of this chapter, you'll learn how to start working with CGI, and where you can turn for more information.

Forms

Form structure

Writing the HTML code to make forms is not any more difficult than creating any other element on your web page. Writing the scripts that interpret the data received is a bit more complicated.

To create a form:

1. Type **<FORM**.

2. Type **METHOD="POST"**. You can also use the GET method.

3. Type **ACTION="script.url"** where *script.url* is the location on the server of the CGI script that will be run when the form is submitted.

4. Create the form elements, as described on the following pages.

5. Create a Submit button, as described on page 161. (You don't need to create a submit button if you're using an active image.)

6. Type **</FORM>** to complete the form.

✔ Tip

■ You can use tables to set up your form elements. For more information, consult Chapter 8, *Tables*.

Figure 10.1 *Every form has three parts: the FORM tag, the actual form elements, where the user enters information, and the SUBMIT tag which creates the button that sends the collected information to the server (or an active image).*

Figure 10.2 *This form has only text and check boxes. It could also contain radio buttons, menus, larger text entry areas, and an active image.*

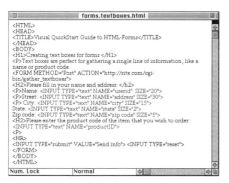

Figure 10.3 *Each text box is defined with its own INPUT line.*

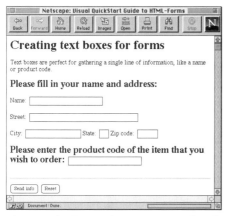

Figure 10.4 *Place text boxes on separate lines by adding a <P> between them.*

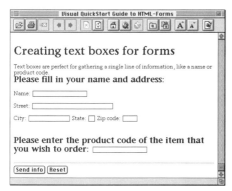

Figure 10.5 *The spacing in Netscape's forms (top) is slightly different from that of Internet Explorer's (bottom).*

Text boxes

Text boxes contain one line of text and are typically used for names, addresses and the like.

To create a text box:

1. Inside the FORM area of your HTML document, type the title of the text box (for example, Name:), if desired.

2. Type **<INPUT TYPE="text"**.

3. Give the text box a name by adding **NAME="name"**. When the data is collected by the server, the information entered in this text box will be identified by the *name*.

4. If desired, define the size of the box on your form, by typing **SIZE="n"**, replacing *n* with the desired width of the box, measured in characters. The default value is 20. Users can add more text than fits in the text box, up to the value defined for MAXLENGTH. (See next step.)

5. If desired, define the maximum number of characters that can be entered in the box by typing **MAXLENGTH="n"**, replacing *n* with the desired maximum length in characters.

6. Finish the text box by typing a final **>**.

Text boxes

Password boxes

A password box is similar to a text box, but when the user types in it, the letters are hidden by bullets or asterisks.

To create password entry boxes:

1. Inside the FORM area of your HTML document, type the title of the password box, if desired. Something like **Enter password** will do fine.

2. Type **<INPUT TYPE="password"**.

3. Give the password box a name by typing **NAME="name"**. When the data is collected by the server, the information entered in this password box will be identified by the *name*.

4. If desired, define the size of the box on your form, by typing **SIZE="n"**, replacing *n* with the desired width of the box, measured in characters.

5. If desired, define the maximum number of characters that can be entered in the box by typing **MAXLENGTH="n"**, replacing *n* with the desired value.

6. Finish the text box by typing a final **>**.

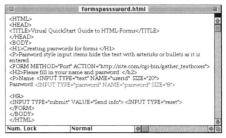

Figure 10.6 *The VALUE tag identifies the data once it is posted to the URL. It may or may not be the same as the identifying text that the user sees on screen.*

Figure 10.7 *When the user enters a password in a form viewed in Netscape, above, or in Internet Explorer, below, the password is hidden with bullets.*

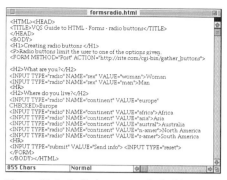

```
formsradio.html
<HTML><HEAD>
<TITLE>VQS Guide to HTML - Forms - radio buttons</TITLE>
</HEAD>
<BODY>
<H1>Creating radio buttons </H1>
<P>Radio buttons limit the user to one of the options given.
<FORM METHOD="Post" ACTION="http://site.com/cgi-bin/gather_buttons">

<H2>What are you?</H2>
<INPUT TYPE="radio" NAME="sex" VALUE="woman">Woman
<INPUT TYPE="radio" NAME="sex" VALUE="man">Man
<HR>
<H2>Where do you live?</H2>
<INPUT TYPE="radio" NAME="continent" VALUE="europe"
CHECKED>Europe
<INPUT TYPE="radio" NAME="continent" VALUE="africa">Africa
<INPUT TYPE="radio" NAME="continent" VALUE="asia">Asia
<INPUT TYPE="radio" NAME="continent" VALUE="austral">Australia
<INPUT TYPE="radio" NAME="continent" VALUE="n-amer">North America
<INPUT TYPE="radio" NAME="continent" VALUE="s-amer">South America
<HR>
<INPUT TYPE="submit" VALUE="Send info"> <INPUT TYPE="reset">
</FORM>
</BODY></HTML>
```
855 Chars   Normal

Figure 10.8 *Radio buttons are linked by a common value for the NAME tag: both elements in the first group have a NAME of* sex *while the elements in the second group have a NAME of* continent.

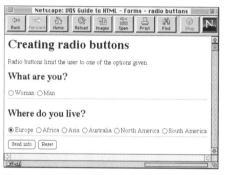

Figure 10.9 *In the first set of radio buttons, there is no "most common" answer; thus, no default has been set with the CHECKED tag.*

Figure 10.10 *If most users of this page are from Europe, it is a good idea to use the CHECKED tag to select it by default. Notice how the lines wrap differently in Netscape (top) vs. in Internet Explorer. (bottom).*

Radio buttons

Remember those old-time car radios with big black plastic buttons? Push one to listen to WAQY; push another for WRNX. You can never push two buttons at once. Radio buttons on forms work the same way (except you can't listen to the radio). Out of all the radio buttons with the same name, only one can be active at a time. In addition, each radio button must have a value.

To create a radio button:

1. In the FORM area of your HTML document, type the introductory text for your radio buttons. You might choose something like *Select one of the following.*

2. Type **<INPUT TYPE="radio"**.

3. Type **NAME="radioset"** where *radioset* identifies each radio button in a particular set. Only one radio button in a set can be checked.

4. You must define a value for each radio button. Type **VALUE="value"**, where *value* is the data that will be sent to the server if the radio button is checked.

5. If desired, type **CHECKED** to make the radio button active by default when the page is opened.

6. Type the final **>** to finish the radio button definition.

7. Type the text that identifies the radio button to the user. This is often the same as VALUE, but needn't be.

8. Repeat steps 2-7 for each radio button in the set.

Radio buttons

Check boxes

While radio buttons can accept only one answer per set, a user can check as many check boxes in a set as they like. Like radio buttons, check boxes are linked by their name.

To create check boxes:

1. In the FORM area of your HTML document, type the introductory text for your check boxes. You might choose something like Select one or more of the following.

2. Type **<INPUT TYPE="checkbox"**. (Notice there is no space in the attribute *checkbox*.)

3. It is a good idea to define a value for each check box. The value will only be sent to the server if the check box is checked (either by the user or by you, see step 4). Type **VALUE= "default value"**. This is often the same as the value shown to the user, but it can be different. (See step 6.)

4. Type **CHECKED** to make the check box checked by default when the page is opened. You (or the user) may check as many check boxes as you wish.

5. Type the final **>** to finish the check box definition.

6. Type the text that identifies the check box to the user. This is often the same as the VALUE, but it doesn't have to be.

7. Repeat steps 2-6 for each check box in the set.

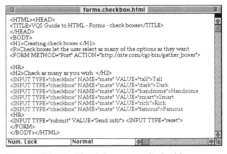

Figure 10.11 *Check boxes are linked by a common NAME.*

Figure 10.12 *Users can check as many of the options in a set of check boxes as they wish. (This is Netscape.)*

Figure 10.13 *This is what this page looks like in Internet Explorer. It is almost identical to that of Netscape (Figure 10.12).*

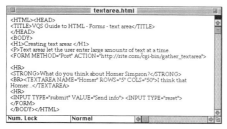

Figure 10.14 *Use a column width of about 50 (COLS="50") if you want the text area to span a normal sized Web page as viewed with Netscape.*

Figure 10.15 *Use default text that helps the user to fill out the rest of the text box. (This is Netscape.)*

Figure 10.16 *A column width of 50 is displayed almost identically in Internet Explorer (here) as in Netscape (Figure 10.15). Notice how Internet Explorer doesn't show the scroll bars until there are enough elements to fill up the text block.*

Text blocks

In some cases, you want to give the user a larger space to respond. Text blocks may be as large as your page, and will expand as needed if the user enters more text than can fit in the display area.

To create text blocks:

1. In the FORM area of your HTML document, type the introductory text for your text area, if desired.

2. Type **<TEXTAREA**.

3. Type **NAME="name"** where *name* is the variable name you give to your text area. The name identifies the data when it is collected by the server.

4. If desired, type **ROWS="n"**, where *n* is the height of the text area in rows. The default value is 4.

5. If desired, type **COLS="n"**, where *n* is the width of the text area in characters. The default value is 40.

6. Type **>**.

7. Type the default text, if any, for the text area. You may not add any HTML coding here.

8. Type **</TEXTAREA>** to complete the text area.

✔ Tip

■ Users can enter up to 32,700 characters in a text area. Scroll bars will appear when necessary.

Text blocks

Menus

Creating menus for your users makes it easy for them to enter information or provide criteria for a search.

To create menus:

1. In the FORM area of your HTML document, type the introductory text for your menu, if desired.

2. Type **<SELECT**.

3. Type **NAME="name"** where *name* is the variable name for the menu that will identify the data when it is collected by the server.

4. Type **SIZE="n"** where *n* represents the number of items that should be initially visible in the menu.

5. If desired, type **MULTIPLE** to allow the user to select more than one option from the menu.

6. Type the final **>** to finish the menu definition.

7. Type **<OPTION**.

8. Type **SELECTED** if you want the option to be selected by default.

9. Type **VALUE="value"** where *value* is the name that will identify the data when it is collected by the server.

10. Type **>**.

11. Type the option name as you wish it to appear in the menu.

12. Repeat steps 7-11 for each option.

13. Type **</SELECT>**.

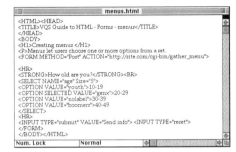

Figure 10.17 *Notice that the option values need not match what the user sees (e.g., youth vs. 10-19). You can use whatever variable name that makes analyzing the information easier.*

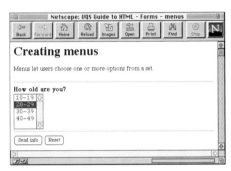

Figure 10.18 *The option with the SELECTED tag is automatically checked when the user jumps to this page. (This is Netscape.)*

Figure 10.19 *When you choose a value for SIZE that is greater than the number of options available, an empty option appears which allows the user to deselect whatever option(s) were previously selected. Again, Internet Explorer only shows scroll bars when necessary.*

```
┌─────────────────────────────────────┐
│▓▓          submit.html           ▓▓│
├─────────────────────────────────────┤
│<HTML><HEAD>                          │
│<TITLE>VQS Guide to HTML · Forms · submit buttons</TITLE>│
│</HEAD>                               │
│<BODY>                                │
│<P>A Submit button sends the entered information to the server.│
│<FORM METHOD="Post" ACTION="http://site.com/cgi-bin/gather_buttons">│
│                                      │
│Sex <INPUT TYPE="radio" NAME="sex" VALUE="woman">Woman│
│<INPUT TYPE="radio" NAME="sex" VALUE="man">Man│
│<HR>                                  │
│Age <SELECT NAME="age" Size="5">     │
│<OPTION VALUE="youth">10-19          │
│<OPTION SELECTED VALUE="genx">20-29  │
│<OPTION VALUE="nolabel">30-39        │
│<OPTION VALUE="boomers">40-49        │
│</SELECT>                             │
│<HR>                                  │
│<INPUT TYPE="submit" VALUE="Send info">│
│<INPUT TYPE="reset" VALUE="Start over">│
│</FORM>                               │
│</BODY></HTML>                        │
├─────────────────────────────────────┤
│Num. Lock      │Normal      │        │
└─────────────────────────────────────┘
```

Figure 10.20 *You can use any text you wish for the Submit button. Just make it clear that a click will send the information gathered to the server.*

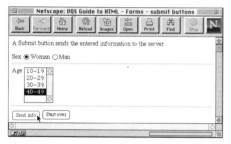

Figure 10.21 *Once the user has entered the appropriate information, they click on the submit button to send the information to the server.*

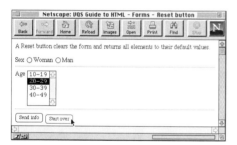

Figure 10.22 *A click on the reset button clears the form and returns all variables to their default values. In this case, there is no default for Sex and so it returns to its unchecked state. The default for Age was 20-29.*

Gathering the information

All the information that your users enter won't be any good to you unless they send it to the server. You should always create a SUBMIT button for your forms so that the user can deliver the information to you. (If you use images as active elements in a FORM area, see page 111.)

To create a submit button:

1. Type **<INPUT TYPE="submit"**.

2. If desired, type **VALUE="submit message"** where *submit message* is the text that will appear in the button. The default submit message is *Submit Query*.

3. Type the final **>**.

Resetting the form

If humans could fill out forms perfectly on the first try, there would be no erasers on pencils and no backspace key on your computer keyboard. You can give your users a Reset button so that they can start over with a fresh form (including all the default values you've set).

To create a Reset button:

1. Type **<INPUT TYPE="reset"**.

2. If desired, type **VALUE="reset message"** where *reset message* is the text that appears in the button. The default reset message is *Reset*.

3. Type **>**.

Hidden elements

At first glance, creating hidden elements in a form seems counter productive. How can the user enter information if they can't see where to put it? Actually, they can't. However, hidden elements can be used by you to store information gathered from an *earlier* form so that it can be combined with the present form's data.

For example, if you ask for a user's name in an earlier form, you can save it in a variable and then add it to a new form as a hidden element so that the name is related to the new information gathered without having to bother the user to enter the name several times.

To create a hidden element:

1. Type **<INPUT TYPE="hidden"**.

2. Type **NAME="name"** where *name* is the name of the information to be stored.

3. Type **VALUE="value"** where *value* is the information itself that is to be stored.

4. Type **>**.

Figure 10.23 *The Hidden element can be placed anywhere in the BODY section of the HTML document.*

Figure 10.24 *Hidden elements are invisible to the user in all browsers, including Netscape (top) and Internet Explorer (bottom).*

Hidden elements

```
formimage.html
<HTML><HEAD>
<TITLE>VQS Guide to HTML - Forms - active image</TITLE>
</HEAD>
<BODY>
<P>You can use an active image to get info from your user with the click of
the mouse.
<HR>
<FORM ACTION="http://site.com/cgi-bin/gather_aimage">
<STRONG>Where are you from?</STRONG> (Click on the map to
answer.)<BR>
<INPUT TYPE="image" NAME="map" SRC="map.gif">
</FORM>
</BODY></HTML>
Num. Lock          Normal
```

Figure 10.25 *You don't need to include a sub-mit button with an active image since a click will automatically submit the data.*

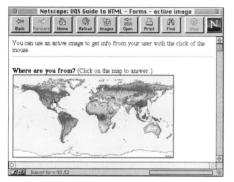

Figure 10.26 *Netscape shows the hand cursor when the user drags it over an active image. In addition, it gives the present coordinates of the mouse in the lower left corner of the window. It is these coordinates that will be sent to the server when the user clicks the mouse button.*

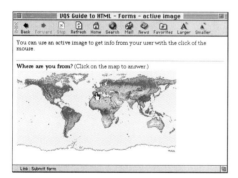

Figure 10.27 *Active images are practically iden-tical in Internet Explorer (shown here), although instead of the hand's coordinates, the status bar simply reads "Link: Submit Form".*

Active images

You may use images as active elements in a FORM area. A click on the image appends the current mouse coordinates (as measured from the top left corner) to the variable name and sends the data to the server.

To create an active image:

1. Create a GIF image and save it in your images directory on your server *(see page 50)*.

2. Type **<INPUT TYPE="image"**.

3. Type **SRC="image_url"** where *image_url* is the location of the image on the server.

4. Type **NAME="name"**. When the user clicks on the image, the x and y coor-dinates of the mouse will be appended to the name defined here and sent to the server.

5. Type the final **>** to finish the active image definition for the FORM.

✔ Tips

■ All the form data is sent automatically when the user clicks on the active image. Therefore, it's a good idea to give instructions on how to use the active image and to place the image at the end of the form so that the user completes the other form elements before clicking the image and sending the data.

■ You can create an entire question-naire out of pictures by making the next question (and active image) appear after the data is sent from the last question to the server.

CGI scripts

A Common Gateway Interface (CGI) script, or gateway program, is an actual program (or batch file) that can be activated by the user with a click on a URL. It may be written in a computer language like C or Pascal, or it may be written in Perl or a shell program, and be a simple executable.

The advantage of using Perl or a shell program is that the script can be easily ported from computer to computer and doesn't need to be compiled. In other words, you can copy a Perl script from someone else, adapt it to your needs by changing the appropriate paths and incorporate it into your page.

One of the principal uses of CGI scripts in HTML documents is to analyze, parse, and store information received from a form, but their more general use is to interact with the server, storing and requesting data, and then offering the results to the user.

The results that are reported back to the user are often formatted as a new HTML document, using the same tags that you've been learning throughout this book.

You need certain permissions to use CGI scripts on particular servers. Any time you open communication between the server and the public (i.e., your users) you are putting the server at a security risk. You should speak to your system administrator about what you need to do to use CGI.

Figure 10.28 *You can test your scripts with a Telnet program. If they don't work here, they won't work when your user points to them.*

Other scripting languages

Some CGI scripts can be replaced by JavaScript or VBScript, scripting languages that tend to be a bit easier to use than CGI.

JavaScript was developed jointly by Sun Microsystems and Netscape Communications. For more information, jump to *http://home.netscape. com/eng/mozilla/Gold/handbook/ javascript/index.html*.

Visual Basic Script, or VBScript for short, was developed by Microsoft. For more information, jump to *http:// www.microsoft.com/vbscript*.

CGI scripts

Figure 10.29 *This is a simple script that creates an HTML page, queries the server for the date, and inserts that date in the HTML page.*

Figure 10.30 *To use the script, create a link to it in your HTML page.*

Figure 10.31 *The simple HTML page in Netscape shows the link to the script.*

Figure 10.32 *Since the script includes HTML coding, the result is an HTML page that contains the date.*

Using CGI scripts

A CGI script is used to activate programs on the server to get information and then to report that information to the user. For example, you could use a CGI script to call the date program on the server and report the results on a Web page.

To create a link to a CGI script:

1. In your HTML document, type **<A HREF="http://www.site.com/** where *www.site.com* is the name of the server that contains the CGI script.

2. Type **cgi-bin**, where *cgi-bin* is the location of CGI scripts on most UNIX servers.

3. Type **/path** where *path* is the path to the cgi-script, if it is not found directly in the main cgi-bin directory. For example, on many servers, each user has their own cgi-bin directory within their personal directory.

4. Type **/cgiscript** where *cgiscript* is the name of the cgiscript that you wish to call.

5. Type **>**.

6. Type the clickable text that the user will click to activate the script.

7. Type **</A>** to complete the link.

Multimedia

One of the things that has made the Web so popular is the idea that you can add graphics, sound and movies to your Web pages. The truth is that today's browsers can only show two kinds of graphic images inline, at most, and that they rely on external applications called *helpers* to open other types of multimedia files. (Of course, the technology is moving so fast that tomorrow's browsers, or perhaps even this afternoon's browsers, may in fact be able to handle more complicated multimedia files without helpers.)

The main problem with multimedia is that the files are generally very large. Ten seconds of average quality sound take up more than 200K, which will take your user three and a half minutes to download before they can hear it with the helper program. Ten seconds of a movie displayed in a tiny 2" x 3" window are considerably larger. Similarly, large still images (even if they are JPEG or GIF format) can exhaust your users.

Finally, since the Web population is diverse, and uses many different kinds of computers, you have to make sure that the files you provide can be read by your users (or the largest number possible of them). This is probably the trickiest part of all.

Helper applications

If a browser cannot handle a certain type of file, it calls up a "helper application" to view the file. A helper application can be any program that is capable of opening the particular format of the file.

For example, a user could conceivably use Adobe Photoshop as a helper application to view TIFF images. But since Photoshop is such a complete program, it takes several seconds to load and view the image—not to mention the fact that it costs $900. Users are generally better off with a small, fast, free, helper application that is good at just one thing: viewing or playing specific file formats. See Table 11.2 for a list of common helper applications.

A browser can only call a helper application if two conditions are met. First, the user must already have the helper application on the computer (*and* have specified which helper application to use for which types of files).

Although helper applications are easily acquired through many FTP servers, not all users have taken the time to download them. If your users don't have the proper helper application, they won't be able to view your files.

Second, you, the page designer, must use the proper extension for the file so that the browser knows which helper application will be necessary to access the file. The system of standardized extensions is known as MIME—Multipurpose Internet Mail Extensions *(see Table 11.1).*

MIME type	Extension(s)
image/gif	.gif
image/jpeg	.jpeg .jpg .jpe
image/pict	.pic .pict
image/tiff	.tif .tiff
image/x-xbitmap	.xbm
audio/basic	.au snd
audio/aiff	.aiff .aif
audio/x-wav	.wav
video/quicktime	.qt .mov
video/mpeg	.mpg .mpeg .mpe
video/x-msvideo	.avi
application/mac-binhex40	.hqx
application/x-stuffit	.sit
application/x-macbinary	.bin
application/octet-stream	.exe
application/postscript	.ai .eps .ps
application/rtf	.rtf
application/x-compressed	.zip .z .gz .tgz
application/x-tar	.tar

Table 11.1: *It is extremely important to use the proper extension to identify your external files. If there is more than one possible extension, you can generally use whichever you prefer, as long as you follow the naming limitations of the server (e.g. DOS servers insist on three letter extensions).*

	Mac	Windows	Unix
Graphics	JPEGView GraphicConverter	LView Pro PaintShop Pro	xv
Sound	SoundMachine SoundApp	Wham Wplany	audiotool audioplayer
Video	Sparkle Fast Player	Media Player mpegplay	mpeg_play xplaygizmo
PostScript	(built-in)	ghostscript ghostview	ghostscript ghostview

Table 11.2: *Some common helper applications.*

Figure 11.3 *Since a user has to take the time to download large images like the one referenced here, you should a 'least give him an idea of how big the image is.*

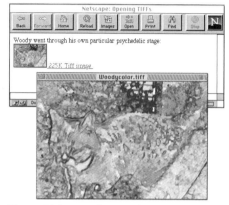

Figure 11.4 *Once the user clicks on the icon, the browser launches the helper application (in this case JPEG View) and the helper application shows the TIFF file.*

Non-supported images

In the current race to be the best browser, both Netscape and Internet Explorer are adding capabilities to view as many types of images as possible internally. If you need to create a link to an image in an as-yet unrecognized format, you'll need to use the proper extension and the user will have to have a helper application that can view the image.

To create a link to a non supported image:

1. Create an image and save it in the desired format with the proper extension. *(See Table 11.1 on page 168.)*

2. In your HTML document where you want the image to appear, type **<A HREF="image.ext">** where *image.ext* is the name of the image file on the server with the appropriate extension.

3. If desired, use a icon to indicate the external image by typing **<IMG SRC="icon.gif">** where *icon.gif* is the location on the server of the icon.

4. Give a description of the image, including its size and format.

5. Complete the link by typing **</A>**.

✔ Tips

■ Why bother with other formats besides GIF or JPEG? Perhaps you want to provide non-expert users with a certain type of graphic image (TIFF, say) and you don't want them to have to bother with converting it.

■ Since non-GIF/JPEG images generally will not appear inline, there is little advantage to using additional image formatting, like ALIGN or LOWSRC.

Non-supported images

169

Sound

As with images, one of the main factors to consider when adding sound to your page is the format. Use a format that few computers can recognize and few users will hear your sound. The most common sound format is au developed by Sun Microsystems. It can be used on Mac, Windows, Unix, and other systems. Unfortunately, the au format only allows for 8 bit sampling, which is certainly at the low end of the quality scale.

The standard format for Macintosh sound is AIFF while Windows machines read sound in the WAV format. You can add sound files to your Web pages in any of these formats, but only those users with the corresponding computer system will be able to download and listen to the sounds right away.

One alternative is to use a conversion program to create several different versions of your sound files and then give your users access to all of them. Then they can download and listen to the one that corresponds to their system.

If your computer has a sound card and microphone (like most Macs and many PCs), and you have a sound editing program, you can create your own sound files.

To create a sound on the Mac:

1. Open the Sound control panel **(Figure 11.5)**.

2. Click Add.

3. Click Record in the dialog box that appears **(Figure 11.6)**.

4. Record your sound.

5. Click Stop and then Save.

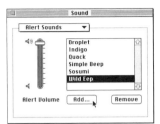

Figure 11.5 *To create a sound with the Macintosh's Sound control panel, click Add.*

Figure 11.6 *Click Record to start recording your sound and Stop when you are finished. Then click Save to save your sound.*

Figure 11.7 *Finally, give your sound a name.*

Figure 11.8 *Once you have created the sound, you can find it in the System icon inside the System folder. Drag it out and place it in the folder with the rest of your HTML files.*

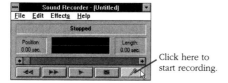

Click here to start recording.

Figure 11.9 *The Sound Recorder main window in Windows.*

Figure 11.10 *Be sure and choose the appropriate format in the pop-up menu when you save your sound.*

6. Give the sound a name and click OK **(Figure 11.7)**.

7. Close the Sound control panel.

8. Open the System Folder and then double click the System icon. You'll find the new sound here **(Figure 11.8)**. Drag it out to the same folder that contains your other HTML files.

To create a sound in Windows:

1. Open Sound Recorder **(Figure 11.9)**.

2. Click on the microphone icon at the far right.

3. Start recording your sound.

4. Click Stop (the button with the square) to finish recording.

5. Choose Save as in the File menu to save your sound file.

6. Choose the appropriate format for the file in the Save as dialog box, and make sure the appropriate extension (.au for au files, .aif for AIFF files, and .wav for WAV files) is added to the file name **(Figure 11.10)**.

✔ Tips

■ Creating sounds for other systems is essentially the same process as outlined here, using the sound editor appropriate to that system.

■ One of the most exciting sound-related improvements to the Web is RealAudio and its ability to download part of a sound, play it, download another piece, play it, and so on, approximating live audio. For more information, check out RealAudio's Web site at *www.realaudio.com.*

Sound

Converting sound formats

Once you have a sound, you need to convert it to the proper format for publication on the Web. Although the au format can be understood by many different kinds of computers, the quality is not that great. Therefore, you may want to provide several versions of your sound file: one in au, one in AIFF for Macintosh, and one in WAV for Windows.

To convert a sound from one format to another:

1. Open SoundApp (for Macintosh) or some other sound conversion program (like Wham for Windows).

2. Choose Convert in the File menu **(Figure 11.11)**.

3. Choose the desired sound document in the dialog box that appears. Select a format in the Convert To pop-up menu **(Figure 11.12)**.

4. Click Open. A progress report appears **(Figure 11.13)**.

5. SoundApp places the converted file in a new folder inside the current folder **(Figure 11.14)**.

6. Add the correct extension to the end of the name (even for Macintosh files). Use .au for au files, .aif for AIFF files and .wav for WAV files.

✔ Tip

■ You can convert files from the Finder with SoundApp. Select the files, hold down the Shift key and drag them onto the SoundApp application. You can change the default destination format (and keyboard shortcut) in the Preferences dialog box.

Figure 11.11 *In SoundApp (for Macintosh), choose Convert in the File menu.*

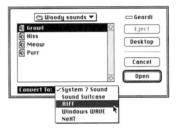

Figure 11.12 *Choose the desired file and the appropriate format in the Convert To menu.*

Figure 11.13 *SoundApp shows you the progress of the file conversion.*

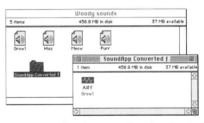

Figure 11.14 *When SoundApp has finished converting the files, it places them in a folder called SoundApp Converted f inside the current folder.*

Converting sound formats

Figure 11.15 *Always include information on your page about the size and recording quality of your sound.*

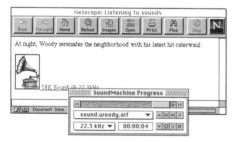

Figure 11.16 *When the user clicks the sound icon (the victrola) or the clickable text description of the sound, the browser downloads the sound and launches the helper application (in this case SoundMachine) which plays the sound.*

Adding external sound to a Web page

Currently there are three main ways to add sound to a page. For Netscape, you can create a sound that can be played from within the page *(see page 174)*. For browsing in Internet Explorer, you can add a background sound that loads automatically when the user jumps to the page *(see page 175)*. Finally, you can create a link to a sound that can be played with a helper application, regardless of the browser the page is viewed with.

To add a sound to your page:

1. Create a small icon that you can use as an inline image on your page to indicate the link to the sound and call it *sound.gif.*

2. Make sure the sound file has the correct extension. Use .au for au files, .aif for AIFF files and .wav for WAV files.

3. In your HTML document where you wish to place the link to the sound file, type **<A HREF="sound.ext">** where *sound.ext* is the location of the sound file, including the correct extension, on the server.

4. Type **<IMG SRC="soundicon.gif">** where *soundicon.gif* is the icon that will indicate the link to the sound.

5. Type the description, size and format of the audio file.

6. Type **</A>** to complete the link.

✔ Tip

■ Give extra information to your user, including the format and size of the audio file, so that they can decide whether or not to download the sound.

Adding internal sound with LiveAudio

 Netscape 3 includes a plug-in that enables the browser to play sound right in the Web page itself, without having to resort to an external helper application. LiveAudio recognizes AIFF, WAV, AU and MIDI formats.

To add sound with LiveAudio:

1. In your HTML document, type **<EMBED SRC=sound.url** where *sound.url* is the complete file name and extension for the sound file.

2. If desired, type **CONTROLS=form** where *form* determines how the sound controls should appear. The available options are *console, small-console, playbutton, pausebutton, stopbutton,* and *volumelever.*

   If you choose a kind of control, type **WIDTH=w HEIGHT=h** where *w* and *h* represent the width and height, respectively, of the type of control.

3. If desired, type **AUTOSTART=true** to make the sound play automatically when the user jumps to the page.

4. If desired, type **LOOP=n** to repeat the sound automatically n number of times. Or type **LOOP=true** to repeat the sound over and over until the user clicks the Stop button (if you've provided one) or jumps to another page.

5. If desired, type **ALIGN=direction** to align the controls on the page. The ALIGN tag works the same for LiveAudio as it does for images. For more information, see page 76.

6. Type the final **>**.

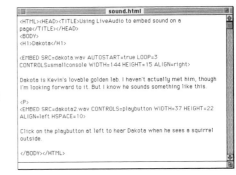

Figure 11.17 *In the top sound, there will be a small console (note the default width and height values). In the bottom sound, I've only included a play button. Notice that although the HSPACE (and VSPACE) attributes are not documented, they work correctly.*

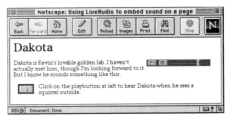

Figure 11.18 *The small console (right) contains, from right to left, a play button, stop button, and progress indicator. The independent play button is shown at bottom left.*

Figure 11.19 *The BGSOUND tag can be placed anywhere on the page. However, since Internet Explorer will play the sound as soon as it encounters the tag so you may want to place the tag at the end of the page so that the user sees the page before hearing the sound.*

Figure 11.20 *Woof, Woof. You can't see sound, but trust me, you can hear it.*

Adding background sound

 Internet Explorer has a special tag that lets you link a sound to a page and have the sound play automatically whenever a user jumps to the page.

To add background sound:

1. In the HTML document, type **<BGSOUND=sound.url** where *sound.url* is the complete file name, including the extension of the sound.

2. If desired, type **LOOP=n** where *n* is the number of times you wish the sound to be played. Use **LOOP=-1** or **LOOP=infinite** to play the sound over and over.

3. Type the final **>**.

✔ Tips

■ You can create a background sound for pages that will be viewed in Netscape by following the instructions on page 174. Omit the CONTROLS, HEIGHT and WIDTH attributes and the sound will be hidden. Then add **AUTOSTART=true** so that the sound plays automatically when the user jumps to the page.

■ Don't use a really obnoxious or annoying sound (or even a particularly loud one) if you want people to come back to your page with any regularity.

■ The BGSOUND tag recognizes WAV, AU or MIDI formatted sounds.

Adding background sound

Video

If you listen to the Web hype long enough, you'll believe you can tune into Paramount's home page and watch previews to their new movies. Unfortunately, thanks to the huge size of video files and the relative minuscule speed of most home modems, although you might be *able* to do this, you might be gray before the opening credits finish rolling.

Nevertheless, it is possible to add links to video on your Web pages. As with sound files, you have to be especially careful to provide video in a format that your users will be able to use: QuickTime and MPEG for Mac and Windows, AVI just for Windows.

Capturing video

If you have an AV Mac or PowerMac or a video capture card for your PC, you can create video files by copying clips from your VCR to your computer. Along with the video-specific hardware, you will need a fast computer and a big, fast, hard disk.

The actual process, although not difficult, is a bit beyond the scope of this book. Your AV Mac or Video card should have instructions on how to digitize video. In my experience, the hardest part is figuring out where to connect all the cables.

Once again, you have to be careful about just what you copy. Most broadcast television is copyrighted and may not be published without permission. Of course, you are welcome to insert videos on your page that you've filmed yourself.

You may also find video files online or in a commercial library on CD-ROM.

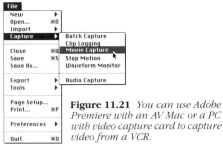

Figure 11.21 *You can use Adobe Premiere with an AV Mac or a PC with video capture card to capture video from a VCR.*

Figure 11.22 *If you don't have your own home movies, you can use copyright free clips included in CD-ROM collections, like this short movie, which is included in the Adobe Premiere Deluxe CD-ROM.*

Figure 11.23 *These tiny menus reveal the simplicity of many video conversion programs. Fast-Player (left) flattens Macintosh QuickTime movies for viewing on Windows machines. AVI->QT (right) converts AVI format movies to QuickTime format.*

Converting video to the proper format

Your users will only be able to download and view your video files if you have saved them in the proper format, with the proper extension.

To convert video to the proper format:

1. Open a video conversion program.

2. Open the video file.

3. Choose Save as in the File menu **(Figure 11.23)**.

4. In the Format submenu, choose QuickTime, AVI or MPEG. QuickTime and MPEG movies can be viewed on both Macintosh and Windows machines. AVI movies are only for Windows.

5. Give the new movie file a distinct name and the proper extension (.qt or .mov for QuickTime, .avi for AVI and .mpeg or .mpg for MPEG).

6. Click Save.

✔ Tip

■ In addition, QuickTime movies need to be *flattened* before they can be viewed on other types of computers besides Macintosh. Use a tool like FastPlayer (for Macintosh) or Qflat (for Windows).

Converting video to the proper format

Adding external video to your page

Although both Internet Explorer and Netscape can display video within a Web page *(see pages 179 and 180)*, they do it in two different ways. To make video accessible to your users regardless of their browser, you might consider using, or at least adding, a link to an external video file. When the user clicks the link, the browser downloads the video file and opens the appropriate helper program which then views the video.

To add a link to external video:

1. Create a small icon that you can use as an inline image on your page to indicate the link to the video and call it *video.gif*.

2. Make sure the video file has the correct extension (even for Macintosh files). Otherwise, the user's browser will not know what kind of file it is and may be unable to open it. (Use .qt or .mov for QuickTime files, .avi for AVI files and .mpeg or .mpg for MPEG files.)

3. In your HTML document, where you wish to place the link to the video file, type **<A HREF="video.ext">** where *video.ext* is the location of the video file, including the correct extension, on the server.

4. Type **<IMG SRC="video.gif">** where *video.gif* is the location of the icon that will indicate the link to the video.

5. Type the size and format of the video file, for example, 5.2 Mb QuickTime movie.

6. Type **</A>** to complete the link to the video file.

Figure 11.24 *It's a good idea to tell your users how big the video file is so that they know how long it will take to download.*

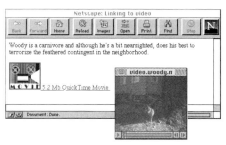

Figure 11.25 *A click by the user on the icon or text downloads the video file, launches the video player, and then plays the video.*

Figure 11.26 *Since videos inserted on a page with the EMBED tag do not have controls, you might want to add the AUTOSTART attribute so that they project automatically. Otherwise, instruct your users to click the video to play it.*

Figure 11.27 *To play a movie that is inserted with the EMBED tag, just click it.*

Figure 11.28 *Internet Explorer can also view videos inserted with the EMBED tag, although it offers more flexibility with the DYNSRC tag described on page 180.*

Adding internal video

Netscape 3 includes a plug-in, called LiveVideo, for viewing video right in the browser window itself. LiveVideo supports only AVI format movies and only runs on Netscape for Windows. Internet Explorer can also view video inserted as described below.

To add internal video:

1. Create a movie in AVI format. You can also convert an existing movie.

2. In your HTML document, type **<EMBED SRC=movie.avi**, where *movie.avi* is the URL for the desired movie file, including the extension.

3. Type **WIDTH=w HEIGHT=h** where *w* and *h* are the width and height, respectively, in pixels, of the movie.

4. If desired, type **AUTOSTART=true** to have the movie play automatically when the user jumps to the page.

5. If desired, type **LOOP=true** to have the movie play continuously until the user clicks on the movie or jumps to a different page.

6. If desired, type **ALIGN=direction**. The ALIGN tag works the same for LiveAudio as it does for images. For more information, see page 76.

✔ Tip

■ Your users must have the LiveVideo plug-in installed for Netscape 3 to display inline movies. There is, as yet, no LiveVideo plug-in for Macintosh. For information on adding links to movies that can be seen on any platform with practically any browser (albeit externally), see page 178.

Adding internal video

Adding video for Internet Explorer

 Internet Explorer recognizes a special attribute of the IMG tag that allows you to insert video on a page.

To add video for Internet Explorer:

1. Create an AVI movie. Create a static image, perhaps of the first frame of the movie.

2. In your HTML document, type **<IMG SRC=image.gif** where *image.gif* is the static image that will be displayed before and after the movie is played.

3. Type **DYNSRC=movie.avi** where movie.avi is the URL of the desired movie.

4. If desired, type **LOOP=n** where n is the number of times the movie should be projected. Use **LOOP=-1** or **LOOP=infinite** to project the movie continuously.

5. If desired, type **CONTROLS** to show the play, pause and stop buttons under the movie.

6. If desired, type **START=event** where event is either **FILEOPEN** to project the movie when the user jumps to the page, or **MOUSEOVER**, to project the movie when the user points at the link with the mouse.

7. Type the final **>**.

✔ Tip

■ To add video that can be accessed by most browsers (although not internally), consult *Adding external video to your page* on page 178.

Figure 11.29 *You can specify a regular image with the SRC attribute as usual. It will be displayed as the movie is loading, as well as in browsers (like Netscape) that don't recognize the DYNSRC attribute.*

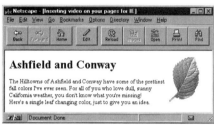

Figure 11.30 *Since Netscape can't view the video, it just shows the static image.*

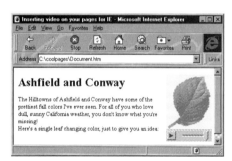

Figure 11.31 *If you use the CONTROLS attribute (see step 5), a play button and progress bar appear below the video.*

Adding video for Internet Explorer

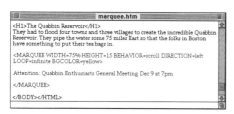

Figure 11.32 *A marquee begins with an opening tag that contains the attributes. It is followed by the text that will scroll and then the closing tag.*

Figure 11.33 *Netscape does not recognize the MARQUEE tag and displays the text without formatting.*

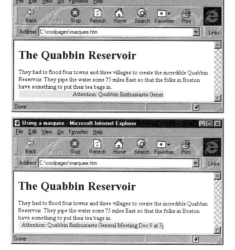

Figure 11.34 *With the attributes BEHAVIOR=scroll and DIRECTION=left, the text begins at the left and then disappears off the right. You can also use the CENTER and FONT tags to change the appearance of the marquee.*

Creating a marquee

A marquee is text that starts at one part of the screen and floats across to the left, rather like the messages that advertise sales in the window of 24 hour gas stations. Internet Explorer lets you put marquees on your Web page.

To create a marquee:

1. Type **<MARQUEE**.

2. If desired, type **BEHAVIOR=type** where *type* is **scroll**, for text that starts at one side of the screen and disappears off the other, **slide** for text that starts at one side of the screen and stops when it reaches the other, or **alternate** for text that starts at one side of the screen and bounces back when it reaches the other side.

3. To determine which direction the text starts from, type **DIRECTION=left** or **DIRECTION=right**.

4. If desired, type **LOOP=n** where n is the number of times the text will pass across the screen. Use **LOOP=infinite** to have the text appear continuously.

5. Type **SCROLLAMOUNT=n** to determine how much space, in pixels, is left between each pass of the text.

6. Type **SCROLLDELAY=n** to determine how much time, in milliseconds, passes before the text scrolls again.

7. Use the **HEIGHT**, **WIDTH**, **HSPACE**, **VSPACE**, **ALIGN** and **BGCOLOR** attributes as usual, if desired.

8. Type the final **>**.

9. Type the scrolling text.

10. Type **</MARQUEE>**.

Creating a marquee

Inserting applets

Java applets are little applications (hence the term *applets*) that can be run in your browser to create special effects on your page, like clocks, calculators, and interactive events. There are whole books devoted to Java; here we'll restrict the topic to how to insert applets on your page once you've written or copied them from another source.

To insert an applet:

1. Type **<APPLET CODE=applet.class** where *applet.class* is the name of the compiled applet.

2. If desired, type **WIDTH=w HEIGHT=h** to specify the applet size in pixels.

3. Type **>**.

4. Type **</APPLET>**.

✔ Tips

■ If you don't know how to write your own applets, you can download freeware applets from many sources on the Web. For starters, try *http://www.gamelan.com*.

■ You can also download the Java Development Kit (JDK) from Sun, its developer *(http://java.sun.com)*. It is available for Mac, Windows, OS2 and others.

■ Even if you don't know how to write Java applets from scratch, the JDK is useful for making minor changes to existing applets. Simply download the source (if it is available), make the desired changes, and then compile the new class file with the Java Compiler that comes with the JDK.

Figure 11.35 *The most important attribute in the APPLET tag is CODE. Make sure that it points to the proper Java compiled applet (not the source).*

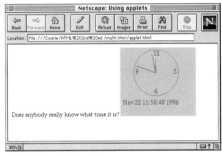

Figure 11.36 *Applets let you create interactive, multimedia effects on your page without having to know how to program or script. Both Netscape 3 for Mac and for Windows support Java applets.*

Figure 11.37 *Internet Explorer for Windows can already view applets. Reportedly, the Mac version will be able to, but at press time, early beta versions still could not.*

Inserting applets

Style Sheets

Styles, in HTML as in regular desktop publishing applications, let you assign several properties at once to a particular kind of element. This makes it easy to give all of your site's pages a common look, without having to define the properties of every word or element individually.

You define styles by assigning properties to HTML tags. For example, you could have all the text marked with a P (paragraph) tag be displayed in red at 14pt.

The style definitions, or markers, discussed in this chapter are part of the standard CSS1 mechanism. CSS stands for Cascading Style Sheets, and means that a designer might specify a style sheet for a document, but that a user can override that style sheet with one of her own, to make the document easier to read, based on her own needs, or on the limitations of the computer she's using.

In fact, a designer can specify styles at three levels: either externally, internally, or locally. Local styles override internal style sheets which, in turn, override external style sheets. In general, designer specified styles take precedence over user's specified styles.

Some properties are inherited from marker to marker, especially for character level tags (EM, B, etc.). For example, if you define H1 tagged text as blue, any text marked with an EM tag that is inside the H1 tag will also be blue. Of course, EM tagged text inside a paragraph defined with P (or any other tag) will not be blue.

Creating an internal style sheet

Internal style sheets are ideal for individual pages with lots of text. They let you set the styles that should be used throughout an HTML document at the top of your page. If you plan to apply the style sheet to more than one page, you're better off using external style sheets *(see page 186)*.

To create an internal style sheet:

1. At the top of your HTML document, after the </HEAD> tag but before the <BODY> tag, type **<STYLE>**.

2. Type the tag whose properties you wish to define.

3. If desired, type **.class**, where class is the subcategory of elements marked with the desired tag.

4. Type **{** to mark the beginning of this tag's properties.

5. Define as many properties as desired for this tag and class, using the steps described on pages 189–197. Separate each property with a semi-colon.

6. Type **}** to mark the end of this tag's properties.

7. Repeat steps 3–6 for each class of the tag.

8. Repeat steps 2–7 for each tag for which you wish to define properties.

9. Type **</STYLE>** to complete the style sheet.

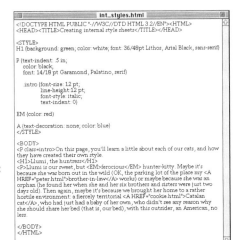

Figure 12.1 *An internal style sheet should be placed between the closing HEAD tag and the opening BODY tag.*

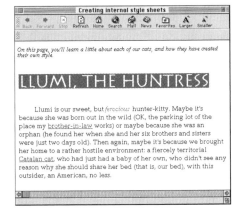

Figure 12.2 *The text marked with tags that are defined in the style sheet displays its new attributes.*

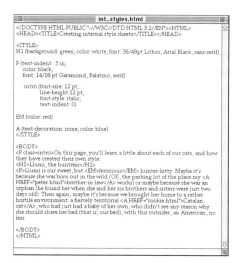

Figure 12.3 *In this example, regular P tags should be indented, black, and in Garamond 14/18pt. However, P tags marked with the intro class should be displayed at 12/12pt, in italic with no indent.*

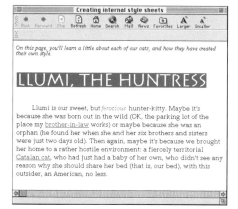

Figure 12.4 *Only the paragraph marked with the P tag as intro class will be formatted as intro. Paragraphs with the P tag without any class will be formatted as usual, as is the case with the last paragraph on this page.*

✔ Tips

■ Each set of properties must begin with an opening curly bracket "{" and end with a closing curly bracket "}". Each style marker and its values must be separated with a semi-colon ";".

■ You can define several classes for a tag—each with its own properties. Each class is based on the properties specified for the tag. Separate each class with a return (or space, if you prefer). In the HTML portion of the document, type **CLASS=classname** within the desired tag to invoke the class' style **(Figures 12.3 and 12.4)**.

■ You can define properties for several tags at once by separating each tag with a comma: **H1, H2, H3 {color:red}** will display the three levels of headers in red.

■ Define the properties for a tag that depends on another by typing the dependent tag after the parent one, separated by just a space: **H1 EM {color:red}** means that all text marked with the EM tag *that is found within the H1 tags* should be shown in red.

■ You can also apply styles individually, simply inserting the properties (as described on pages 189–197) into individual tags in the body of the HTML document.

■ Add comment tags after (**<!--**) the initial <STYLE> tag and before (**-->**) the final </STYLE> tag to hide the style sheet from browsers that don't yet understand it, and to keep them from showing it to your users. For more information on comments, consult *Adding comments to your pages* on page 30.

Creating an internal style sheet

Creating an external style sheet

External style sheets are ideal for giving all the pages on your Web site a common look. Instead of getting their styles from individual internal style sheets, you can set each page to look at the external sheet, thus, ensuring that each will have the same settings.

To create an external style sheet:

1. Create a new text document.

2. Type the tag whose properties you wish to define.

3. If desired, type **.class**, where class is the subcategory of elements marked with the desired tag.

4. Type { to mark the beginning of this tag's properties.

5. Define as many properties as desired for this tag and class, using the steps described on pages 188–206. Separate each property with a semi-colon.

6. Type } to mark the end of this tag's properties.

7. Repeat steps 3–6 for each class of the tag.

8. Repeat steps 2–7 for each tag for which you wish to define properties.

9. Save the document in text only format. Give the document the extension .css to designate the document as a cascading style sheet.

✔ Tip

■ All of the tips listed on page 185 also apply to external style sheets.

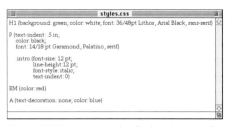

Figure 12.5 *An external style sheet is a text document and starts right in with the style definitions. No HTML tags are necessary.*

Figure 12.6 *An external style sheet is linked to a particular Web page with the LINK tag.*

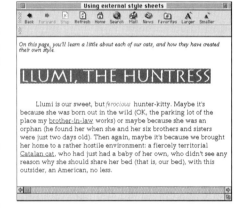

Figure 12.7 *A page linked to an external style sheet looks just as it would if the style sheet were right in the page itself (see Figure 12.2).*

Creating an external style sheet

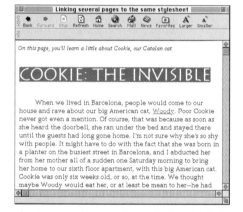

```
ext2.html
<!DOCTYPE HTML PUBLIC "-//W3C//DTD HTML 3.2//EN"><HTML>
<HEAD>
<LINK REL=stylesheet TYPE="text/css" HREF="styles.css">
<TITLE>Linking several pages to the same stylesheet</TITLE></HEAD>
<BODY>
<P class=intro>On this page, you'll learn a little about Cookie, our Catalan cat.
<H1>Cookie: the invisible</H1>
<P>When we lived in Barcelona, people would come to our house and rave
about our big American cat, <A HREF="woody.html">Woody</A>. Poor Cookie
never got even a mention. Of course, that was because as soon as she heard the
doorbell, she ran under the bed and stayed there until the guests had long gone
home. I'm not sure why she's so shy with people. It might have to do with the
fact that she was born in a planter on the busiest street in Barcelona, and I
abducted her from her mother all of a sudden one Saturday morning to bring
her home to our sixth floor apartment, with this big American cat. Cookie was
only six weeks old, or so, at the time. We thought maybe Woody would eat her,
or at least be mean to her--he had never been with other cats, and he was so big
that he could've done what he wanted. Or so we thought.
<P>What happened of course, was very different. Tiny little Cookie, no bigger
than Woody's front paw (well, maybe a little bigger), hissed at poor Woody and
bopped him on the head and he quickly ran from her room. They got to be
friends after a while, she often mistaking his tail for a venomous snake, he
getting over his initial shock and wrestling with her as often as she would let
him.
```

Figure 12.8 *Here is a second page that we will link to the same external style sheet.*

```
Linking several pages to the same stylesheet
Back  Forward  Stop  Refresh  Home  Search  Mail  News  Favorites  Larger  Smaller

On this page, you'll learn a little about Cookie, our Catalan cat.

COOKIE: THE INVISIBLE

        When we lived in Barcelona, people would come to our
house and rave about our big American cat, Woody. Poor Cookie
never got even a mention. Of course, that was because as soon as
she heard the doorbell, she ran under the bed and stayed there
until the guests had long gone home. I'm not sure why she's so shy
with people. It might have to do with the fact that she was born in
a planter on the busiest street in Barcelona, and I abducted her
from her mother all of a sudden one Saturday morning to bring
her home to our sixth floor apartment, with this big American cat.
Cookie was only six weeks old, or so, at the time. We thought
maybe Woody would eat her, or at least be mean to her--she had
```

Figure 12.9 *The second page displayed with the same styles as the first (see Figure 12.7).*

Using an external style sheet

In order for a page to use an external style sheet, it has to know where the style sheet is. The easiest way is to create a LINK tag in the HTML document that points to the external style sheet. You can also import the style sheet into the page.

To link an external style sheet to a page:

In each HTML page in which you wish to use the style sheet, type **<LINK REL=stylesheet TYPE="text/css" HREF=url.css>**, where *url.css* is the name you used in step 9 on page 186.

To import an external style sheet into a page:

1. After the </HEAD> tag but before the initial BODY tag, type **<STYLE TYPE="text/css">**.

2. Type **@import url(styles.css)**, where *styles.css* is the name of the document you created in step 9 on page 186.

3. Type **</STYLE>**.

✔ Tip

■ You can link an external style sheet, import a style sheet, include an internal style sheet, and include local styles all in the same HTML document. Local styles override internal style sheets which, in turn, override external style sheets.

Special tags for styles

There are two tags that are particularly useful for applying styles. The first is DIV, which applies to one or more sections of your document. The second is SPAN, which can be applied to a few words of text. Given a class, each of these tags can be used to apply custom styles to any part of your document.

To use the DIV tag:

1. At the beginning of the desired section of your document, type **<DIV**.

2. Type **CLASS=classname**, where *classname* identifies the type of section.

3. If desired, type **ALIGN=direction**, where *direction* is left, right, or center.

4. Type the final **>**.

5. Create the contents of this section.

6. At the end of the desired section, type **</DIV>**.

To use the SPAN tag:

1. At the beginning of the desired words, type **<SPAN**.

2. Type **CLASS=classname**, where *classname* identifies the type of text.

3. Type the final **>**.

4. Create the text you wish to affect.

5. Type **</SPAN>**.

✔ Tip

■ The DIV and SPAN tags let you create custom styles without co-opting any existing tags and their corresponding styles.

Figure 12.10 *By defining classes for the DIV and SPAN tags, you create custom paragraph and character styles, respectively.*

Figure 12.11 *The DIV tags define sections or paragraphs of the page. The SPAN tags define words or phrases.*

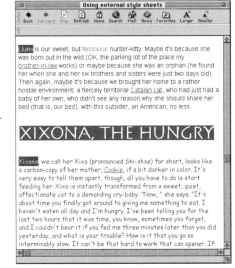

Figure 12.12 *The DIV tags changed the font for each description. The SPAN tags created the reverse background around the name of each cat.*

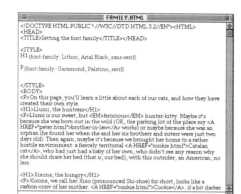

Figure 12.13 *For the header, Lithos is the first choice. If the user doesn't have Lithos, Arial Black will be used. And if Arial Black is not available, a sans-serif font will be chosen. Similarly for P paragraphs, Garamond is the first choice, Palatino is the second choice, and a generic serif font is the last choice.*

Figure 12.14 *On this system, both first choices were available: Lithos for headers and Garamond for the P paragraphs.*

Choosing a font family

Because not everyone has the same set of fonts, the font-family marker has a special characteristic: you can specify more than one font, in case the first is not available in the user's system. You can also have a last ditch attempt at controlling the display in the user's system by specifying a generic font style like *serif* or *monospace*.

To set the font family:

1. Type **font-family: familyname**, where *familyname* is your first choice of font.

2. If desired, type **, familyname2**, where *familyname2* is your second font choice. Separate each choice with a comma and a space.

3. Repeat step 2 as desired.

✔ Tips

■ It's a good idea to specify at least two font choices, one of them a common font, so that you maintain some control over how the document is displayed. Common fonts in Macintosh systems are Times, Palatino for serif fonts and Helvetica for sans-serif. Most Windows systems contain Times as well, but Arial is more prevalent as a sans-serif choice.

■ You can use the following generic font names—**serif**, **sans-serif**, **cursive**, **fantasy**, and **monospace**—as a last attempt to influence which font is used for display.

■ You can set the font family, font size and line height all at once, using the general font style *(see page 193).*

■ You can use very specific font names, like *Futura Condensed Bold Italic.*

Choosing a font family

189

Choosing a font style and weight

Although you can choose a font style and weight by selecting a specific font like Garamond Bold Italic with the font-family tag as described on page 189, you can also set these characteristics separately, and more globally.

To set the font style:

1. Type **font-style:**.

2. Type **normal** for roman text, **oblique** for oblique text, or **italic** for italic text.

✔ Tip

■ If you set the font style as italic and there is no italic style available, the browser should try to display the text in oblique style.

To set the font weight:

1. Type **font-weight:**.

2. Type a weight for the text. You may choose from **normal**, **bold**, **bolder**, **lighter**, or from **100** to **900**, where 400 represents a book weight font and 700 represents bold.

✔ Tips

■ Since the way weights are defined varies from font to font, the numeric values may not be relative from font to font. They are designed to be relative within a given font family.

■ If the font family has less than nine weights, or if they are concentrated on one end of the scale, it is possible that some numeric values correspond to the same font weight.

Figure 12.15 *In this example, we've tried to set the header as bold and the intro P style as italic.*

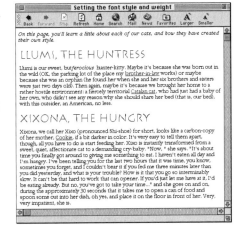

Figure 12.16 *The paragraph marked with the P tag and intro class (the one at the top of the page) is indeed shown in italics. The headers, however, have mysteriously gotten lighter. That's a bug.*

Choosing a font style and weight

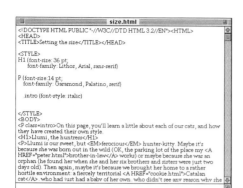

Figure 12.17 *You can set the font size as an absolute value in points, as shown here, or as a relative value with respect to a parent style.*

Figure 12.18 *The new font sizes make the headers stand out and the text easier to read.*

Setting the font size

You can set the font size of text marked with a particular HTML tag (or class) by specifying an exact size in points or pixels, or with descriptive words, or by specifying a relative size, with respect to a parent element.

To set the font size:

1. Type **font-size:**.

2. Type an absolute font size: **xx-small**, **x-small**, **small**, **medium**, **large**, **x-large**, or **xx-large**.

Or type a relative font size: **larger** or **smaller**.

Or type an exact size: **12pt** or **15px**.

Or type a percentage relative to any parent style: **150%**.

✔ Tips

■ The relative values (larger, smaller and the percentage) depend on the size of the parent style. For example, if we defined a value of 150% for the P tag's intro class, it would mean 150% of 14pt, the defined size for the P tag in general, or 21pt.

■ You can set font size, line height and the font family all at once with the general font style.

Setting the font size

Setting the line height

Line height refers to a paragraph's leading, that is, the amount of space between each line in a paragraph. Using a large line height can sometimes make your body text easier to read. A small line height for headers often makes them look classier.

To set the line height:

1. Type **line-height:**.

2. Type **n**, where *n* is a number that will be multiplied by the font-size to obtain the desired line height.

Or type **p%** where *p%* is a percentage of the font size.

Or type **a**, where *a* is an absolute value in points, pixels, or whatever.

✔ **Tips**

■ You can specify the line height together with the font size and font family using the font style, as described on page 193.

■ If you use a number to determine the line height, this factor is inherited by all child items. If you use a percentage, only the resulting size is inherited, not the percentage factor.

Figure 12.19 *The only crucial element between each style definition is the semi-colon. I've also inserted a return and spacing to make it look good.*

Figure 12.20 *Notice the added space around the headers.*

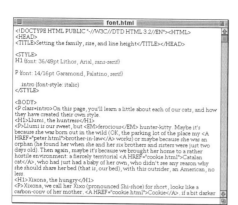

Figure 12.21 *For the font tag, first comes the font size and line height divided by a slash, and then the list of preferred fonts separated by a*

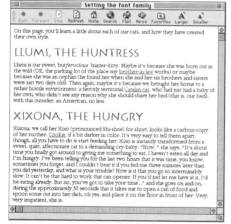

Figure 12.22 *The three criteria take effect in the same as way as if they were applied individually.*

Setting font size, line height and family

You can set font size, line height and family all at once.

To set font size, line height and family all at once:

1. Type **font:**.

2. Type **fontsize**, using the possible values given in step 2 on page 191.

3. If desired, type **/lineheight**, where line height is expressed in the same form as the font size *(see page 191)*.

4. Type a space followed by the desired font family or families, in order of preference, separated by commas, as described on page 189.

✔ Tip

- You can set the font size separately. For more information, consult *Setting the font size* on page 191. For information on setting the font family separately, consult *Choosing a font family* on page 189. For more information on setting the line height, consult *Setting the line height* on page 192.

Setting the color

You can change the color of any tagged text, whether it be an entire paragraph, or just a few words.

To set the color:

1. Type **color:**.

2. Type **colorname**, where colorname is one of the 16 predefined colors.

Or type **#rrggbb**, where rrggbb is the hexadecimal representation of the desired color.

Or type **rgb(r, g, b)** where *r*, *g*, and *b* are integers from 0-255 that specify the amount of red, green, or blue, respectively, in the desired color.

Or type **rgb(r%, g%, b%)** where *r*, *g*, and *b* specify the percentage of red, green, and blue, respectively, in the desired color.

✔ Tip

■ If you type a value for r, g, or b higher than 255 it will be replaced with 255. Similarly a percentage higher than 100% will be replaced with 100%.

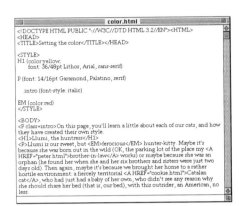

Figure 12.23 *You can use either color names, like* yellow, *in this example, or hexadecimal representations of colors.*

Figure 12.24 *These headers are really yellow!*

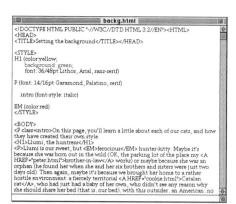

Figure 12.25 *In this example, the background of just the headers is set to green to offset the yellow text.*

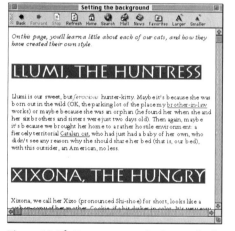

Figure 12.26 *Be sure to use a background color that contrasts enough with the color of the text and the background of the page itself.*

Setting the background properties

The background refers not to the background of the entire page, but to the background of the specified tag. In other words, you can change the background of just a few paragraphs or words, by setting the background of those words to a different color.

To set the background properties:

1. Type **background:**.

2. Type **transparent** or **color**, where *color* is a color name or hex color.

3. If desired, type **url(image.gif)**, to use an image for the background.

If desired, type **repeat** to tile the image both horizontally and vertically, **repeat-x** to tile the image only horizontally, **repeat-y** to tile the image only vertically and **no-repeat** to not tile the image.

If desired, type **fixed** or **scroll** to determine whether the background should scroll along with the canvas.

If desired, type **x y** to set the position of the background image, where *x* and *y* can be expressed as a percentage of distance, an absolute distance. Or use values of *top*, *center*, or *bottom* for *x* and *left*, *center*, and *right* for *y*.

✔ **Tip**

■ You can specify both a color and a URL for the background. The color will be used until the URL is loaded, and will be seen through any transparent portions of the background image.

Setting the background properties

195

Controlling spacing

You can add more space between words (tracking) or between letters (kerning). You can also add a chunk of space, or an indent, before particular paragraphs.

To specify tracking:

1. Type **word-spacing:**.

2. Type **length**, where length is a numerical value in pixels, points, ems, etc.

To specify kerning:

1. Type **letter-spacing:**.

2. Type **length**, where length is a numerical value in pixels, points, ems, etc.

To add indents:

1. Type **text-indent:**.

2. Type a value for the text indent, either as an absolute value (either positive or negative) or as a percentage.

✔ Tips

■ You may use negative values for word and letter spacing, although the actual display always depends on the browser's capabilities.

■ Word and letter spacing values may also be affected by your choice of alignment.

■ Use a value of normal to set the letter and word spacing to their defaults.

■ To avoid gaping holes in justified text, use a value of 0 for letter spacing.

Figure 12.27 *You can specify tracking and kerning by using the letter-spacing and word-spacing tags, respectively. Indenting is defined with the text-indent marker.*

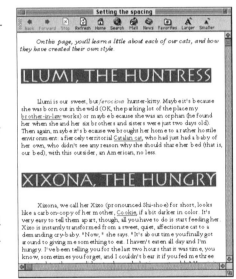

Figure 12.28 *Only indents are currently supported by Internet Explorer. At press time, the word-spacing and letter-spacing tags are still unrecognized.*

Controlling spacing

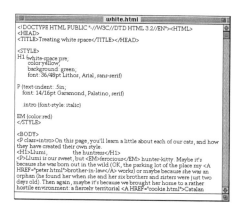

```
                  white.html
<!DOCTYPE HTML PUBLIC "-//W3C//DTD HTML 3.2//EN"><HTML>
<HEAD>
<TITLE>Treating white space</TITLE></HEAD>

<STYLE>
H1 {white-space:pre;
    color:yellow;
    background: green;
    font: 36/48pt Lithos, Arial, sans-serif}

P {text-indent: .5in;
    font: 14/16pt Garamond, Palatino, serif}

 .intro {font-style: italic}

EM {color:red}
</STYLE>

<BODY>
<P class=intro>On this page, you'll learn a little about each of our cats, and how
they have created their own style.
<H1>Llumi,          the huntress</H1>
<P>Llumi is our sweet, but <EM>ferocious</EM> hunter-kitty. Maybe it's
because she was born out in the wild (OK, the parking lot of the place my <A
HREF="peter.html">brother-in-law</A> works) or maybe because she was an
orphan (he found her when she and her six brothers and sisters were just two
days old). Then again, maybe it's because we brought her home to a rather
hostile environment: a fiercely territorial <A HREF="cookie.html">Catalan
```

Figure 12.29 *A value of pre for white space means that the browser will conserve all extra spaces and returns that you type in the HTML document—as if you had formatted the text with the PRE tag, but without the monospace font.*

Setting white space properties

Normally browsers will simply ignore any extra spaces or returns that you type in an HTML document. You can set certain tags to behave like the PRE tag, taking into account all this extra white space.

To set white space properties:

1. Type **white-space:**.

2. Type **pre** to have browsers take all extra spaces and returns into account.

   Or type **nowrap** to keep all elements on the same line, except where you've inserted BR tags.

   Or type **normal** to treat white space as usual.

Aligning text

You can set up certain HTML tags to be always aligned to the right, left, center, or to be justified, as desired.

To align text:

1. Type **text-align:**.

2. Type **left** to align the text to the left.

Or type **right** to align the text to the right.

Or type **center** to center the text in the middle of the screen.

Or type **justify** to align the text on both the right and left.

✔ Tip

■ If you choose to justify the text, be aware that the word spacing and letter spacing may be adversely affected. For more information, consult *Controlling spacing* on page 196.

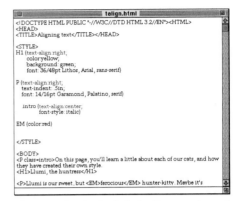

Figure 12.30 *Set the default alignment for each tag by using the text-align marker.*

Figure 12.31 *The affected paragraphs (all of them in this example), are aligned to the right.*

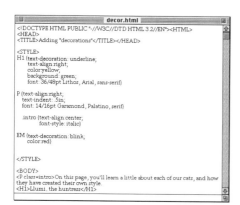

```
                decor.html
<!DOCTYPE HTML PUBLIC "-//W3C//DTD HTML 3.2//EN"><HTML>
<HEAD>
<TITLE>Adding "decorations"</TITLE></HEAD>

<STYLE>
H1 {text-decoration: underline;
    text-align: right;
    color: yellow;
    background: green;
    font: 36/48pt Lithos, Arial, sans-serif}

P {text-align: right;
   text-indent: .5in;
   font: 14/16pt Garamond, Palatino, serif}

.intro {text-align: center;
        font-style: italic}

EM {text-decoration: blink;
    color: red}


</STYLE>

<BODY>
<P class=intro>On this page, you'll learn a little about each of our cats, and how
they have created their own style.
<H1>Llumi, the huntress</H1>
```

Figure 12.32 *Personally, I think underlining should be left for links. But I suppose it can be useful for making headers stand out.*

Figure 12.33 *Then again, the effect of underlining is so ugly it is to be avoided at all costs! And as you can see, the blink marker, added to the EM tag, does not yet work.*

Adding text decorations

Text decorations make the text stand out in an unconventional way. The current options let you add lines above, below, or through the text, or make it blink.

To add text decorations:

1. Type **text-decoration:**.

2. For plain text, type **none**.

For underlined text, type **underline**.

For a line above the text, type **overline**.

To strike out the text, type **line-through**.

To make the text blink, type **blink**.

✔ Tips

■ Theoretically, you can use the *none* option for text-decoration to keep links from being underlined. However, I think you'll just confuse your audience.

■ At press time, Internet Explorer did not yet recognize the *overline* and *blink* options.

Adding text decorations

Changing the text case

You can add a text case to your style by using the text-transform marker. In this way, you can display the text either with initial capital letters, in all capital letters, in all small letters or as it was typed.

To change the text case:

1. Type **text-transform:**.

2. Type **capitalize** to put the first character of each word in upper case.

Or type **uppercase** to change all the letters to upper case.

Or type **lowercase** to change all the letters to lower case.

Or type **none** to leave the text as is (possibly canceling out an inherited value).

Many fonts have a corresponding small caps variant that includes upper case versions of the letters proportionately reduced to small caps size. You can call up the small caps variant with the font-variant marker.

To use a small caps font:

1. Type **font-variant:**.

2. Type **small-caps**.

✓ Tips

■ To stop using the small caps variant for a dependent style, use **font-variant: none**.

■ Unfortunately, Internet Explorer doesn't recognize the text-transform or font-variant markers yet.

```
                    transf.html
<STYLE>
H1 {text-align:right;
     color:yellow;
     background: green;
     font-variant: smallcaps;
     font: 36/48pt Lithos, Arial, sans-serif}

P {text-align:right;
     text-indent: .5in;
     font: 14/16pt Garamond, Palatino, serif}

.intro {text-align:center;
          font-style: italic}

EM {text-decoration: blink;
     color:red}

SPAN {background:blue;
       color: white;
       text-transform: uppercase}

</STYLE>

<BODY>
<P class=intro>On this page, you'll learn a little about each of our cats, and how
they have created their own style.
<H1>Llumi, the huntress</H1>

<P><SPAN>Llumi</SPAN> is our sweet, but <EM>ferocious</EM> hunter-kitty.
Maybe it's because she was born out in the wild (OK, the parking lot of the place
my <A HREF="peter.html">brother-in-law</A> works) or maybe because she was
an orphan (he found her when she and her six brothers and sisters were just two
days old). Then again, maybe it's because we brought her home to a rather
```

Figure 12.34 *Here, the desired result is that the SPAN tag show all text in capital letters, and that it use the small caps variant of the font for the headers.*

Changing the text case

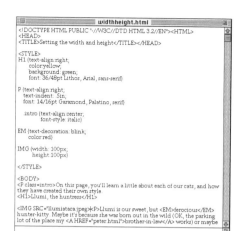

```
                widthheight.html
<!DOCTYPE HTML PUBLIC "-//W3C//DTD HTML 3.2//EN"><HTML>
<HEAD>
<TITLE>Setting the width and height</TITLE></HEAD>

<STYLE>
H1 {text-align:right;
    color:yellow;
    background: green;
    font: 36/48pt Lithos, Arial, sans-serif}

P {text-align:right;
   text-indent: .5in;
   font: 14/16pt Garamond, Palatino, serif}

  .intro {text-align:center;
          font-style: italic}

EM {text-decoration: blink;
    color:red}

IMG {width: 100px;
     height:100px}

</STYLE>

<BODY>
<P class=intro>On this page, you'll learn a little about each of our cats, and how
they have created their own style
<H1>Llumi, the huntress</H1>

<IMG SRC="llumiataca.jpeg><P>Llumi is our sweet, but <EM>ferocious</EM>
hunter-kitty. Maybe it's because she was born out in the wild (OK, the parking
lot of the place my <A HREF="peter.html">brother-in-law</A> works) or maybe
```

Figure 12.35 *Generally, it makes most sense to set the width and height of images.*

Setting the height or width for an element

If you have several images on a page that are the same size, you can set their height and width simultaneously. This information helps browsers set aside the proper amount of space necessary and thus view the rest of the page—generally, the text—more quickly.

To set the height or width for an element:

1. Type **width:w**, where *w* is the maximum width of the element, and can be expressed either as an absolute value or as a percentage of the window width.

2. Type **height:h**, where *h* is the maximum height of the element, and can be expressed only as an absolute value.

✔ Tip

■ The height and width markers are not yet recognized by Internet Explorer.

Positioning elements vertically

If you have similar images on your page that you would like aligned in the same way, you can use the vertical-align marker to set the IMG tag, or a class of the IMG tag, accordingly.

To position text:

1. Type **vertical-align:**

2. Type **baseline** to align the element's baseline with the parent's baseline.

Or type **middle** to align the middle of the element with the middle of the parent.

Or type **sub** to position the element as a subscript of the parent.

Or type **super** to position the element as a superscript of the parent.

Or type **text-top** to align the top of the element with the top of the parent.

Or type **text-bottom** to align the bottom of the element with the bottom of the parent.

Or type **top** to align the top of the element with the top of the tallest element on the line.

Or type **bottom** to align the bottom of the element to the bottom of the lowest element on the line.

Or type a percentage of the line height of the element, which may be positive or negative.

✔ Tip

■ Internet Explorer doesn't recognize the vertical-align marker yet.

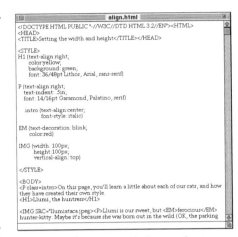

Figure 12.36 *The vertical-align marker is generally used with images. Of course, you could just use it with a class of the IMG tag.*

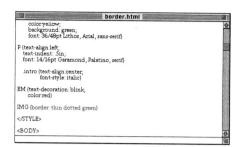

```
                 border.html
        color:yellow;
        background: green;
        font: 36/48pt Lithos, Arial, sans-serif)

P {text-align:left;
   text-indent: .5in;
   font: 14/16pt Garamond, Palatino, serif)

   .intro {text-align:center;
           font-style: italic)

EM {text-decoration:blink;
    color:red)

IMG {border: thin dotted green)

</STYLE>

<BODY>
```

Figure 12.37 *You can set the border's width, style, and color with the border marker.*

Setting the border

You can create a border around an ele-ment and then set its thickness, style, and color. If you've specified any padding *(see page 204)* the border encloses both the padding and the element itself.

To set the border:

1. Type **border**.

2. Type **-top**, **-bottom**, **-left**, or **-right**, depending on where you wish to add the space.

3. If desired, type **thin**, **medium**, **thick**, or an absolute value to determine the thickness of the border. Medium is the default.

4. If desired, type **none**, **dotted**, **dashed**, **solid**, **double**, **groove**, **ridge**, **inset**, or **outset** to determine the border style.

5. If desired, type **color**, where *color* is either one of the 16 predefined color names or is expressed as described on page 194.

✔ Tip

■ Internet Explorer doesn't yet under-stand the border marker.

Setting the space around an element

The margin is the amount of invisible space between one element and the next, in addition to and outside of any padding or border around the element. The padding is the space between the element and the border.

To set an element's margins or padding:

1. Type **margin** or **padding**, depending on which value you wish to adjust.

2. Type **-top**, **-bottom**, **-left**, or **-right**, depending on where you wish to add the space.

3. Type **:x**, where x is the amount of desired space to be added, expressed in units or as a percentage of the width of the corresponding value of the parent element.

✔ Tips

■ You can also use **{margin:t, r, b, l}** or **{padding:t, r, b, l}** to set all four values at once. Or **{margin:v, h}** or **{padding:v, h}** to set the top and bottom values equally and the right and left values equally. Or type **{margin:a}** or **{padding:a}**, where *a* is the value to be used for all sides.

■ The values may be expressed in absolute terms or as a percentage of the corresponding width in the parent element.

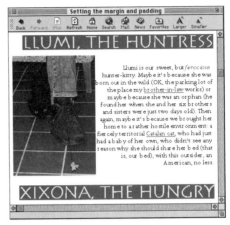

Figure 12.38 *This is the page before any margin or padding have been added.*

Figure 12.39 *Twenty pixels of margin space are added at the top of each image, the other values are not yet recognized and so will be ignored.*

Figure 12.40 *There is now extra space between the header and the image.*

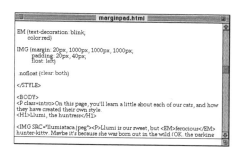

```
┌─────────── marginpad.html ───────────┐
│ EM {text-decoration:blink;            │
│     color:red}                        │
│                                       │
│ IMG {margin: 20px, 1000px, 1000px, 1000px; │
│     padding: 20px, 40px;              │
│     float: left}                      │
│                                       │
│ .nofloat {clear: both}                │
│                                       │
│ </STYLE>                              │
│                                       │
│ <BODY>                                │
│ <P class=intro>On this page, you'll learn a little about each of our cats, and how │
│ they have created their own style.    │
│ <H1>Llumi, the huntress</H1>          │
│                                       │
│ <IMG SRC="llumiataca.jpeg"><P>Llumi is our sweet, but <EM>ferocious</EM> │
│ hunter-kitty. Maybe it's because she was born out in the wild (OK, the parking │
└───────────────────────────────────────┘
```

Figure 12.41 *If you want all your images to have text wrapped around them, use the float marker. In this example, I've also created a class of images (nofloat) that will not allow text to wrap around on either side.*

Wrapping text around elements

You can define your images so that text always wraps around them to the left or right, or down both sides, or never at all.

To wrap text around elements:

1. Type **float:**.

2. Type **left** if you want the element on the left and the text to flow to its right.

Or type **right** if you want the element on the right and the text to flow to its left.

To stop text wrap:

1. Type **clear:**.

2. Type **left** if you don't want floating elements to appear to the left.

Or type **right** if you don't want float-ing elements to appear to the right.

Or type **both** to keep floating ele-ments from floating to the right or left.

Or type **none** to allow floating ele-ments

✔ Tip

■ The use of the clear style is analogous to the BR tag with the CLEAR attribute *(see page 73).*

Setting list properties

There are several bullet styles for unordered lists, and several number styles for numbered lists. You can set these styles globally with the list-style marker.

To set list properties:

1. Type **list-style:**.

2. If desired, to set the list item marker to a solid, round circle, type **disc**.

Or type circle to use an empty, round **circle**.

Or type **square** to use a solid square.

Or type **decimal** to use arabic numerals (1, 2, 3, etc.)

Or type **lower-alpha** to use lowercase letters (a, b,c, etc.)

Or type **upper-alpha** to use uppercase letters (A, B, C, etc.)

Or type **lower-roman** to use lowercase Roman numerals (i, ii, iii, etc.)

Or type **upper-roman** to use uppercase Roman numerals (I, II, III, etc.)

Or type **url(image.gif)**, *image.gif* is the URL of the image that you want to use as a marker for your lists.

3. If desired, type **outside** to format list items with the marker hanging to the left. Type inside to align the marker flush left, with all the other lines in the list item paragraph.

✔ Tip

■ So far as I can tell, the list-style marker has not been implemented in Internet Explorer (or Netscape) yet.

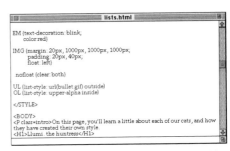

Figure 12.42 *In this example, all unordered lists will use a special image (bullet.gif) for the bullet which will be a hanging indent to the left of each line item. The ordered lists will all use uppercase letters (A, B, C, etc.) and will be aligned flush left.*

Extras

In this chapter, you'll find a collection of special touches you can give your Web pages to set them apart from the crowd (or to make them fit in better by following the latest trends).

Perhaps the best advice included in this chapter *(see page 208)* is to take a gander around the Web and see what other designers are up to. With each passing day, Microsoft and Netscape Communications add more extensions to their already burgeoning HTML specifications, enabling designers to push beyond current limits. By keeping your eye on the Web, you'll be among the first to find out about these new tags, and about the new ways to combine them on your pages.

Next, don't take anything at face value. Tables are a perfect example. In the printed world, they're perfect for conveying rows and columns of numbers. In the Web world, they can do so much more *(see pages 211, 212, and 213)*. Many other HTML tags can also be stretched beyond their original use. Be creative! Hopefully, this chapter will give you a good start.

Extras

The inspiration of others

One of the easiest ways to expand your HTML fluency is by looking at how other page designers have created *their* pages. Luckily, HTML code is easy to view and is not copyrighted. However, text content, graphics, sounds, video, and other external files may be copyrighted. As a general rule, use other designers' pages for inspiration with your HTML, and then create your own contents.

To view other designers' HTML code:

1. Open their page with any browser.

2. Choose View Source (in the View menu in Netscape), or View (in the View menu in Internet Explorer).

3. The browser will open the helper application you have specified for text files and show you the HTML code for the given page.

4. If you wish, save the file with the text editor for further study.

✔ Tip

■ You can also save the source code by selecting Save as in the File menu and then Source or HTML in the Format pop-up menu in the dialog box that appears.

Figure 13.1 *This is one of my favorite pages on the Web. It can be found at http://www.artsan-tafe.com/sfm/sfmmap.html.*

Figure 13.2 *When you select View Source, the assigned text editor opens with the page's HTML code.*

The inspiration of others

Figure 13.3 *Use the ALIGN=LEFT tag to wrap the text around the drop cap.*

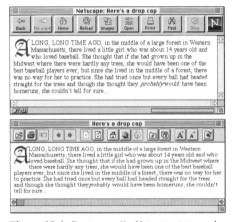

Figure 13.4 *Drop caps (in Netscape, top, and Internet Explorer, bottom) are ideal for books or stories.*

Creating drop caps

Some of the best tricks are the simplest. Since HTML doesn't let you choose a font to set off a drop cap, you can create an image file of the capital letter, make it transparent, and insert it before the rest of the paragraph.

To create a drop cap:

1. In an image editing program, create the capital letter, in any font you choose, for your drop cap. Save it in GIF format and make it transparent *(see pages 50 and 52)*.

2. In your HTML document where you want the drop cap to appear, type **<IMG SRC="dropcap.gif"** where *dropcap.gif* is the location on the server of the image created in step 1.

3. Type **ALIGN=left** so that the text that follows wraps around the drop cap.

4. Type the final **>** to finish the IMG definition.

5. Type the text that should appear next to the drop cap. Generally, next to a drop cap, it is a good idea to type the first few words in all caps.

Creating drop caps

Using vertical rules

It's easy to create horizontal rules in an HTML document. Creating vertical rules, along the left or right margin, for example, is only slightly more complicated.

To create a vertical rule:

1. In Photoshop, or other image editing program, create a bar of the desired color, 5 pixels wide and 500 pixels high.

2. In the HTML document, place the cursor above the text that should be alongside the vertical bar.

3. Type **<IMG SRC="verticalbar.gif"** where *verticalbar.gif* is the location on the server of the vertical bar created in step 1.

4. *Either* type **ALIGN=left** to place the vertical bar along the left margin *or* type **ALIGN=right** to place it along the right margin.

5. Type the final **>** to complete the IMG definition.

6. Type the text that should appear alongside the vertical rule.

✔ Tips

■ You can narrow the body of text by inserting a transparent vertical rule on either side of the body of your page. You can also use transparent GIFs to adjust the spacing between paragraphs, and even between words.

■ Another easy way to make a vertical rule is to create a two-column table and then specify a background color for the left column.

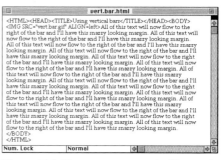

Figure 13.5 *You can create a vertical bar on the left side of the page by inserting an image and using the ALIGN=left attribute.*

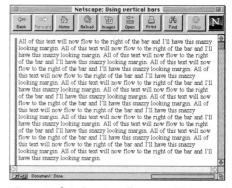

Figure 13.6 *It doesn't really matter if the vertical bar is longer than the text. It will simply continue down the page.*

```
                 buttons.html
<!DOCTYPE HTML PUBLIC "-//W3C/DTD HTML 3.2//EN">
<HTML><HEAD><TITLE>Buttons</TITLE></HEAD>
<BODY BGCOLOR=#fce503>
<TABLE CELLPADDING=5 CELLSPACING=0 WIDTH=100%>
<TR>
<TH BGCOLOR="#F3D7E3" NOWRAP><A HREF="openingpage.html">City
Tour</A>
<TH BGCOLOR="#F6D5C3" NOWRAP><A HREF="market1.html">Market</A>
<TH BGCOLOR="#D8E9D6" NOWRAP><A
HREF="arch1.html">Architecture</A>
<TH BGCOLOR="#D1C9DF" NOWRAP><A HREF="sports1.html">Sports</A>
<TH BGCOLOR="#D4EBF9" NOWRAP><A
HREF="natlism1.html">Nationalism</A>
<TH BGCOLOR="#CECDB4" NOWRAP><A
HREF="language1.html">Language</A>
</TR>
</TABLE>
```

Figure 13.7 *In this example, all the text is black, but each cell/button is a different color.*

Figure 13.8 *The cells of the one-row table, when colored differently, look just like little buttons— but they load much more quickly than images. This page is used in the examples described in Chapter 9, Frames.*

Creating buttons with tables

Buttons made out of images sometimes take a maddening amount of time to appear on the screen. If your user has images turned off, they may never appear at all. One solution is to create navigational buttons with tables. The technique is simple: create a table and change the background color of each cell, that is, button.

To create buttons with tables:

1. Create a table as described in Chapter 8, *Tables.*

2. The button cells might look like this:
**<TD BGCOLOR=red ALIGN=middle>
<A HREF="link.html"><FONT SIZE=+3
COLOR=black>Click me</A></TD>.**

✔ Tips

■ Make sure the text that should appear in the cell is large enough to stand out. For more information, consult *Changing the color of a few letters* on page 44 and *Changing a cell's color* on page 132.

■ Use contrasting colors for both the background and the text that appears in the cell. For more information, consult *Changing the color of a few letters* on page 44 and *Using background color* on page 90.

■ Use a different colored background or image for each cell.

Creating buttons with tables

Creating designs from tables

By using the BGCOLOR attribute in the BODY, TABLE, TR, TH, or TD tags, you can create a design without any images at all—thereby speeding up the loading time considerably.

✔ Tips

■ There are an unlimited number of ways to combine the table cells in a pleasing pattern. Experiment!

■ Don't forget that the color or image specified in the BODY tag will show through the empty cells in the table. You can use this to your advantage.

■ Fill empty table cells with a <BR>. Otherwise, the cell won't appear at all.

■ Use the WIDTH and HEIGHT attributes to control the size of cells, rows, and of the table itself.

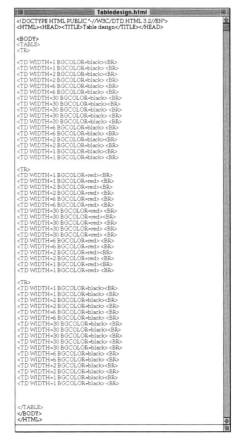

Figure 13.9 *None of the cells contain anything, they are simply colored differently.*

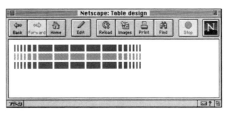

Figure 13.10 *You can create images out of tables that load much more quickly than regular images. Hopefully, you'll be slightly more artistic than I am.*

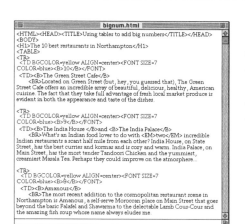

Figure 13.11 *You can change the alignment, font size, font color, and background color of a cell. All of these properties help define that area of your page.*

Figure 13.12 *You could get this effect with images and text wrapped around them, but each time you changed the text, you'd have to adjust the images. In the table, the number cells adjust automatically according to how much text is used in the cell/paragraph to its right.*

Using tables for layout

Tables are ideal for spacing elements on your page exactly as you wish. You can use them like an invisible grid supporting your elements. For example, you might want to make a numbered list, with over-sized numbers aligned with each section.

✔ Tips

- Use the ALIGN attribute within cell definitions to control how the contents will appear in the cell.

- You can divide information visually by a judicious use of background color for the cells. Don't be afraid to change the text color as well.

- Tables also have the advantage of expanding to fit the window when it's resized, something images won't do.

- Generally, when using tables for layout, you shouldn't use a border. That way, the table is invisible to the user while the structure of the table keeps the elements on the page in tune.

Using tables for layout

A shortcut for creating HTML tables in Word

Creating tables by hand can be a pain. It's hard to see where to put each element and you have to type TD and TR over and over again. Here's a clever way to convert a table from Word (both Mac and Windows versions) into an HTML table.

To convert a Word table into HTML:

1. Create a table in a separate document using Microsoft Word (for Macintosh or Windows).

2. Select the entire table and choose Table to text in the Format menu.

3. In the dialog box that appears, choose Tab delimited. Your table now consists of individual paragraphs (which correspond to each row) separated by returns. Each element is separated by a tab.

4. With the cursor at the top of the document, select Find/Change in the Edit menu (Command-H).

5. In the Find box, type **^p** to search for every occurrence of a new paragraph (that is a new row).

6. In the Change box, type **</TD> </TR>^p<TR>** (without spaces). The ^p is optional, since extra returns will be ignored by the browser. It simply makes the HTML document easier to read (and edit).

7. Click Change all.

8. In the Find box, type **^t** to search for every occurrence of a tab (a new element).

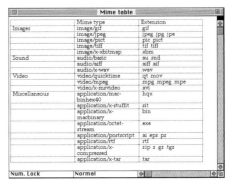

Figure 13.13 *It is much easier to create a table in Microsoft Word than with Table tags.*

Figure 13.14 *Select Table to text in the Insert menu.*

Figure 13.15 *Choose Tab delimited in the Table to text dialog box.*

Figure 13.16 *Each row of the table is converted into a separate paragraph. The elements in each row are separated by tabs.*

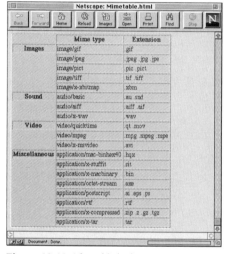

```
                    Mimetable.html
<TABLE BORDER>
<TR><TH></TH><TH>Mime type</TH><TH>Extension</TH></TR>
<TR><TH>Images</TH><TD>image/gif</TD><TD>.gif</TD></TR>
<TR><TD></TD><TD>image/jpeg</TD><TD>.jpeg .jpg .jpe</TD></TR>
<TR><TD></TD><TD>image/pict</TD><TD>.pic .pict</TD></TR>
<TR><TD></TD><TD>image/tiff</TD><TD>.tif .tiff</TD></TR>
<TR><TD></TD><TD>image/x-xbitmap</TD><TD>.xbm</TD></TR>
<TR><TH>Sound</TH><TD>audio/basic</TD><TD>.au .snd</TD></TR>
<TR><TD></TD><TD>audio/aiff</TD><TD>.aiff .aif</TD></TR>
<TR><TD></TD><TD>audio/x-wav</TD><TD>.wav</TD></TR>
<TR><TH>Video</TH><TD>video/quicktime</TD><TD>.qt
.mov</TD></TR>
<TR><TD></TD><TD>video/mpeg</TD><TD>.mpg .mpeg
.mpe</TD></TR>
<TR><TD></TD><TD>video/x-msvideo</TD><TD>.avi</TD></TR>
<TR><TH>Miscellaneous</TH><TD>application/mac-
binhex40</TD><TD>.hqx</TD></TR>
<TR><TD></TD><TD>application/x-stuffit</TD><TD>.sit</TD></TR>
<TR><TD></TD><TD>application/x-
macbinary</TD><TD>.bin</TD></TR>
<TR><TD></TD><TD>application/octet-
stream</TD><TD>.exe</TD></TR>
<TR><TD></TD><TD>application/postscript</TD><TD>.ai .eps
.ps</TD></TR>
<TR><TD></TD><TD>application/rtf</TD><TD>.rtf</TD></TR>
<TR><TD></TD><TD>application/x-compressed</TD><TD>.zip .z .gz
.tgz</TD></TR>
<TR><TD></TD><TD>application/x-tar</TD><TD>.tar</TD></TR>
</TABLE>
Num. Lock            Normal
```

Figure 13.17 *After a few search and replace operations, the table is transformed into HTML code.*

Figure 13.18 *The table looks great in Netscape.*

9. In the Change box, type **</TD><TD>**.

10. Click Change all.

11. At the very beginning of the document, type **<TABLE>**. Include any table attributes, as desired. (See pages 89–98.)

12. Type **<TR><TD>**.

13. At the very end of the document, you may find extra blank lines of TRs and TDs. Eliminate them. Then type **</TABLE>** after the final </TD></TR>.

14. Change the TDs of your header cells to THs as needed (yes, sorry, by hand).

15. Choose Save as in the File menu and Text Only in the Format submenu of the dialog box that appears. Click OK.

16. Copy the table back into your HTML document.

17. View your table to make sure that everything is the way you want it. You may want to adjust the alignment or text formatting of individual cells.

✔ **Tip**

■ Save frequently and sequentially! If you decide to add a column to your table, it will help to have a copy of the Word table still lying around.

A shortcut for creating HTML tables in Word

Creating an automatic slide show

This isn't really an extra, but it's so unusual, I didn't know quite where else to put it. You can use a special feature of the META attribute, within the BODY tag, to automatically move the reader from one page to another. If you set up a series of pages in this way, you create a Web slide show.

To create an automatic slide show:

1. In the first page, within the HEAD section, type **<META HTTP-EQUIV= "Refresh"**. (That's a regular hyphen between *HTTP* and *EQUIV.*)

2. Type **CONTENT="n;** where *n* is the number of seconds the current page should display on the screen.

3. Type **URL=nextpage.html">** where *nextpage.html* is the URL of the next page that you want to the user to jump to automatically.

4. Repeat these steps for each page in the series.

✔ Tips

■ Make sure you use a display time long enough for all of your pages to appear on screen.

■ This use of the META tag works with Netscape and Internet Explorer (and may work with other browsers as well), both on Windows machines and Macs.

■ This is a great way to show a portfolio or other series of images without having to create a lot of links and buttons.

Figure 13.19 *The META tag must be in the HEAD section. It won't work if you place it anywhere else.*

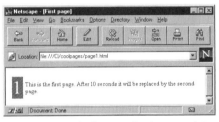

Figure 13.20 *The first page loads as usual. But wait ten seconds, and...*

Figure 13.21 *...the second page loads automatically. Wait ten more seconds and...*

Figure 13.22 *...the third page loads automatically. If you wait ten more seconds, it'll go back to page 1 (Figure 13.20) and start the whole process all over again. Of course, if you don't want it to, just leave the META tag out of the last page.*

Creating an automatic slide show

Publishing

Once you've finished your masterpiece and are ready to present it to the public, you have to publish your page on a server and help your public find a way to your door.

Your first step is to organize your files, designate a home page and then test everything and make sure it works like you planned.

Then you're ready to transfer the files to the server and to change the permissions so that the files are open to the public.

Finally, you should use the services available on the Web to advertise your page so that your readers know where to find you.

Chapter 14

Organizing files for transfer

Before transferring your files to the server, you should organize them in one or more folders or directories.

To organize your files for transfer:

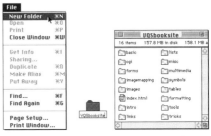

Figure 14.1 *On the Mac, select New Folder, give the folder a name, and then drag each HTML document to the new folder.*

1. Create a central folder or directory to hold all the material that will be available at your Web site. (On the Mac, choose New Folder in the File menu in the Finder. On Windows, choose Create Directory in the File menu of the File Manager. In DOS, type **mkdir**.)

Figure 14.2 *In Windows, select Create Directory in the File menu...*

2. Give the folder or directory a short, descriptive name.

Figure14.3 *...give the new directory a name...*

3. Drag all the HTML files, images and external files that belong to your Web site to the new folder/directory. (In DOS, use the move command.)

4. Organize the central folder/directory. You may decide to create a separate folder for HTML documents, one for images and one for other external files. If you have a large site with many pages, you may wish to divide the site into categories or chapters as I've done here, placing the images in the individual folders.

Figure 14.4 *...and then drag the HTML documents to the new directory.*

5. The names and paths should correspond to the links you have established in your pages.

✔ Tip

■ Use simple, one-word names without symbols or punctuation for your files and folders. Use a consistent scheme of capital and small letters. This helps make your URLs easier to type and your pages easier to reach.

Organizing files for transfer

218

Figure 14.5 *On a Mac, change the name of the home page to* index.html *and place it in the main folder of the Web site.*

Figure 14.6 *In Windows, change the name of the home page to index.htm and place it in the main directory of the Web site.*

Figure 14.7 *A good home page draws the users right into the material, giving them easy, quick access to all the parts of the site.*

Designating a home page

A home page is the one that a user will see if they use a URL without a file name. That is, if your site's principal directory on the server is *www.site.com/flintstone/website1*, and a user points to *http://www.site.com/flintstone/website1/*, with a trailing forward slash but no file name, the browser will look for the default or home page. The most common home page name is *index.html* but varies from server to server. Ask your server administrator to be sure.

To designate one page as the home page:

1. Change the file name of the page to *index.html* (or whatever the default home page name is for your server).

2. Place the home page in the principal directory of your web

✔ Tips

■ Your home page should have links to all the other information available at your Web site. Your home page should be a table of contents to your site, not just the first page.

■ If you want your users to be able to reach the other pages in your site, make your home page clean, neat and fast **(Figure 14.7)**.

■ If you work on a Windows or DOS machine and with a UNIX server, you will have to transfer the file to the server first, and then add the four letter extension.

Testing your page

Even if you use a validation command in a special HTML editor (see page 150) to check your HTML documents for proper syntax, you should always test your HTML pages in at least one browser. It is not necessary to connect to the server to test your pages. Instead, use the Open Local or Open File command to open the pages from your local computer.

Inevitably you will have to make adjustments to your HTML code. You only need to forget one angle bracket for your page to look completely different from what you expected. Other times what you thought might look OK looks awful.

To test your HTML pages:

1. Before you copy your file to the server, view it locally on your own computer by choosing Open Local or Open File **(Figure 14.8)** in the browser's File menu. (Viewing files locally saves connection charges.)

2. Go through the whole page and make sure it looks exactly the way you want it **(Figures 14.9 and 14.10)**. For example:

Is the formatting like you wanted?

Does each of your URLs point to the proper document? (You can check the URLs by clicking them if the destination files are located in the same relative position on the local computer.)

Are your images aligned properly?

Have you included your name and e-mail address (preferably in a mailto URL) so that your users can contact you with comments and suggestions?

Figure 14.8 *Use the Open File command (the name may be slightly different depending on the browser and platform you use) from the File menu in order to open the page on your local computer and test it.*

Figure 14.9 *Check your document for typographical errors, missing angle brackets, and other mistakes.*

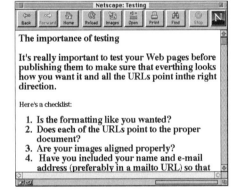

Figure 14.10 *Can you tell what's making this page look so bad?*

Figure 14.11 *As long as you have enough memory, you can keep the browser and the text editor open at the same time so that you can see what effects your changes are having.*

Figure 14.12 *You must save the changes to your HTML document before reloading, or else the changes will not appear in the browser.*

Figure 14.13 *Select Reload (in the View menu), or click the Reload button on the toolbar in order to show the changes.*

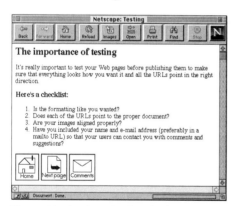

Figure 14.14 *After reloading the fixed HTML document, everything appears as it should—artistic deficiencies aside.*

3. Without closing the page on the browser, open the text or HTML editor and the corresponding HTML document. You should be able to simultaneously edit the HTML document with one program and view it with another **(Figure 14.11)**.

4. Save the changes **(Figure 14.12)**.

5. Switch back to the browser and choose Reload (usually Command-R) to see the changes **(Figures 14.13 and 14.14)**.

6. Repeat steps 1-5 until you are satisfied with your Web page. Don't get discouraged if it takes several tries.

7. Transfer the files to the server and change the permissions, if you haven't done so already *(see page 222)*.

8. Test all your URLs to make sure that they work correctly from the server.

✔ **Tip**

■ Use several browsers to test your HTML documents. You never know what browser your user is going to use. The three principal browsers are discussed on page 16.

Testing your page

Transferring files to the server

The steps you need to take to transfer files to the server depend on the type of server you are working with and where it is located. Most people use UNIX servers at a remote location. The easiest way to transfer your HTML files to this kind of server is an FTP program, like Fetch for Macintosh (see below), or WS_FTP for Windows *(see page 224)*. For details on publishing files to AOL or CompuServe, see page 226.

To transfer HTML files to the server with Fetch:

1. Open your Internet connection.

2. Open Fetch or some other FTP program.

3. Choose Preferences in the Customize menu **(Figure 14.15)**, Uploading in the Topics menu of the Preferences box that appears and make sure the Add file format suffixes option is not checked **(Figure 14.16)**.

4. Select Open Connection in the main window to show the Open Connection window **(Figure 14.17)**.

5. Enter the server name in the Host text box, your user name in the User ID box, your password in the Password box and the path to the directory where you plan to save the Web pages in the Directory box **(Figure 14.18)**.

6. Click OK to open the connection. Fetch will make the connection to the server you requested and open the designated directory.

7. Make sure the correct directory where you wish to place your set of HTML files is showing in the main Fetch window **(Figure 14.19)**.

Figure 14.15 *Choose Preferences in Fetch's Customize menu to open the Preferences dialog box.*

Figure 14.16 *Choose Uploading in the Topic menu and then unmark the Add file format suffixes option.*

Figure 14.17 *Click the Open Connection button or select Open Connection in the File menu to display the Open Connection window.*

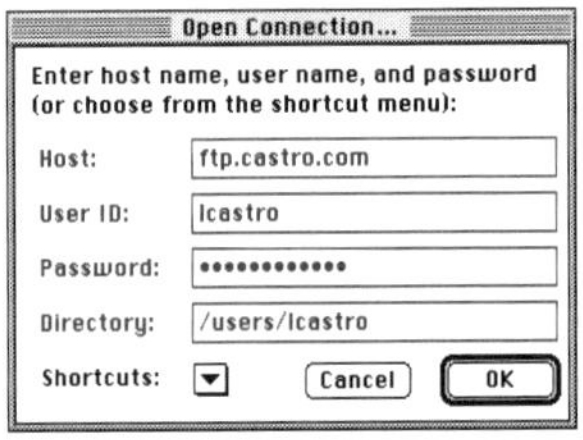

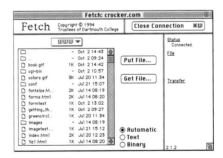

Figure 14.18 *In the Open Connection window, type the server name (Host), your User ID and password, and the directory where you want to transfer the files.*

Figure 14.19 *Make sure the proper directory on the server (where you want to transfer the files) is showing in the Fetch window before transferring the files (in this case, WWW).*

Figure 14.20 *Choose Put Folders and Files in the Remote menu. (To transfer just one file, you can click the Put File button in the main Fetch window.)*

Figure 14.21 *Select each folder or file that you wish to transfer to the server and click Add. When you've finished choosing folders and files, click Done.*

Figure 14.22 *Choose the Text format for Text files and the Raw Data format for Other Files.*

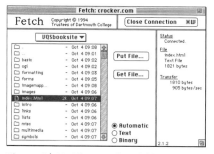

Figure 14.23 *The transferred files maintain the same hierarchy that they had on the Mac. Click Close Connection to close the connection to the server.*

8. Choose Put Folders and Files in the Remote menu **(Figure 14.20)**.

9. In the dialog box that appears, choose the files that you wish to transfer to the server and click Add. The files will appear at the bottom of the dialog box. When you have selected all the files you wish to transfer, click Done **(Figure 14.21)**.

10. In the Choose formats dialog box that appears, select the appropriate formats for the files. Use Text for HTML and other text documents and Raw Data for other kinds of files **(Figure 14.22)**.

11. Click OK. The files will be transferred to the server and will maintain the hierarchy that they had on the local system **(Figure 14.23)**. If folders already exist with the same names as those that you are transferring, the folders on the servers will be used (and their contents preserved, unless the files transferred also have the same names).

12. Click Close Connection to close the connection to the server.

✔ Tip

■ If you have used relative URLs *(see page 21)*, these will be maintained when you transfer the entire folder or directory from your computer to the server. If you have used absolute URLs *(see page 20)*, you will have to change them to reflect the files' new locations.

Transferring files to the server

To transfer files to the server with WS_FTP:

1. Open WS_FTP.

2. In the Session Profile dialog box that appears **(Figure 14.24)**, click New to create a new set of preferences (or select an existing profile if you've already created it.)

3. Give the profile a name in the Profile Name box.

4. Enter the Host name of the server, the Host type (Automatic detect, if you're not sure), your User ID and Password.

5. Enter the desired directory on the server where you plan to transfer the files in the Remote Host area at the bottom of the dialog box. If you like, you can also enter the directory on the local PC from which you will transfer the files.

6. Click Save to save the profile.

7. Click OK to open the connection.

8. Click Options at the bottom of the WS_FTP window **(Figure 14.25)**.

9. Click the Extensions button **(Figure 14.26)**.

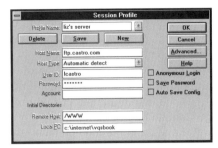

Figure 14.24 *After clicking New in WS_FTP, enter the information necessary for connecting to the server, including the server's name (Host Name), the Host type, your User ID and password.*

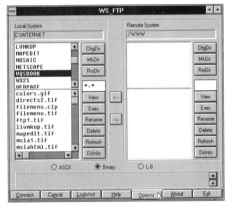

Figure 14.25 *Click Options in the bottom part of the main WS_FTP window.*

Figure 14.26 *Click the Extensions button in the Options dialog box.*

Transferring files to the server

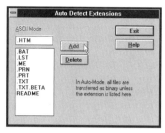

Figure 14.27 *Type .htm in the text box and then click Add so that the HTML documents will be transferred in ASCII format, even with Binary format selected in the main window.*

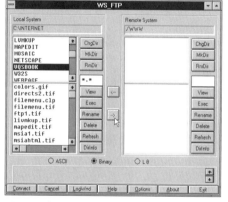

Figure 14.28 *Select the desired directory (or directories) and then click the right pointing arrow in the middle of the dialog box.*

10. Type **.htm** in the text box and click Add so that your HTML documents will be transferred in ASCII format **(Figure 14.27)**.

11. Click Exit in both dialog boxes to return to the main window.

12. Make sure the Binary option is selected at the bottom of the main window. This applies to all files with extensions not appearing in the Auto Detect Extensions dialog box.

13. Choose the files that you wish to transfer from the left side of the window by clicking on them. You may have to create directories on the server with the MkDir button.

14. Click the right pointing arrow to begin the transfer **(Figure 14.28)**.

15. Repeat steps 13-14 as needed.

16. Close the connection to the server.

Transferring files to the server

225

Transferring files to AOL or CompuServe

Even if you are a member of AOL or CompuServe you can still use the techniques described in this book to create your Web page. The only difference is how to transfer your files to the service.

To transfer files to AOL:

1. Go to keyword **myplace**.

2. Click the Upload button.

3. Type the exact name of the file, and its extension (but not the path). Click ASCII for text documents and Binary for images. Then click Continue.

4. Click Select File, and then choose the corresponding file from your hard disk and click OK.

5. Click Send to upload the file.

To transfer files to CompuServe:

1. Download and then open Publishing Wizard for Mac (GO MACPUB) or for Windows (it's included in the Home-Page Wizard; GO HPWIZ).

2. Follow the directions on each screen, choosing the files you want to upload.

✔ Tips

■ The URL of your pages on AOL is *http://members.aol.com/screenname/ filename*. You can publish up to 2Mb *per screenname* (for a total of 10Mb).

■ On CompuServe, your URL is *http:// ourworld.compuserve.com/home-pages/username*, where *username* is specified with the Publishing Wizard. You can publish up to 2Mb of files.

Figure 14.29 *Go to keyword* myplace *and then click the Upload button at the bottom of the screen.*

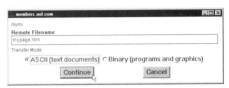

Figure 14.30 *Type the name of the file, choose ASCII or Binary, depending on the nature of the file, and then click Continue.*

Figure 14.31 *Click Select File to choose the file that you want to upload from your hard disk. Its name appears in the File box at the bottom of the screen. Then click Send to upload the file to AOL.*

Figure 14.32 *CompuServe's Publishing Wizard takes you through transferring process step by step. Fill out each screen and click Next to continue.*

Figure 14.33 *After opening the connection with the File menu, log in by typing your user name and password.*

Figure 14.34 *Use the cd command to go to the directory that contains the files or directories whose permissions you wish to change.*

Figure 14.35 *Type* **chmod o+rx** *followed by the name of the file or directory whose permissions you wish to change.*

Changing permissions

Whether you transfer the files from a Mac or PC, or even another UNIX machine, if your server is a UNIX machine, often you will have to change the permissions of the transferred files to open access to your pages to the public. However, you may not have the necessary privileges to change the permissions. In that case, contact your server administrator.

To change permissions:

1. Open a Telnet program, like NCSA Telnet for Mac or Ewan for Windows.

2. Enter the server name in the Host box and click Connect. You will be connected to the server as if you were at a local terminal.

3. Log in with your User ID and Password **(Figure 14.33)**. Generally, you will find yourself automatically in your personal directory on the server.

4. If necessary, type **cd directory** where *directory* is the desired directory you wish to view **(Figure 14.34)**. Type **ls** to list the directory's contents.

5. Type **chmod o+rx name** where *name* is the name of the directory or file whose permissions will be changed **(Figure 14.35)**.

6. Type **lo** to log out.

✔ Tips

■ Type **man chmod** for more information about the chmod command.

■ HTML files and images need *read-only* permission (the *r* in o+rx); CGI scripts need *execute* permission (the *x* in o+rx).

Advertising your site

Before you start talking up your site in public, you should test it once again *(see page 220)* and make sure that everything works as it should. Once you are satisfied you can begin to recruit users.

To advertise your site:

1. Use the Add URL fill in forms at search and indexing services like Yahoo, Altavista, and Lycos **(Figures 14.36 and 14.37)**:

Yahoo: *http://add.yahoo.com/fast/add?+*

AltaVista: *http://altavista.digital.com/cgi-bin/query?pg=tmpl&v=addurl.html*

Lycos: *http://www.lycos.com/addasite.html*

(There are no spaces in any of these URLs. The symbols are *not* optional.)

2. Pay a company to advertise your page for you.

3. Post a note in the moderated UseNet newsgroup *comp.infosystems.www. announce* or the unmoderated *comp.internet.net-happenings* or in newsgroups that have similar interests as your Web site.

4. Send e-mail to your associates and friends. (You can include the URL for your site in all your correspondence in a signature.)

5. Send e-mail to the creators of other sites with similar interests or topics.

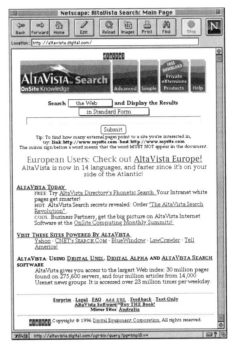

Figure 14.36 *Go to the indexing service's home page and click the Add URL link. This is AltaVista. Its Add URL link is at the bottom of its home page.*

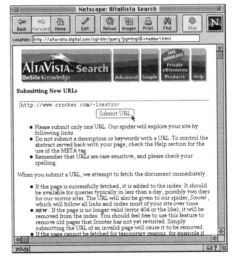

Figure 14.37 *Follow the directions on the Add URL page. In AltaVista, type the URL of your home page and then click Submit URL.*

Advertising your site

HTML Tools

The lists on the following pages are by no means exhaustive. There are literally hundreds of programs, some commercial, some shareware, and some freeware, of varying quality, that you can use as you design and create your Web pages. If you don't find what you're looking for on these pages, jump to any search service on the Web (e.g., *http://altavista.digital. com*) and look for "Web Tools".

HTML Editors

You can use *any* text editor to write HTML, including SimpleText or TeachText on the Macintosh, Write for Windows, or vi in Unix systems. The HTML code produced with these simpler programs is no different from the HTML produced by more complex HTML editors.

A simple text editor is like the most basic SLR 35 mm camera. You have to set your f-stop and aperture manually, and then focus before shooting. The dedicated HTML editors are point-and-shoot cameras: just aim and fire, for a price. They are more expensive, and generally less flexible.

What HTML editors offer	Disadvantages of HTML editors
Dedicated HTML editors offer the following advantages over simple text editors (of course, not every HTML editor has every feature): • they insert opening and closing tags with a single click • they check and verify syntax in your HTML and typos in your text • they allow you to add attributes by clicking buttons instead of typing words in a certain order in a certain place in the document • they offer varying degrees of WYSIWYG display of your Web page • they correct mistakes in existing HTML pages • they simplify the use of special characters	These extra features come at a price, however. Some things that may annoy you about HTML editors is that • they don't all recognize new or non-standard HTML codes (like Netscape extensions) • they don't all support forms, frames, and tables • they are more difficult to learn, and less intuitive than they promise • they are expensive (all simple text editors are included free with the respective system software) • they use up more space on disk and more memory • they add proprietary information (like *their* name, for example) to the HTML document

HTML Editors

HTML Editors

Name	Description	URL
Claris Home Page (M, W)	WYSIWYG Editor from Claris Corporation. Free beta available.	http://www.claris.com/products/ claris/clarispage/clarispage.html *demo:* http://www2.claris.com/ forms/homepagedownload.html
Microsoft FrontPage (M, W)	WYSIWYG Editor from Microsoft Corporation.	http://www.microsoft.com/ frontpage/
Adobe PageMill (M; W soon)	$100, Probably the most popular WYSIWYG editor for Macintosh. Soon for Windows.	http://www.adobe.com/ prodindex/pagemill/ overview.html
SoftQuad HoTMetaL (M, W)	$200, not quite WYSIWYG, but creates standard, universal HTML.	http://www.sq.com/products/ hotmetal/ *demo:* http:// www.sq.com/products/hotmetal/ hm-ftp.htm
AOLpress (M, W)	America Online, WYSIWYG HTML Editor (Formerly GNNpress)	http://www.aolpress.com/press/ index.html *demo:* http://www. aolpress.com/download.html
BBEdit (M)	Bare Bones Software, Text Editor +, $120, demo available	http://www.barebones.com/ bbedit.html *demo:* ftp:// ftp.barebones.com/pub/demos/ BBEdit_4.0)Demo.hqx
BBEdit HTML Extensions (M)	Carles Bellver, free, for HTML editing with BBEdit	http://nti.uji.es/software/bb-html-ext/
BBEdit HTML Tools (M)	Lindsay Davies, free. Latest version included with BBEdit.	http://www.barebones.com/ html.html
World Wide Web Weaver (W)	Miracle Software, $80	http://www.miracleinc.com/ Commercial/W4/index.html *demo:* ftp://zappa.northnet.org/ pub/best/W4_Demo202.hqx
Aardvark Pro (W)	Distributed by TMGNetwork, $60	http://www.tmgnet.com/ aardvark/ *demo:* http:// www.tmgnet.com/aardvark/ aarddown.htm
ANT-HTML (W)	Jill Swift, $40; template for use with Microsoft Word 6	http://telacommunications. com/ ant/antdesc.htm *demo:* ftp:// ftp.mcia.com/pub/windows/ant/ ant_demo.zip
HotDog Professional (W)	Sausage Software, $80, shareware version also available	info: http://www.sausage.com/ hotdog32.htm *demo:* http:// www.sausage.com/ dog32dwn.htm
Internet Assistant (W)	Microsoft, works with Word 6 for Windows, free	http://www.microsoft.com/word/ internet/ia/ *download:* http:// www.microsoft.com/word/ internet/ia/sysreq.htm

Free-use images for your pages

Name	Description	URL
Terry Gould's Graphics	Collection of background images, and other graphics	http://webstrands.nas.net/list1.html
Hawkeye's Land of Backgrounds	Collection of background images	http://johnh.wheaton.edu/~sgill/backgrounds.html
Paul Medoff's Hall of Doodads	Backgrounds, icons, bullets, graphics	http://ousd.k12.ca.us/munck/iconpage.html
Lycos list of Graphics sites	List of sites that contain free use graphics	http://a2x.lycos.com/Internet/Web_Publishing_and_HTML/Graphics,_Image_and_Wallpaper_Archives/

Graphics Tools

Name	Description	URL
GraphicConverter (M)	Thorsten Lemke ($35) image editor for Macintosh. Reads and writes an incredible array of graphics formats, including Progressive JPEG, GIF89a (Animated), etc.	http://members.aol.com/lemkesoft/index.html
Adobe Photoshop (M, W)	$900 commercial image editing program. Version 4 supports Progressive JPEG, PNG, PDF, as well as GIF89a.	http://www.adobe.com/prodindex/photoshop/main.html
PaintShop Pro (W)	JASC Software.. Powerful image editing program for Windows. Commercial and shareware versions available. Supports JPEG, PNG, GIF.	http://www.jasc.com/psp.html; download: http://www.jasc.com/pspdl.html
LView Pro (W)	CD-ROM edition available for popular shareware graphics program ($40).	http://www.lview.com/lvcd.htm; download: http://www.lview.com/lvdload.htm

Image Map Tools

Name	Description	URL
WebMap (M)	Rowland Smith, $25.	http://home.city.net/cnx/software/webmap.html
MapEdit	Thomas Boutell, $25.	http://sunsite.unc.edu/pub/packages/infosystems/WWW/tools/mapedit/

Special Symbols

You can type any letter of the English alphabet or any number into your HTML document and be confident that every other computer system will interpret it correctly. However, if your Web page contains any accents, foreign characters or special symbols, you may have to use a special code to make sure they appear correctly on the page.

The ISO Latin-1 character set is the standard for the World Wide Web. It assigns a number to each character, number or symbol in the set. In addition, some characters, especially the accented letters, have special names.

However, some computer systems, especially Macintosh and DOS, do not use the standard character set. That means that you could type a *é* in your HTML document and have it appear as a | (a straight vertical line) on your Web page.

To make sure accented characters and special characters appear correctly, no matter what system you write on, use the steps described on page 158 to enter them into your HTML document.

Special symbols

Using special symbols

The symbols numbered 32 to 126—which include all the letters in the English alphabet, the numbers and many common symbols—can be typed directly from the keyboard of any system. The symbols numbered 127 to 255 should be entered as described below.

To use special symbols:

1. Place the cursor where you wish the special character to appear.

2. Type **&**.

3. *Either* type **#n** where *n* is the number that corresponds to the desired symbol *or* type **name** where *name* is the code that corresponds to the desired symbol *(see pages 235 and 236)*.

4. Type **;**.

5. Continue with your HTML document.

✔ **Tips**

■ All characters have a corresponding number. Not all characters have a corresponding name. It doesn't matter which one you use.

■ Netscape 1.1 doesn't recognize *í* code. To insert a small *í*, use the number *í*.

■ The character names are case sensitive. Type them exactly as they appear in the tables.

■ Although this system is supposed to eliminate differences across platforms, the tables illustrate that it is not 100% effective.

Typing a ç on a Mac gets you a Ÿ. (In DOS, you'd get a ‡.)

`<H1>Visca el Barça</H1>`

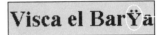

The number code for ç

`<H1>Visca el Bar&#231;a</H1>`

In the Web page

The name code for ç

`<H1>Visca el Bar&ccedil;a</H1>`

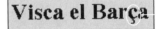

In the Web page

Figure B.1 *To display a ç properly, you must use either its number or name. It looks awful in your HTML document, but on the Web page, where it counts, it's beautiful.*

Table I: Characters

To get this…	…type this…	…or this.	To get this…	…type this…	…or this.
à	&#224;	&agrave;	ò	&#242;	&ograve;
á	&#225;	&aacute;	ó	&#243;	&oacute;
â	&#226;	&acirc;	ô	&#244;	&ocirc;
ã	&#227;	&atilde;	õ	&#245;	&otilde;
ä	&#228;	&auml;	ö	&#246;	&ouml;
å	&#229;	&aring;	ø	&#248;	&oslash;
æ	&#230;	&aelig;	œ	&#156;	*
À	&#192;	&Agrave;	Ò	&#210;	&Ograve;
Á	&#193;	&Aacute;	Ó	&#211;	&Oacute;
Â	&#194;	&Acirc;	Ô	&#212;	&Ocirc;
Ã	&#195;	&Atilde;	Õ	&#213;	&Otilde;
Ä	&#196;	&Auml;	Ö	&#214;	&Ouml;
Å	&#197;	&Aring;	Ø	&#216;	&Oslash;
Æ	&#198;	&AElig;	Œ	&#;	*
è	&#232;	&egrave;	ù	&#249;	&ugrave;
é	&#233;	&eacute;	ú	&#250;	&uacute;
ê	&#234;	&ecirc;	û	&#251;	&ucirc;
ë	&#235;	&euml;	ü	&#252;	&uuml;
È	&#200;	&Egrave;	Ù	&#217;	&Ugrave;
É	&#201;	&Eacute;	Ú	&#218;	&Uacute;
Ê	&#202;	&Ecirc;	Û	&#219;	&Ucirc;
Ë	&#203;	&Euml;	Ü	&#220;	&Uuml;
ì	&#236;	&igrave;	ÿ	&#255;	&yuml;
í	&#237;	&iacute;	Ÿ	&#159;	*
î	&#238;	&icirc;	ç	&#231;	&ccedil;
ï	&#239;	&iuml;	Ç	&#199;	&Ccedil;
Ì	&#204;	&Igrave;	ß	&#223;	&szlig;
Í	&#205;	&Iacute;	ñ	&#241;	&ntilde;
Î	&#206;	&Icirc;	Ñ	&#209;	&Ntilde;
Ï	&#207;	&Iuml;			

* These characters don't have a name code.

Table II: Symbols

To get this...	...type this...	...or this.	To get this...	...type this...	...or this.
"	&#34;	&quot;	©	&#169;	*
#	&#35;	*	®	&#174;	*
&	&#38;	&amp;	@	&#64;	*
<	&#60;	&lt;	…	&#133;	*
>	&#62;	&gt;	"	&#147;	*
%	&#37;	*	"	&#148;	*
‰	&#137;	*	•	&#149;	*
¢	&#162;	*	°	š[1]	*
$	&#36;	*	§	&#167;	*
£	&#163;	*	¶	&#182;	*
¥	&#165;	*	º	&#186;	*
™	&#153;	*	ª	&#170;	*

* These characters don't have a name code.

[1] To get this character in Windows, type the number code º.

Colors in Hex

You can choose the color for the background of your page as well as for the text and links. Both Netscape and Internet Explorer understand sixteen predefined color names: Silver, Gray, White, Black, Maroon, Red, Green, Lime, Purple, Fuchsia, Olive, Yellow, Navy, Blue, Teal, and Aqua. Some browsers also recognize Magenta (same as Fuchsia) and Cyan (same as Aqua). Consult the inside back cover for a look at these colors.

You can also specify any color by giving its red, green and blue components—in the form of a number between 0 and 255. To make things really complicated, you must specify these components with the hexadecimal equivalent of that number. The table on page 239 gives the corresponding hexadecimal number for each possible value of red, green or blue.

Check the inside back cover for a full-color table of many common colors, together with their hexadecimal codes.

Finding a color's RGB components—in hex

The inside back cover contains a full-color table of many common colors and their hexadecimal equivalents. If you don't see the color you want, you can use Photoshop (or other image editing program) to display the red, green, and blue components of the colors you want to use on your page. Then consult the table on page 239 for the hexadecimal equivalents of those components.

To find a color's RGB components:

1. In Photoshop, click one of the color boxes in the tool box **(Figure C.1)**.

2. In the Color picker dialog box that appears, choose the desired color.

3. Write down the numbers that appear in the R, G, and B text boxes. These numbers represent the R, G and B components of the color **(Fig. C.2)**.

4. Use the table on the next page to find the hexadecimal equivalents of the numbers found in step 3.

5. Assemble the hexadecimal numbers in the form *#rrggbb* where *rr* is the hexadecimal equivalent for the red component, *gg* is the hexadecimal equivalent for the green component, and *bb* is the hexadecimal equivalent of the blue component.

✔ Tip

■ You can find instructions for specifying the background color on page 90, for specifying the text color on pages 43 and 44, and for specifying the links' color on page 45.

Figure C.1 *In Photoshop, click on one of the color boxes in the toolbox to make the Color Picker dialog box appear.*

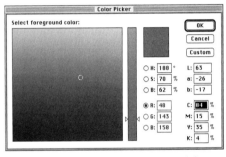

Figure C.2 *Choose the desired color and then jot down the values shown in the R, G, and B text boxes. This color, a teal blue, has an R of 48 (hex=30), a G of 143 (hex=8F) and a B of 158 (hex=9E). Therefore, the hexadecimal equivalent of this color would be #308F9E.*

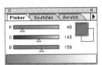

Figure C.3 *You can also use the Picker palette to choose colors and see their RGB components.*

Hexadecimal equivalents

#	Hex.	#	Hex.	#	Hex.	#	Hex.	#	Hex.	#	Hex.	#	Hex.	#	Hex.
0	0	32	20	64	40	96	60	128	80	160	A0	192	C0	224	E0
1	1	33	21	65	41	97	61	129	81	161	A1	193	C1	225	E1
2	2	34	22	66	42	98	62	130	82	162	A2	194	C2	226	E2
3	3	35	23	67	43	99	63	131	83	163	A3	195	C3	227	E3
4	4	36	24	68	44	100	64	132	84	164	A4	196	C4	228	E4
5	5	37	25	69	45	101	65	133	85	165	A5	197	C5	229	E5
6	6	38	26	70	46	102	66	134	86	166	A6	198	C6	230	E6
7	7	39	27	71	47	103	67	135	87	167	A7	199	C7	231	E7
8	8	40	28	72	48	104	68	136	88	168	A8	200	C8	232	E8
9	9	41	29	73	49	105	69	137	89	169	A9	201	C9	233	E9
10	A	42	2A	74	4A	106	6A	138	8A	170	AA	202	CA	234	EA
11	B	43	2B	75	4B	107	6B	139	8B	171	AB	203	CB	235	EB
12	C	44	2C	76	4C	108	6C	140	8C	172	AC	204	CC	236	EC
13	D	45	2D	77	4D	109	6D	141	8D	173	AD	205	CD	237	ED
14	E	46	2E	78	4E	110	6E	142	8E	174	AE	206	CE	238	EE
15	F	47	2F	79	4F	111	6F	143	8F	175	AF	207	CF	239	EF
16	10	48	30	80	50	112	70	144	90	176	B0	208	D0	240	F0
17	11	49	31	81	51	113	71	145	91	177	B1	209	D1	241	F1
18	12	50	32	82	52	114	72	146	92	178	B2	210	D2	242	F2
19	13	51	33	83	53	115	73	147	93	179	B3	211	D3	243	F3
20	14	52	34	84	54	116	74	148	94	180	B4	212	D4	244	F4
21	15	53	35	85	55	117	75	149	95	181	B5	213	D5	245	F5
22	16	54	36	86	56	118	76	150	96	182	B6	214	D6	246	F6
23	17	55	37	87	57	119	77	151	97	183	B7	215	D7	247	F7
24	18	56	38	88	58	120	78	152	98	184	B8	216	D8	248	F8
25	19	57	39	89	59	121	79	153	99	185	B9	217	D9	249	F9
26	1A	58	3A	90	5A	122	7A	154	9A	186	BA	218	DA	250	FA
27	1B	59	3B	91	5B	123	7B	155	9B	187	BB	219	DB	251	FB
28	1C	60	3C	92	5C	124	7C	156	9C	188	BC	220	DC	252	FC
29	1D	61	3D	93	5D	125	7D	157	9D	189	BD	221	DD	253	FD
30	1E	62	3E	94	5E	126	7E	158	9E	190	BE	222	DE	254	FE
31	1F	63	3F	95	5F	127	7F	159	9F	191	BF	223	DF	255	FF

The Hexadecimal system

"Regular" numbers are based on the base 10 system, that is, there are ten symbols (what we call numbers): 0, 1, 2, 3, 4, 5, 6, 7, 8, and 9. To represent numbers greater than 9, we use a combination of these symbols where the first digit specifies how many *ones,* the second digit (to the left) specifies how many *tens,* and so on.

In the hexadecimal system, which is base 16, there are sixteen symbols: 0, 1, 2, 3, 4, 5, 6, 7, 8, 9, a, b, c, d, e, and f. To represent numbers greater than *f* (which in base 10 we understand as *15*), we

again use a combination of symbols. This time the first digit specifies how many ones, but the second digit (again, to the left) specifies how many sixteens. Thus, 10 is one *sixteen* and no *ones,* or simply *16* (as represented in base 10).

In addition to colors, you can use hexadecimal numbers to represent special symbols in URLs. Find the corresponding number in the table on pages 235–236, convert it to hexadecimal with the above table and precede it with a percent sign (%). Thus, the space, which is number 32, and has a hexadecimal equivalent of 20, can be represented as %20.

239

HTML and Compatibility

Like many of the pages you'll find out on the Web, HTML is a language under construction. There are three main driving forces that determine what HTML will look like tomorrow: the World Wide Web Consortium (W3C), Netscape Communications, and Microsoft.

Theoretically, both Netscape and Microsoft have agreed to abide by the decisions of the W3C (of which they are members) in an attempt to maintain HTML's universality. However, the reality is a bit different. These two companies are in a heated battle to determine whose browser is used by the Web-surfing public. If a new extension to HTML will tip the balance in their favor, their agreement with the W3C may be at least momentarily forgotten.

On the following pages, you'll find a list of the HTML tags and attributes described in this book. In the "Vers." or *version* column, I've indicated if the tag or attribute belongs to HTML 3.2, or if it is only recognized by Netscape, by Internet Explorer, or by both. That way, you can decide if a given tag is "universal enough" for your page. If you use a tag that is not part of standard HTML 3.2, you might want to warn users who jump to the page that it is best viewed with a particular browser.

HTML Tags

HTML Tags

TAG/ATTRIBUTE	DESCRIPTION	VERS.
!--	For inserting invisible comments (p. 30)	3.2
!DOCTYPE	Required. For indicating version of HTML used (p. 24)	3.2
A	For creating links and anchors (p. 91)	3.2
HREF	For specifying URL of page or name of anchor that link goes to (p. 91)	3.2
NAME	For marking specific area of page that a link might jump to (p. 95)	3.2
TARGET	For specifying particular window or frame that link should be displayed in (pp. 94, 105, 149)	N
APPLET	For inserting applets (p. 182)	3.2
CODE	For specifying URL of applet's code	3.2
WIDTH, HEIGHT	For specifying width and height of applet	3.2
AREA	For specifying coordinates of image maps (p. 104)	3.2
COORDS	For giving coordinates of area in image map	3.2
HREF	For specifying destination URL of link in area in image map	3.2
NOHREF	For making a click in image map have no effect.	3.2
SHAPE	For specifying shape of area in image map	3.2
TARGET	For specifying window or frame that link should be displayed in	3.2
B	For displaying text in boldface (p. 33)	3.2
BASE	For specifying URL of document that will be used to generate any relative URLs within (p. 92)	3.2
BASEFONT	For changing font specifications throughout entire page (p. 39)	N+IE
SIZE	For changing size of text throughout page	N+IE
BGSOUND	For inserting background sound to page (p. 175)	IE
LOOP	For specifying how many times sound should play	IE
SRC	For specifying URL of sound	IE
BIG	For making text bigger than surrounding text (p. 41)	3.2
BLOCKQUOTE	For setting off block of text on page (p. 37)	3.2
BODY	For enclosing main section of page (p. 25)	3.2
ALINK, LINK, VLINK	For specifying color of active links, new links, and visited links (p. 45)	3.2
BACKGROUND	For specifying a background image (p. 77)	3.2
BGCOLOR	For specifying the background color (p. 90)	3.2
LEFTMARGIN, TOPMARGIN	For specifying left and top margins (p. 82)	IE
TEXT	For specifying color of text (p. 43)	3.2
BR	For creating a line break (p. 29)	3.2
CLEAR	For stopping text wrap on one or both sides of an image (p. 73)	3.2
CAPTION	For creating a caption for a table (p. 124)	3.2
ALIGN	For placing caption above or below table	3.2
CENTER	For centering text, images, or other elements (p. 88)	3.2
CITE	For marking text as a citation (p. 33)	3.2

Page numbers are omitted for those attributes discussed on the same page as the tag to which they belong

TAG/ATTRIBUTE	DESCRIPTION	VERS.
CODE	For marking text as computer code (p. 33)	3.2
COLGROUP	For joining several columns in a table into a column group (p. 120)	IE
ALIGN	For specifying alignment of columns in column group	IE
SPAN	For specifying number of columns in column group	IE
DD	For marking a definition in a list (p. 112)	3.2
DIV	For dividing a page into logical sections (p. 188)	3.2
ALIGN	For aligning a given section to left, right, or center	3.2
CLASS	For giving a name to each of the sections	3.2
DL	For creating a definition list (p. 112)	3.2
DT	For marking a term to be defined in a list (p. 112)	3.2
EM	For emphasizing text, usually with italics (p. 32)	3.2
EMBED	For adding multimedia (and others) to pages (pp. 174, 179)	N+IE
ALIGN	For aligning controls	N+IE
AUTOSTART	For making multimedia event begin automatically	N+IE
CONTROLS	For displaying play, pause, rewind buttons	N+IE
LOOP	For determining if multimedia event should play more than once	N+IE
SRC	For specifying URL of multimedia file	N+IE
WIDTH, HEIGHT	For specifying size of controls	N+IE
FONT	For changing the size, face, and color of individual letters or words	3.2
COLOR	For changing text color (p. 44)	3.2
FACE	For changing text font (p. 42)	3.2
SIZE	For changing text size (p. 40)	3.2
FORM	For creating fill-in forms (p. 154)	3.2
ACTION	For giving URL of CGI script for form	3.2
METHOD	For determining how form should be processed	3.2
FRAME	For creating frames (p. 136)	N+IE
BORDER	For determining thickness of frame borders (p. 145)	N
BORDERCOLOR	For determining color of frame borders (p. 144)	N
FRAMEBORDER	For displaying or hiding frame borders (p. 146)	N+IE
FRAMESPACING	For adding space between frames (p. 148)	IE
NAME	For naming frame so it can be used as target (p. 136)	N+IE
NORESIZE	For keeping users from resizing a frame (p. 147)	N+IE
MARGINWIDTH, MARGINHEIGHT	For specifying a frame's left and right, and top and bottom margins (p. 142)	N+IE
SCROLLING	For displaying or hiding a frame's scrollbars (p. 143)	N+IE
SRC	For specifying initial URL to be displayed in frame (p. 136)	N+IE
FRAMESET	For defining a frameset (p. 136)	N+IE
BORDER	For determining thickness of frame borders (p. 145)	N
BORDERCOLOR	For determining color of frame borders (p. 144)	N
COLS	For determining number and size of frames (pp. 138, 139)	N+IE
FRAMEBORDER	For displaying or hiding frame borders (p. 146)	N, IE

Page numbers are omitted for those attributes discussed on the same page as the tag to which they belong

HTML Tags

TAG/ATTRIBUTE	DESCRIPTION	VERS.
FRAMESPACING	For adding space between frames (p. 148)	IE
ROWS	For determining number and size of frames (pp. 136, 139)	N+IE
Hn	For creating headers (p. 27)	3.2
ALIGN	For aligning headers	3.2
HEAD	For creating head section of page (p. 25)	3.2
HR	For creating horizontal rules (p. 79)	3.2
ALIGN	For aligning horizontal rules	3.2
NOSHADE	For displaying horizontal rules without shading	3.2
SIZE	For specifying height of horizontal rule	3.2
WIDTH	For specifying width of horizontal rule	3.2
HTML	For identifying a text document as an HTML document (p. 24)	3.2
I	For displaying text in italics (p. 33)	3.2
IFRAME	For creating floating frames (p. 141)	IE
ALIGN	For aligning floating frames	IE
FRAMEBORDER	For displaying or hiding frame borders (p. 146)	IE
HSPACE, VSPACE	For specifying amount of space above and below, and to each side of floating frame	IE
WIDTH, HEIGHT	For specifying size of floating frame	IE
SCROLLING	For displaying or hiding scrollbars (p. 143)	IE
SRC	For specifying the URL of the page that should initially be displayed in the frame	IE
IMG	For inserting images on a page (p. 66)	3.2
ALIGN	For aligning images (p. 76) and for wrapping text around images (pp. 71, 72)	3.2
ALT	For giving alternative text that will be displayed if image is not (p. 67)	3.2
CONTROLS	For displaying or hiding video controls (p. 180)	IE
DYNSRC	For specifying URL of video file (p. 180)	IE
HSPACE, VSPACE	For specifying amount of space above and below, and to the sides of image (p. 74)	3.2
LOOP	For specifying number of repeats of video file (p. 180)	IE
LOWSRC	For specifying URL of low resolution version of image (p. 70)	3.2
SRC	For specifying URL of image (p. 66)	3.2
START	For determining when video should begin (p. 180)	IE
USEMAP	For specifying the image map that should be used with the referenced image (pp. 104–105)	3.2
WIDTH, HEIGHT	For specifying size of image so that page is loaded more quickly, or for scaling (pp. 68, 75)	3.2
INPUT	For creating form elements (pp. 155–158, 161–163)	3.2
CHECKED	For marking a radio button or check box by default (pp. 157, 158)	3.2
MAXLENGTH	For determining maximum amount of characters that can be entered in form element (pp. 155-156)	3.2
NAME	For identifying data collected by this element (pp. 155-157, 162–163)	3.2
SIZE	For specifying width of text or password box (pp. 155-156)	3.2

Page numbers are omitted for those attributes discussed on the same page as the tag to which they belong

HTML Tags

TAG/ATTRIBUTE	DESCRIPTION	VERS.
SRC	For specifying URL of active image (p. 163)	3.2
TYPE	For determining type of form element (p. 155–158, 161–163)	3.2
VALUE	For specifying initial value of form element (pp. 157, 158)	3.2
KBD	For marking keyboard text (p. 34)	3.2
LI	For creating a list item (p. 108)	3.2
TYPE	For determining which symbols should begin the list item	3.2
VALUE	For determining the initial value of the first list item	3.2
LINK	For using an external style sheet (p. 187)	3.2
MAP	For creating a client-side image map (p. 104)	3.2
NAME	For naming map so it can be referenced later	3.2
MARQUEE	For creating moving text (p. 181)	IE
BEHAVIOR	For controlling how the text should move (scroll, slide, alternate)	IE
DIRECTION	For controlling if the text moves from left to right or right to left	IE
LOOP	For specifying how many times the text should come across the screen	IE
SCORLLAMOUNT	For specifying amount of space between each marquee repetition	IE
SCROLLDELAY	For specifying amount of time between each marquee repetition	IE
ALIGN, BGCOLOR, HEIGHT, WIDTH, HSPACE, VSPACE,	For specifying the alignment, background color, size, and space around the marquee, respectively.	IE
META	For creating automatic jumps to other pages (p. 216)	3.2
NOBR	For keeping all the enclosed elements on one line (p. 89)	N+IE
NOFRAMES	For providing alternatives to frames for browsers that don't recognize them (p. 152)	N+IE
OL	For creating ordered lists (p. 108)	3.2
TYPE	For specifying the symbols that should begin each list item	3.2
START	For specifying the initial value of the first list item	3.2
OPTION	For creating the individual options in a form menu (p. 160)	3.2
SELECTED	For making a menu option be selected by default in a blank form	3.2
VALUE	For specifying the initial value of a menu option	3.2
P	For creating new paragraphs (p. 28)	3.2
ALIGN	For aligning paragraphs	3.2
PRE	For displaying text in a monospaced font, including all the enclosed spaces and returns (p. 38)	3.2
S	(Same as STRIKE) For displaying text with a line through it (p. 35)	3.2
SAMP	For displaying sample text—in a monospaced font (p. 34)	3.2
SELECT	For creating menus in forms (p. 160)	3.2
NAME	For identifying the data collected by the menu	3.2
MULTIPLE	For allowing users to choose more than one option in the menu	3.2
SIZE	For specifying the number of items initially visible in the menu	3.2
SMALL	For decreasing the size of text (p. 41)	3.2
SPAN	For creating custom character styles (p. 188)	3.2

Page numbers are omitted for those attributes discussed on the same page as the tag to which they belong

HTML Tags

HTML Tags

TAG/ATTRIBUTE	DESCRIPTION	VERS.
CLASS	For naming individual custom character styles	3.2
STRIKE	(Same as S) For displaying text with a line through it (p. 35)	3.2
STRONG	For emphasizing text logically, usually in boldface (p. 32)	3.2
SUB	For creating subscripts (p. 36)	3.2
SUP	For creating superscripts (p. 36)	3.2
TABLE	For creating tables (p. 116)	3.2
BORDER	For specifying the thickness, if any, of the border (p. 121)	3.2
BORDERCOLOR	For specifying a solid color for the border (p. 121)	IE
BORDERCOLORDARK	For specifying the darker (shaded) color of the border (p. 121)	IE
BORDERCOLORLIGHT	For specifying the lighter (highlighted) color of the border (p. 121)	IE
CELLPADDING	For specifying the amount of space between a cell's contents and its borders (p. 125)	3.2
CELLSPACING	For specifying the amount of space between cells (p. 125)	3.2
FRAME	For displaying external borders (p. 122)	IE
RULES	For displaying internal borders (p. 123)	IE
WIDTH, HEIGHT	For specifying the size of the table (p. 126)	3.2
TBODY	For identifying the body of the table (p. 119)	IE
TD; TH	For creating regular and header cells, respectively, in a table (p. 116)	3.2
ALIGN, VALIGN	For aligning a cell's contents horizontally or vertically (pp. 130, 131)	3.2
BGCOLOR	For changing the background color of a cell (p. 132)	3.2
COLSPAN	For spanning a cell across more than one column (p. 128)	3.2
NOWRAP	For keeping a cell's contents on one line	3.2
ROWSPAN	For spanning a cell across more than one row (p. 129)	3.2
WIDTH, HEIGHT	For specifying the size of the cell (p. 127)	3.2
TEXTAREA	For creating text block entry areas in a form (p. 159)	3.2
NAME	For identifying the data that is gathered with the text block	3.2
ROWS, COLS	For specifying the number of rows and columns in the text block	3.2
TFOOT	For identifying the footer area of a table (p. 119)	IE
THEAD	For identifying the header area of a table (p. 119)	IE
TITLE	Required. For creating the title of the page in window title bar area (p. 26)	3.2
TR	For creating rows in a table (p. 116)	3.2
ALIGN, VALIGN	For aligning contents of row horizontally or vertically (p. 119)	3.2
BGCOLOR	For changing color of entire row (p. 132)	3.2
TT	For displaying text in monospaced font (p. 34)	3.2
U	For displaying text with line underneath it (p. 35)	3.2
UL	For creating unordered lists (p. 110)	3.2
TYPE	For specifying the type of symbols that should precede each list item	3.2
WBR	For creating discretional line breaks in text enclosed in NOBR tags (p. 89)	N+IE

Page numbers are omitted for those attributes discussed on the same page as the tag to which they belong

Index

Index

Index

margins
 of elements, setting with style sheets 204
 of frames 142
 of page 82
 of text 210
MARGINWIDTH attribute, in FRAME tag 142
MARQUEE tag 181
marquees, creating 181
MAXLENGTH attribute, in INPUT tag
 for password boxes 156
 for text boxes 155
Medoff, Paul 232
menus (in forms) 160
META tag 216
METHOD attribute, in FORM tag 154
Microsoft Corporation 164, 231
Microsoft FrontPage 231
Microsoft Internet Explorer 16
Microsoft Word 231
 and tables 214–215
MIME 168
miniatures (of large, external images)
 creating 62
 using 69
Miracle Software 231
MIT 15
modems, and loading time 13
monospaced fonts 34
movies. See video
moving text (marquee) 181
MPEG format 178
MULTICOL tag 87
multimedia 167–182
 applets 182
 file size 167
 marquees 181
 non-supported images 169
 sound 170–175
 video 176–180
MULTIPLE attribute, in SELECT tag 160
Multipurpose Internet Mail Extensions. See MIME
myplace, keyword in AOL 226

N

NAME attribute
 in A tag 95
 in FRAME tag 136
 in INPUT tag
  for active images 163
  for hidden elements 162
  for password boxes 156
  for radio buttons 157
  for text boxes 155

 in MAP tag 104
 in SELECT tag, for menus 160
 in TEXTAREA tag, for text blocks 159
name/value pairs 153
naming frames 136
navigational buttons 102
 out of tables 211
NCSA Telnet, for changing permissions 227
nested
 framesets 151
 lists 113
Netscape Communications 164
Netscape Communicator. See Netscape Navigator
Netscape extensions 15
 and HTML editors 230
Netscape Navigator 16
newsgroups
 and advertising 228
 links to 101
NOBR tag 89
NOFRAME tag
 and BODY 25
NOFRAMES tag 152
NOHREF attribute, in AREA tag 105
non-supported images 169
NORESIZE attribute, in FRAME tag 147
NOSHADE attribute, in HR tag 79
Notepad 17
NOWRAP attribute, in TH or TD tags 133
number symbol (#), use of 96

O

OL tag 108
OPTION tag 160
ordered lists 108
organizing
 frames 135
 pages 27
 tables 134
overlining text, with style sheets 199

P

P tag 23, 28
 and block quotes 37
 and lists 109, 111
padding cells 125
page layout 81–90
 background color 90
 blocks of space 85
 centering 88
 columns 87
 indents 83
 line breaks 89
 margins 82

pixel shims 86
 spacing between paragraphs 84
 using tables for 213
PageMill. See Adobe PageMill
pages
 limited control of appearance 14
 organizing 27
 typical width 78
PaintShop Pro 232
 and images 47
palettes, Netscape's standard 57
paragraphs
 aligning 28
 centering 28, 88
 space between 84
 starting new 28
parsing information 164
password boxes 156
passwords, and links to FTP sites 98
paths, in URLs 20
Paul Medoff's Hall of Doodads 232
perl scripts 153, 164
permissions, changing 227
photographs 48
physical formatting 33
Piguet, Yves 59
pixel shims 86
pixels, size of 83, 84
placing images on page 66
poems, and BR tag 29
Portable Network Graphics. See PNG format
portfolio, showing automatically 216
positioning elements, with style sheets 202
POST method for forms 154
pound sign (#), use of 96
PRE tag 38
 and monospaced fonts 34
preformatted text 38
processing forms 165
programmer limitations 14
protocol 19
publishing 217–228
 on AOL 226
 on CompuServe 226

Q

Qflat (for Windows) 177
QuickTime format for video 177
QuickTime movies 177
quotation marks 18, 22
 and anchor names 95
quotations, setting off 37

Index

Index

More from Peachpit Press

JavaScript for the World Wide Web: Visual QuickStart Guide

Ted Gesing and Jeremy Schneider

Once you've got HTML nailed, you're ready for JavaScript. Designed for users without much programming experience, JavaScript allows you to create even more compelling Web pages with powerful interactive features. *$17.95 (192 pages)*

Netscape Communicator for Windows: Visual QuickStart Guide
Netscape Communicator for Macintosh: Visual QuickStart Guide

Elizabeth Castro

The fastest way to learn Communicator, the enhanced version of Navigator, the Web's leading browser. Its components include: Navigator 4; Messenger, Netscape's email program; Collabra, for group discussions; Composer, for easily editing HTML; and Conference, for sharing information instantly across the Internet. *$16.95 (300 pages)*

Internet Explorer 3 for Windows 95/NT: Visual QuickStart Guide

Steven Schwartz

This hands-on guide enables even those with little past browsing experience to get up and running quickly. Readers with some Internet Explorer experience will pick up valuable tips on using new plug-ins such as ActiveX and JavaScript. *$16.95 (208 pages)*

Shocking the Web, Macintosh Edition
Shocking the Web, Windows Edition

Cathy Clarke, Lee Swearingen, David K. Anderson

The authoritative hands-on guide by the creators of Macromedia's Shockwave Web site shows Director developers how to create high impact, low-bandwidth movies and high-quality graphics for the Internet. Using detailed case studies and step-by-step design examples, the authors show CD-ROM and other multimedia authors how to unleash the Shockwave's full power. The accompanying CD-ROM is packed with design examples, case studies, tutorials, reusable template files, setup software, and a clip-art and sound-effects sampler. *$44.95 (464 pages)*

Getting Hits

Don Sellers

Building a world-class web site doesn't mean people will stampede to your door. Successful web sites must be promoted. *Getting Hits* guides you through the entire advertising and promotion process: posting your site to a search engine; creating links that give the biggest hits; producing hits offline; creating your own web campaign; and keeping visitors coming back. *$19.95 (200 pages)*

Web Graphics Tools and Techniques

Peter Kentie

An indispensable resource for web site creators needing to master a variety of authoring and graphics tools. It begins with HTML and the latest HTML-editing tools. It then moves deeper into graphics techniques, explaining the use of such tools as Photoshop, Painter, Poser, KPT Welder, GIF Construction Set, and Director. Advanced issues covered include frames, clickable maps, 3-D images, and interactivity. *$39.95 (320 pages)*

Elements of Web Design

Darcy DiNucci with Maria Giudice and Lynne Stiles

This book introduces traditional designers to the Web's opportunities and pitfalls. Every step of Web design is covered from practical issues such as pulling together a Web team to the design issues of HTML, graphics, interactivity, and dealing with the ever-changing nature of Web pages. *$39.95 (176 pages)*

For ordering information on these titles, contact Peachpit Press at:
USA 800-283-9444 • 510-548-4393 • CANADA 800-387-8028
or find us on the World Wide Web at http://www.peachpit.com